Please remember that this is a library book,
and that it belongs only temporarily to each
person who uses it. Be considerate. Do
not write in this, or any, library book.

WITHDRAWN

The Pequot War

A VOLUME IN THE SERIES

Native Americans of the Northeast:
Culture, History, and the Contemporary

Edited by
Colin G. Calloway and Barry O'Connell

The Pequot War

ALFRED A. CAVE

University of Massachusetts Press
Amherst

Copyright © 1996 by
The University of Massachusetts Press
All rights reserved
Printed in the United States of America
LC 95-47282
ISBN 1-55849-029-9 (cloth); 030-2 (pbk.)
Designed by Jack Harrison
Set in Adobe Minion with Adobe Walbaum display by dix!
Printed and bound by Thomson-Shore, Inc.

Library of Congress Cataloging-in-Publication Data
Cave, Alfred A.
The Pequot War / Alfred A. Cave.
p.   cm.—(Native Americans of the Northeast)
Includes bibliographical references and index.
ISBN 1-55849-029-9 (cloth : alk. paper).
—ISBN 1-55849-030-2 (pbk.)
1. Pequot War, 1636–1638.   2. Pequot Indians—History—17th century.
3. Pequot Indians—Government relations.
4. Indians, Treatment of—New England—History—17th century.
5. Puritans—New England—History—17th century.
I. Title. II. Series.
E83.63.C37   1996
973.2'2—dc20   95-47282
CIP

British Library Cataloguing in Publication data are available.

To Mary Sue

Contents

Acknowledgments

In reflecting on the many debts, both professional and personal, that I have incurred in the preparation of this study, I am particularly grateful to my wife, Mary Sue Deisher Cave, whose constant support and encouragement over the years have meant so much. Special mention must also be made of Marvin L. Michael Kay, my colleague, office mate, and close friend at the University of Toledo who patiently read several drafts of the manuscript and offered trenchant criticisms that led to both stylistic and substantive improvements. I am grateful also for the superb critical assistance of the editors of this series, Barry O'Connell and Colin Calloway, and to Neal Salisbury, whose report on an earlier version was of great value in resolving some problems of organization and emphasis. Thanks are also due to editor Janet Benton and other staff members at the University of Massachusetts Press. I am grateful also to Will Alpern, Joseph Michael Becker, Michael McGiffert, and Alden Vaughan, all of whom read and critiqued some of my earlier work on the Pequot War. The University of Toledo administration provided support for my research activities in the form of two sabbatical leaves and several travel grants. Particular thanks are expressed to the late James D. McComas, former president of the University of Toledo, to William N. Free, former vice president for academic affairs, to William Hoover, former chair of the Department of History at the University of Toledo, and to Carol Menning, present chair, for their support and encouragement. And last but hardly least, thanks to Louise Celley of the Department of History who typed the manuscript not only with great accuracy but with unfailing good humor.

Toledo, Ohio
August 1995

The Pequot War

Introduction

The Pequot War of 1636–37 paved the way for the establishment of English hegemony in southern New England. For that reason, historians have generally agreed that it "is one of the most important events in early American history."[1] Over the past quarter of a century, this war has been the subject of extensive scholarly discussion and controversy. But despite the wealth of insights into various aspects of the Puritan quarrel with the Pequots contained in the writings of Alden Vaughan, Francis Jennings, Neal Salisbury, and others, we still lack a detailed narrative history of the events leading up to the conflict and of its course and aftermath.[2] There is no modern work to which a reader may turn for an accurate and complete account of the interaction of Puritans and Pequots in the crucial years between 1634 and 1637. This book attempts to meet the need for a full-scale study of New England's first Anglo-Indian war. The author hopes to resolve some of the more controversial questions about this crucial episode by reassessing the events that led to conflict in the light of present-day knowledge of the cultural values and attitudes of Pequots as well as Puritans.

Most of the basic facts about the war itself are not at issue. It is a matter of record that the English assaulted the Pequots after the failure of efforts to persuade them to apprehend and surrender to Puritan justice those Indians believed to be responsible for the deaths of Captain John Stone and other Englishmen. The record also reveals that immediately before the outbreak of hostilities English negotiators pressed new

1

demands upon the Pequot sachems, specifically, that they pay a substantial indemnity and send Pequot children to Boston to serve as hostages to guarantee future good behavior. Puritan chroniclers freely admitted that their military offensive against the Pequot Indians was highly punitive, deliberately intended to inflict the maximum number of casualties. Pequot resistance was broken by a surprise attack on a fortified village near the Mystic River. The commanders at that engagement wrote detailed descriptions of the deliberate slaughter of Pequot noncombatants, many of them burned alive when their homes were put to the torch by English troops. They related that they spared neither women nor children but ordered their men to shoot or impale those survivors who escaped the flames. One recalled that dead and dying Indians in the fields surrounding Fort Mystic were "so thick in some places that you could hardly pass along." Their accounts of the mopping-up operations following the Mystic massacre speak of the summary execution of prisoners of war and of the enslavement of their surviving women and children. The more fortunate captives were given to Mohegan and Narragansett sachems who had assisted the Puritans in their war against the Pequots. The less fortunate were sold to Caribbean slave traders. At the war's end, the victorious English terminated Pequot sovereignty and outlawed use of the tribal name.[3]

The facts enumerated above are well documented, but the causes of the war and the reasons for the Puritans' brutal treatment of noncombatants as well as warriors remain obscure and controversial. The historiography of the Pequot War is often more polemical than substantive. Puritan apologists justified their savagery by demonizing the victims. Contemporary chroniclers and later historians sympathetic to the Puritans painted a portrait of the Pequots as a "cruell, barbarous and bloudy" people. That portrait reflected a long-standing stereotype of the New World "savage" as irrational, unpredictable, malicious, treacherous, and inhumane. Drawing upon a body of lore from the previous century that described Native American religious practices as a form of satanism, Puritan writers declared that the Pequots were "the Devil's instruments" and charged them with masterminding a plot to exterminate all Christians in New England. The Puritans and their later apologists asserted that the English colonists had no choice but to strike first. They also argued that, given the savagery of their adversary, they were under no obligation to respect the rules of civilized warfare. In his chronicle of the war, Captain John Underhill proclaimed that God himself demanded that the Pequots suffer "the most terriblest death that may be" in punishment for their sins. "Sometimes," he wrote, "the scripture declareth that women and children must perish with their parents. . . . We had sufficient light from the Word of God for our proceedings." Despite their distrust of the good captain's presumed antinomianism in other matters, his fellow Puritans enthusiastically echoed Underhill's defense of righteous violence.[4]

As we shall see, the Puritan explanations of the war will not stand close scrutiny. Their allegation that the Pequots threatened the security of Puritan New England cannot be confirmed. A close reexamination of the Puritans' own testimony suggests that it was without any foundation whatsoever. In their justifications of the war, Puritan writers advanced interpretations of Pequot character and intentions based on prejudice and supposition rather than hard evidence. Nonetheless, with very few exceptions, writers for three centuries uncritically echoed Puritan fantasies about Pequot malevolence. The eighteenth-century Connecticut poet Timothy Dwight, in "Greenfield Hill," described the Pequots as "murderous fiends" inspired by "vindictive rage." In commemoration of their victims, Dwight wrote:

> *First, hapless Stone! they bade thy bosom bleed,*
> *A guiltless offering at th'infernal shrine:*
> *Then, gallant Norton! the hard fate was thine,*
> *By ruffians butcher'd, and denied a grave:*
> *Thee, generous Oldham! next the doom malign*
> *Arrested; nor could all thy courage save;*
> *Forsaken, plunder'd, cleft, and buried in the wave.*[5]

In the next century, the historian Francis Parkman declared that the Pequots were "far worse than wolves or rattlesnakes."[6] John Gorham Palfrey maintained that the massacre at Mystic taught all the Indians "a salutary lesson" and thereby freed New England of "savage violence" for forty years.[7] John Fiske, invoking the precepts of Social Darwinism in his analysis of the issues at stake, urged his readers not to fault the Puritans for their "savage fierceness" against the Pequots, as "the world is so made that it is only in this way that the higher races have been able to preserve themselves and carry on their progressive work."[8]

Although Fiske's vision of racial conflict was shared by many nine-teenth-century commentators on Indian wars, not all writers were will-ing to commend Puritan conduct in the Pequot War. Thomas Hutchinson, in his *History of the Colony and Province of Massachusetts Bay* (1783), had suggested that Puritan reprisals against Pequot noncom-batants were both excessive and dishonorable.[9] Richard Hildreth in 1849 carried the criticism of the Puritans a bit further by expressing reserva-tions about their claim that the Pequots threatened English security.[10] In a more radical reversal of the usual stereotypes, William Apess, a Meth-odist minister of Pequot ancestry, declared that all of New England's Indians, including the Pequots, had acted "like men acquainted with the principles of integrity and good faith . . . while the English, with perfidi-ous craft, were preparing to imitate savages in their revenge and cruelty." His claim that the Pequots were not the savages portrayed in history and myth for the most part fell on deaf ears.[11]

Twentieth-century writers have generally been reluctant to accept ear-lier rationalizations for racial massacre. Most accounts of the Pequot War published during the past century have faulted the Puritans for their "wholesale slaughter and enslavement" of Indian adversaries.[12] But until quite recently most writers have also accepted the premise that, in their war against the Pequots, the Puritans were acting in self-defense. Criti-cism of their conduct was thus usually limited to suggestions that they were overly harsh in their dealings with hostile Indians. In most accounts of New England's Indian wars, the Pequots, not the Puritans, were portrayed as the aggressors. Alden Vaughan's *New England Frontier* (1965) provided the most comprehensive restatement of the traditional interpretation of the Pequot War. Vaughan declared that "the Pequot tribe had incurred by its forced intrusion into New England the enmity of its Indian neighbors and it had won a notorious reputation for brutal-ity." He concluded that the Pequot War was not a racial conflict but rather a salutary example of Anglo-Indian cooperation in resisting ag-gression. Although he granted that Puritan conduct toward the Pequots was hardly above reproach, Vaughan found that the burden of responsi-bility for the conflict rested with the Pequots.[13]

During the past two decades, the assumption of Pequot culpability has been challenged by revisionist scholars who have found the war's origins not in Pequot malevolence but in Puritan greed, prejudice, and bigotry. The revisionists are not entirely agreed in their explanations of the reasons for the Puritan assault on the Pequots. Some have advanced an economic interpretation of the conflict. Francis Jennings, in *The Invasion of America: Indians, Colonialism, and the Cant of Conquest* (1975), argues that annexation of Pequot land, control of Connecticut trade, access to the rich wampum resources of Long Island Sound, and the outflanking of other ambitious English claimants to those sources of wealth were the real motives behind the Massachusetts Bay Colony's assault on the Pequots. Jennings portrays Puritan Indian killings as cold-blooded expressions of self-interest. He conjectures that the "decisive" factor in precipitating the Pequot War was the quarrel between the Massachusetts Bay Colony and the Connecticut settlers over control of "colonizing in New England." Both the Bay Colony and the Connecticut towns hoped to win title to the Pequot country by right of conquest. The Pequots, Jennings believes, were caught in the middle of an English power struggle over the spoils of colonization.[14] Though some revisionists find this aspect of Jennings's thesis overly speculative, a number agree with his emphasis on material considerations. Richard Drinnon declares that "the Pequots were early victims of a process that Marxists would later call 'primitive accumulation.' "[15] The popular historian Alvin Josephy, drawing on the work of the anthropologist Lynn Ceci, maintains that wresting control of wampum-producing areas from the Pequots was the basic objective of the Massachusetts Bay Colony's offensive. Wampum, Josephy reminds us, served as money in the English colonies in the 1630s, and Pequot domination of the wampum mints of eastern Long Island Sound thus had serious economic implications for Puritan New England.[16] William Cronon concurs, noting that "exacting a regular military tribute in wampum proved a safer and more reliable source of supply than trading guns for it."[17]

Some scholars, however, have cautioned against seeking to explain the Pequot War in purely economic terms. Neal Salisbury, in *Manitou and Providence: Indians, Europeans, and the Making of New England, 1500–1643* (1982), writes of the English desire to control trade and annex Pequot land but argues that the war also served to provide a means of reestablishing unity within the contentious Puritan community by reminding the English of their divine mission to smite Canaanites and drive them from the promised land. "The (re)discovery that God had a purpose in mind for the settlers and that that purpose could be happily reconciled with their desire to spread out and expropriate Indians lands,"

Salisbury writes, "marked a significant adjustment of tensions within the New England Puritan movement between individual and communal goals."[18] Gary Nash strikes a similar note: "The Puritan leaders talked morbidly about God's anger at seeing his chosen people subvert the City on a Hill. In this sense, the Puritan determination to destroy the Pequots and the violence manifested at Mystic Fort can be partially understood in terms of the self doubt and guilt that Puritans could expiate only by exterminating so many of 'Satan's Agents.' Dead Pequots were offered to God as atonement for Puritan failings."[19]

Larzer Ziff sees in the slaughter of Pequots a means of resolving tensions and frustrations generated by the Antinomian Controversy. The Pequot War, in his analysis, "provided the militia with an unambiguous outlet for [their] sense of righteousness."[20] Anne Kibbey, a feminist scholar, finds the meaning of both the Pequot War and the Antinomian Crisis in the sanctioning of righteous violence. "The events of 1637," Kibbey writes, "established the legitimacy of genocidal war against non-white peoples and the sanctity of prejudicial attitudes towards women, granting theological sanction to the rhetoric of threat in Puritan men's speech." Kibbey concludes that both the Pequot War and the silencing of Anne Hutchinson and her followers were part of "a struggle to institute a particular kind of social order by defining acceptable forms of prejudicial violence and beliefs."[21] The Pequot War, in Kibbey's analysis, is to be understood as an expression of the patriarchal need to justify violence as a means of control.

Other writers have stressed the primacy of the irrational factors driving English Indian policy. Karen Kupperman finds the key to the English penchant for "preemptive strikes" such as the Pequot War in the "rage and hostility" prompted by feelings of both guilt and vulnerability in their dealings with Native Americans.[22] Richard Slotkin regards the Pequot War as an outgrowth and expression of Puritan fears of "the power of darkness in the wilderness." In his very provocative study of the contemporary war chronicles, Slotkin finds that "the wilderness was seen as a Calvinist universe in microcosm and also as an analogy of the human mind. Both were dark, with hidden possibilities for good and evil. Through the darkness the Indians flitted, like the secret Enemy of Christ or like the evil thoughts that plague the mind on the edge of consciousness. Like the devil, Indians struck where the defenses of good were the weakest and, having done their deed, retreated into hiding.

Often they carried off good men and pure virgins into hellish captivity and sexual temptation, as an evil thought will carry a good man forever out of the light." The Pequot War was thus the expression of a mind-set that "presumed no common ground between the groups" and "transferred the sphere of contention to a deeper psychological plane and brought unconscious fears and desires more overtly into play."[23]

The work of revisionist historians critical of Puritan Indian policy, combined with a growing sensitivity to past injustices committed against Native Americans, has led to a partial transformation of the Pequot image. Pequots are now often celebrated rather than excoriated for their resistance to English expansionism.[24] Even Alden Vaughan, their severest modern critic, confesses in the second edition of *New England Frontier* (1979) that "I am less certain than I was fifteen years ago that the Pequots deserve the burden of the blame." Most recently, Vaughan, in a 1995 revision of an article on the causes of the Pequot War first published thirty years earlier, concluded that while the Pequots must bear some share of the blame for the conflict, having provoked Puritan reprisals through their refusal to extradite Indians guilty of murdering Englishmen, they were clearly not "solely or even primarily responsible. . . . The Bay colony's gross escalation of violence and of excessive demand for prisoners and reparations made all-out war unavoidable; until then, negotiation was at least conceivable."[25] Nonetheless, belief that the Pequots were somehow unlike other Indian groups in New England and that their presence in Connecticut did somehow endanger the fledgling English colonies persists. Such misconceptions still find expression in the writings of historians who generally reject the overall anti-Indian bias that motivated the savage portrayals of Pequots penned by earlier writers. To cite some conspicuous examples, the author of a well-regarded textbook on American Indian history published in 1980 describes the Pequots as "a threat to the security of New England."[26] A major study of New England Puritanism published in 1989 reminds readers of a long-standing belief that the Pequot name "was the Algonquian word for 'destroyers of men'" and suggests that "the historiographic pendulum has swung too far" in exonerating Pequots and blaming Puritans.[27] A writer in the *New England Quarterly* in 1991 declares categorically that the Pequots were planning "to destroy European settlement."[28]

In the pages that follow, I will seek to demonstrate that the documentary evidence and ethnohistorical data available to us not only do not support the Puritans' more extreme allegations that Pequots plotted the extermination of all Christians in New England but also discredit the commonly accepted assumption that the Pequots were obstacles to English expansion in the Connecticut River valley. Instead, the record indicates that they actively sought European trading partners and that their aggressive actions were aimed primarily at Indian trade rivals, not English colonists. There is no evidence that the Pequots were guilty of any acts of violence against English settlers in Connecticut prior to John Endecott's initiation of hostilities. The Pequots neither desired nor anticipated war with the Puritans. The origins of the Pequot War are to be found in the actions of the Massachusetts Bay Colony which, for reasons not yet fully explained, pressed demands that the Pequots clearly could not honorably accept and then resorted to violence in an effort to force Pequot compliance.

I believe that the key to understanding the English provocation of the Pequot War in 1637 lies in recapturing, as best we can, their sense of the meaning and implication of the specific events that transpired in the years immediately preceding hostilities. With that in mind, I have read and reread all of the primary sources of the Pequot War period: letters, journals, legal records, historical narratives. As I have reflected on these Puritan accounts of their conflicts with the Pequots, I have often been reminded of Roy Harvey Pearce's characterization of the idea of savagism as "one of those unattractive 'isms' which taught our forebears how to make up their minds and also how to act." "For the Puritan," as Pearce has noted, "history was everywhere cosmically and eternally meaningful. A Satanic principle was part of that meaningfulness; and New England Indians somehow embodied that principle. . . . God had meant the savage Indians' lands for the civilized English, and, moreover, had meant the savage state as a sign of Satan's power and savage warfare as a sign of earthly struggle and sin."[29] From my own reading of the Puritan texts I am persuaded that Pearce's explication of the Puritan view of the Indian as agent of the "Satanic principle" in history provides us with an eminently sound point of departure for our efforts to understand the context within which the leaders of the Puritan colonies conducted their dealings with the Pequots. Unlike many eminent students of the "New England mind," Pearce realized that the meanings that Puritans attached to their encounters with Indians were of vital importance in the ongoing formulation of their conception of their "errand into the wilderness." Later scholars have supplemented Pearce's work in important ways and probed dimensions of the problem he left untouched. In response to their work, Pearce has commented that, were he to rewrite *Savagism and Civilization*, he would place greater emphasis upon both material factors and "psychological needs." But Pearce's original insight about the central role the concept of savagery played in shaping Puritan perceptions of their Indian neighbors remains valid.[30]

Mindful of Pearce's admonition, I have endeavored to weigh and balance material, ideological, and psychological considerations in assessing Puritan explanations of their action against the Pequots. My conclusions concerning the origins of the Pequot War depart somewhat from the main thrust of much recent revisionism. The difference is one of emphasis. I do not believe that accounts of the war's origins that point primarily or exclusively to English greed, to the desire to annex land and seize fur, slaves, and wampum, provide us with an adequate explanation of Puritan behavior. Although revisionist scholars have done much to demythologize the Pequot War, they have often placed too much weight on economic motivations and have accordingly ignored or slighted the ideological assumptions that drove Indian policy and determined reactions to immediate events. One cannot, of course, separate ideology from its specific context of interests and power relationships, and any interpretation of causation that simply addresses one segment of the equation runs the risk of falling into reductionism. Moreover, the relationship between ideology and self-interest is often a rather subtle one. Though ideology in the abstract serves to grant "legitimacy to the interests of hegemonic groups," in practice the ideas, prejudices, symbols, images, and myths that compose it do not necessarily need to be activated by some particular immediate economic objective in order to color and distort perceptions of events.[31]

For that reason, we must pay close attention to Puritan expectations about the behavior of "savages" and to their conception of the Indians' place in a sacred history shaped by divine providence. It is ironic that, while historians of the early contact period generally accept the ethnohistorians' warning that one must comprehend and weigh the cultural values of Native Americans in order to understand their reaction to the European presence, they sometimes understate the extent to which sixteenth-and seventeenth-century Europeans were driven by beliefs and assumptions rather unlike our own. Quite simply, the Pequot War must be placed in the context of Puritan assumptions about intercultural encounters in the wilderness. Though our present-day understanding of the culture of New England's Algonquian peoples lends no support to the Puritan portrayals of the Pequots as murderous savages determined to exterminate all Christians, or of other Indian groups as potential collaborators in that scheme, we must remember that seventeenth-century English conceptions of Indian character, and of historical processes, led to very different interpretations of Indian behavior. We must also remember that, then as now, prejudices were often highly resistant to modification by experience and that misconceptions rather than realities often drive historical events. When prejudices are part of a hegemonic ideology, and are woven into a complex of beliefs that rationalize and sustain claims to power and justify expropriation of resources, they prove particularly intractable. Such was the case with Puritan ideas about savagery.

Puritan commitment to certain notions about savages and their role in history led to serious misinterpretations of both past Pequot actions and future Pequot intentions. Puritan provocation of the Pequot War was consistent with the basic assumptions that drove their Indian policy. As Sacvan Bercovitch has noted, Puritan documents dealing with Indians "show the astonishing capacity of myth not only to obscure but to invert reality. What they tell us, in effect, is that there are two parties in the new world, God's and the Devil's; and that God's party is white, Puritan and entrusted with a world-redeeming errand, while Satan's party is dark-skinned, heathen and doomed."[32] It was of little consequence that the ordinary events that marked the day-to-day interactions of Englishmen and Algonquians in the early years of colonization failed to conform to that dramatic scenario. As Breitwieser remarks, "Puritan representation was particularly adept at subduing fact with category."[33] The absence of tangible evidence of Indian malevolence did not remove belief in its reality. In the Puritans' vision of the New World as a spiritual battleground between the Elect and the Forces of Darkness, the survival of the New World Zion required decisive action to nip in the bud the Indian conspiracies whose existence, though intangible, was necessary to fulfill Puritan ideological expectations. Thus, based on nothing more substantial than rumors of dubious origin, Puritans came to see the Pequots as conspirators who threatened their survival. The tensions generated by the Antinomian Controversy and the greed of opportunists covetous of Pequot land, peltry, and wampum, so heavily stressed by recent revisionist historians, probably contributed to the determination to humble the Pequots. But neither, in my judgment, was the "cause" of the war. Both must be placed within an ideological context that legitimized, indeed required, the use of violence to protect Christians through the intimidation of savages. New England's Puritans did not anticipate permanent peaceful coexistence with the indigenous inhabitants. In their earliest reflections on their conflicts with Indians, Puritan intellectuals saw war as God's means of punishing heathens. They later came to believe that it also enabled the Almighty to chastise wayward Saints and test the mettle of his own people. But, from the beginning, they regarded armed confrontations with savage peoples in league with Satan as predictable, necessary events.

In understanding the origins of the Pequot War, it must be borne in mind that Puritan ideology embraced images and stereotypes of Indians and their motives and behavior that led easily to misreadings of the meaning of events, misreadings that, I will argue, tragically cast the Pequots in an unwarranted role of aggressor. In reviewing Puritan explanations of their attack on the Pequots, one is struck by their repeated insistence that they acted defensively to counter a satanic plot to destroy Christ's church in the wilderness. It is tempting to dismiss such pronouncements as wartime propaganda or sanctimonious prattle. But, as I will seek to demonstrate in the first chapter of this study, the Puritan view of Indian character and, by extension, their misgivings about Pequot intentions were the outgrowth of beliefs that not only were not formulated on the spot to justify the Pequot War but, in their broad outlines, long predated the founding of the Puritan colonies. The New England Puritans' concept of savagery as a manifestation of the Devil in history and their suspicion that the history of God's people in the wilderness would be marked by recurrent conflicts with the Devil's minions had deep roots.

What of the role of economic self-interest in precipitating the Pequot War? Although the conflict cannot be explained in purely economic terms, it does not follow that the Puritan leaders were unmindful of the material advantages that would accrue to them after a successful campaign against Sassacus and his people. The records indicate that the magistrates were keenly interested in land, wampum, and Indian slaves, and they profited greatly from the Pequot War. Greed alone did not inspire the attack on the Pequots, but it was hardly absent and it was certainly not a deterrent. Human conflicts are driven by complex and mixed motives, and New England's Puritans were hardly exceptions to the rule. Their misinterpretations of Pequot actions and intentions, stemming from deep-seated prejudices and preconceptions about "savages," led to concerns about security that prompted and justified a war that also expressed and advanced their desire to subdue the American wilderness and profit from its exploitation. Ideology and self-interest went hand in hand. The former legitimized the latter, as holy war opened the way to territorial acquisition and personal self-aggrandizement. The Pequots were victims not only of their adversaries' preconceptions and fears but also of their ambition.

The greatest challenge facing the historian of the Pequot War is not the interpretation of English motives and intentions. The written records permit a reasonably full reconstruction of the Puritan side of the story. The Pequots' perspective is far more difficult to recapture. They left no written records. Most, if not all, of their leaders perished in the war or were executed by the English or their Indian allies shortly thereafter. Most of our information about the Pequots comes from Puritan sources. But that does not mean that we are left completely in the dark about their role in this conflict. A critical reading and comparison of various Puritan texts discredit much Puritan mythology about Pequot motives and behavior. Moreover, insights gained from the work of the past generation of ethnohistorians provide a new basis for critical analysis of source materials. Recent findings regarding the languages, culture, customs, values, and behavior of New England's Algonquian peoples generally and of the Pequots in particular place the Anglo-Pequot conflict in a new perspective. Although some aspects of our reconstruction of their history remain conjectural, we nonetheless have ample evidence to correct the inaccuracies and misrepresentations that have marred past accounts of their early encounters with the Puritans. Through a reexamination of the English sources relating to the Pequot War, combined with some of the newer insights of ethnohistory, we can now correct many of the misconceptions that have led to misunderstanding of this crucial episode in Puritan New England's formative years.

1

Preconceptions and Misperceptions

We begin our story of the Pequot War not by recounting events but by describing a state of mind, for Puritan preconceptions about the indigenous inhabitants of New England shaped their assessments of Pequot motives and intentions. Some of those preconceptions antedated the Puritan movement, lingering remnants of old rumors about monsters, wild men, and savages. Early European accounts of the New World, eagerly read by learned Englishmen, were filled with tales of encounters with people so fierce and brutal that, as Peter Martyr declared, "there is no man able to behowlde them, but he shall feele his bowelles grate with a certen horroure." The impact of those stories on the English imagination is well illustrated by the writings of the mid-sixteenth-century Anglican bishop John Jewell, who declared the Americans a "wild and naked people" who lived "without any civil government, offering up men's bodies in sacrifice, drinking men's blood . . . sacrificing boys and girls to certain familiar devils."[1]

Though later English voyages to the New World removed some of those misconceptions, the idea that Native Americans were satanists persisted.[2] To cite a few examples from Richard Hakluyt's massive compendia of travel reports, Sir Francis Drake was convinced that the Indians whom he observed cavorting around a fire on a South American beach in 1577 were endeavoring to summon the devil to sink his ship. He gave thanks to God for thwarting their satanic efforts. The chronicler of Martin Frobisher's third voyage in 1578 claimed that the natives of

Newfoundland "made us to understand, lying groveling with their faces upon the ground, and making a noise downeward, that they worship the devill under them." The report of John Davis's second voyage in search of the Northwest Passage in 1586 related an encounter with a race of "idolaters" and "witches" who employed "many kinds of inchantments." The narrator suggested that their diabolical incantations failed only because of God's special protection of Christians. Sir George Peckham, summarizing reports from Newfoundland, wrote that the inhabitants of the coast were continually at war with "a cruell kinde of people, whose food is mans flesh, and have teeth like dogges, and doe pursue them with ravenous mindes to eate their flesh, and devoure them." Peckham also believed that in the interior lurked devil worshipers who practiced human sacrifice and immolated their own progeny. He urged English occupation of North America on the grounds that "by this meanes many of their poore innocent children shall be preserved from the bloody knife of the sacrificer, a most horrible and detestable custom in the sight of God and man." The chroniclers of Raleigh's ill-fated Roanoke venture (1584–87) at first believed that they had found a "people most gentle, loving and faithful, voide of all guile and treason . . . such as live after the manner of the golden age." But they later concluded that many of the Indians were devil worshipers whose efforts to use witchcraft against the English had prompted God to punish "their witches" by sending a plague that had decimated the offending villages.[3]

The founding of a permanent English colony in Virginia in 1607 was attended by a resurgence of reports of Indian satanism. Captain John Smith, whose reports were later studied with particular care by New England's Puritans, described the indigenous inhabitants of America as devil worshipers who groveled before idols shaped "with such deformity as may well suit with such a god." Smith mistakenly assumed that Indians participating in a puberty ceremony were sacrificing their own children to the devil. His overall assessment of Indian character was harsh. Though he granted that they possessed a certain quickness of wit and an innate shrewdness, Native Americans, in Smith's view, were basically cruel and irrational. Easily angered and extremely vengeful, they were also, he warned, unpredictable, mercurial, treacherous, and malicious and must therefore never be trusted. Although aid from Powhatan and his people had rescued many of the hapless Jamestown settlers from starvation, Smith explained away their generosity by claiming that the Almighty had intervened to soften their hearts, as charity was alien to savage nature. The security of the English colonies in North America, Smith warned, could not be based on goodwill but must instead be maintained by force. Colonists, he admonished, must inspire in the Indians a "greate fear" or perish at their hands. Smith's imperative was endorsed by the Reverend Alexander Whitaker, missionary to Virginia's Indians, who warned that no progress could be made in delivering Virginia from the devil unless the Indians first "stoode in fear of us." The founders of Puritan New England, as we shall see, made that maxim a guiding principle of their Indian policy.[4]

As the Jamestown settlers struggled with their fears of a satanic presence in the wilderness, Englishmen at home perused a popular survey of world geography written by George Abbot, future archbishop of Canterbury, that claimed that the natives of the Americas were worshipers of "vile spirits" and regularly engaged in incest, sodomy, witchcraft, and cannibalism. Striking the same note, Sir Walter Raleigh in his *History of the World*, written in the Tower of London in the early 1600s, asserted that, some centuries before, the Americans had been "brought by the devil under his fearful servitude." The belief that the New World was the devil's domain was commonly accepted in early seventeenth-century England. Placing that belief in the context of sacred history, the eminent theologian Joseph Mede declared that, shortly after the advent of Christianity, Satan induced the ancestors of North America's Indians to migrate with him to America, "where they might be hid, and not be disturbed in the idolatrous and abominable, or rather diabolical, service he expected from those his followers." Though Mede hoped for the conversion of the Indians, he thought it more likely that they would join the legions of Gog and Magog predestined to assail God's people in the final days.[5]

The founders of Puritan New England carried that notion across the Atlantic and assumed that as Christians they enjoyed a measure of divine favor denied to godless savages. Their colonies at Plymouth and at Massachusetts Bay were planted on land largely depopulated by the pandemic of 1617–19. Neither understanding how disease is transmitted nor comprehending the Indians' lack of immunity to microorganisms of European origin, the Saints, as one of their early chroniclers noted, gave thanks for "this wonderous work of the great Jehovah" in "wasting the naturall Inhabitants with deaths stroke" in order to make room in the wilderness for God's own people.[6]

Since the New World literature available to them described Indians as cruel savages given to diabolical practices, it is not surprising that the founders of Puritan New England were skeptical about the possibility of peaceful coexistence. From their writings we learn that many of the early settlers of New England were troubled by premonitions of violent death at the hands of "savage and brutish men." William Bradford recalled that the Pilgrims, sighting land off Cape Cod in 1620, gazed with foreboding upon "a hideous and desolate wilderness, full of wild beasts and wild men." He added this reflection: "It is recorded in Scripture as a mercy to the apostle and his shipwrecked company, that the barbarians showed them no small kindness in refreshing them, but these savage barbarians . . . were readier to fill their sides full of arrows than otherwise. . . . What could now sustain them but the spirit of God and His grace?" Edward Johnson, the chronicler of the Massachusetts Bay Colony, recorded that as the Puritans boarding the *Arbella* in 1630 bade farewell to their friends and loved ones in England they were reminded by one well-wisher that, "after two, three, or foure moneths spent with daily expectation of swallowing Waves and cruell Pirates, you are to be Landed amongst barbarous Indians famous for nothing but cruelty." Commenting on morale among the colonists during the first decade, Johnson declared that "their lonesome condition . . . very grievous to some . . . was much aggravated by continuall feare of the Indians approach, whose cruelties were much spoken of."[7]

The Pilgrims in Holland, prior to their embarkation for the New World, had exchanged Indian atrocity stories. Bradford, echoing Peter Martyr, recorded that "the very hearing of these things could not but move the bowels of men to grate within them and make the weak to quake and tremble." As the Separatist leaders pondered the question of relocation of their congregation to North America, some who opposed the move grimly predicted that those who survived the hardships of the Atlantic crossing and the risks of "famine and nakedness . . . sore sickness and grievous diseases" in a distant and inhospitable wilderness would die in agony as captives of savages, "who are cruel, barbarous, and most treacherous . . . most furious in their rage, and merciless where they overcome." In meetinghouse and by fireside the members of the

Pilgrim congregation reflected upon the dangers of life in a land inhabited by a brutal people whose chief "delight" was to "torment men in the most bloody manner that may be, flaying some alive with the shells of fishes, cutting off the members and joints of others by piecemeal and broiling on the coals," and finally devouring "collops of their flesh in their sight whilst they live, with other cruelties horrible to be related."[8]

The Indians of New England did not visit those horrors upon the first colonists but rather extended aid indispensable to their survival. But experience did not alter the Puritans' assessment of Indian character. While promotional tracts published to encourage immigration to the New World often described Native Americans as "gentle and loving," English colonists in the early contact period were far more inclined to see them as sinister and menacing. William Bradford, for example, believed that, shortly after his party had landed on Cape Cod in the late fall of 1620, the "savages" had assembled in a "dark and dismal swamp" and for three days and three nights had labored, through fearful conjurations, to raise the devil. It was only after the failure of their hellish invocations that the Indians decided, reluctantly, to go "to the English and make friendship."[9] Bradford's colleague Edward Winslow, in a tract published in London in 1624, maintained that, had the Almighty not intervened to fill "the hearts of the savages with astonishment and fear of us," the fledgling colony would have soon perished, the victim of their "many plots and treacheries."[10]

Before we deal with the specific ways in which the Puritans' preconceptions about Indian character led to misperceptions of both their culture and their behavior, the persistence of savage stereotypes in the face of evidence that might well have led to a more realistic and humane view of Native Americans requires some explanation, as it is central to an understanding of the origins of the Pequot War. At one level, characterization of Indians as savages devoid of virtues such as pity and compassion confirmed Christian Europe's sense of moral superiority and justified not only occupation and dispossession but also the violence and cruelty toward indigenous peoples that often accompanied the founding of colonies. It clearly occupies a crucial place among the ideas that were part of the hegemonic ideology of early modern capitalism and colonialism. But in addition to its obvious usefulness as a rationale for empire building, the idea of savagery also possessed a powerful psychic appeal. Images of primitive peoples living in a state of lawlessness, unfettered by the restraints that bound civilized men, aroused strong emotions. While to some Christians the savage appeared primarily as an errant human being to be lifted up and given the blessings of civility in this life and salvation in the world to come, to most he inspired more fear than compassion, for he represented the dark side of man's nature— lawless, cruel, rapacious, and licentious.[11] Puritans, in common with other Englishmen, defined themselves in part by contrast with others who represented the antitheses of the values they affirmed and embodied. Catholics and those who covertly aided and abetted their "Papistic schemes" symbolized, in the Puritan mind, the degradation of Christianity; the natives of America, whom they commonly described as "the worst of the heathens," evoked fears of the total negation of civilized values. The Native American was cast, in a radical sense, into the role of the Other, the living example of what civilized men had transcended and of all that Christians must resist in their encounters with the wilderness and its denizens. The idea of savagery in opposition to civilization was thus an essential part of the English colonizers' sense of identity.

The preservation and extension of civil and Christian values on alien soil defined the English understanding of their colonial mission. The dangers Indians posed to that undertaking were primarily spiritual and stemmed from their presumed role as the devil's agents in the New World wilderness. Bernard Sheehan has noted the widespread belief that "proximity to savagism" placed Christians "in danger of losing their souls and their civility." English Puritans and Anglicans reacted to reports from the New World in much the same way. In 1622, in a treatise on the importance of establishing schools in the colonies, the Puritan sympathizer John Brinsley noted widespread concern that association with Indians would lead to a "falling away from God to Sathan" as Christian colonists removed from the constraints of civilization became "utterly savage." The Anglican cleric Richard Eburne advocated settlement in Newfoundland on the grounds that the sparsity of native inhabitants there greatly reduced the danger "of corruption of language or blood."[12] The idea that Indians were a potential source of corruption was sometimes justified through appeals to biblical authority. Some New England Puritans, in their efforts to locate Indians within the grand historical scheme they believed to be embodied in the Old and New

Testaments, gave credence to speculation, originating with Anglican promoters of the Jamestown venture, that Indians were descendants of Ham, the son of Noah who, according to the Book of Genesis, had provoked the wrath of the Almighty by looking upon the nakedness of his drunken father. Driven into exile and condemned to wander the earth under God's curse, Ham and his progeny were said to have degenerated into devil worshipers.[13] John White of the Massachusetts Bay Company believed that he had found in Indian creation myths and in some of their "Legal Observations" evidence of their origin in the world described in the Old Testament and their subsequent degeneration.[14]

For the most part, English Puritan reactions to the Indian as the Other —as the antithesis of the civilized Christian—were neither original nor unique. But certain aspects of Puritan belief gave the concept of a conflict of savagery and Christian civilization in the North American wilderness a particular force and resonance. As Andrew Delbanco suggests, in the absence of the opposition and persecution they had faced in England, New England's Puritans felt impelled to create "new enemies . . . Indians, Antinomians, eventually Quakers and 'witches.'"[15] The inner logic of Puritan ideology required that the Saints be beleaguered and besieged in this world, and Indians could play the role of foes of God's own people quite admirably. Puritan divines taught that, as successors to the Israelites in God's special favor, the faithful could also expect to be the special objects of the devil's blandishments and of God's frequent testing and chastisement. A fundamental element in the Puritans' founding myth was the belief that the wilderness was a place of darkness and peril to the soul, inhabited by savages and devils, ideally suited for testing both the faith and the mettle of the righteous. An early eighteenth-century New England preacher captured the essence of that myth when, in celebration of the courage and faith of founders of the Plymouth Colony, he declared: "But O how horrid and dismal do these new-found regions appear! On the shores and rivers, nothing but sights of wretched, naked and barbarous nations, adorers of devils—the earth covered with hideous thickets that require infinite toils to subdue—a rigorous winter for a third of the year—not a house to live in—not a Christian to see— none but the heathen of a strange and hard language to speak with—not a friend within three thousand miles to help in any emergency—and a vast and dangerous ocean to pass over to this."[16]

Puritan divines worried that the proximity of the wilderness, which

they conceptualized more in spiritual and moral than in strictly geo-
graphical terms, placed Christians in constant danger of reversion to
savagery through the embracing of such presumed "Indian vices" as
sloth, self-indulgence, deceit, blasphemy, devil worship, and concupis-
cence. With regard to the latter, the Plymouth Colony's outrage at the
trader Thomas Morton's alleged cohabitation with Indian women was
the first but hardly the last indication of Puritan fear of Indian sexuality.[17] Later Puritan portrayals of Native Americans sometimes falsely
assumed that they were sexually unrestrained and could therefore be
expected to rape captives. As we will note later in this study, John
Underhill, in interrogating some young girls who had been held captive
by the Pequots in 1637, was quite preoccupied with their sexual experiences and rejoiced that, although they had been solicited to "uncleanness" by their dusky captors, the girls had called upon God and
thereby preserved their chastity. Although later New England captivity
narratives would offer no support for the image of the Indian as sexually
abandoned, the preoccupation with forbidden interracial sexuality persisted. Writing in 1706, Cotton Mather acknowledged that English expectations of Indian sexual misconduct had been unfounded but attributed
the protection of the chastity of captives to "a wonderful restraint from
God upon the Brutish Salvages."[18] The Indian in Puritan eyes thus
remained licentious by nature, his good conduct explained away as a
special "providence" of God. Once again, experience had little impact on
the Puritan conception of savagery. To Cotton Mather, as to other Puritans, the idea itself transcended the mundane, factual record. The concept of savagery was essential to their definition of their "errand into the
wilderness." They were therefore insensitive to ambiguities and contra-
dictions in the pattern of intercultural interaction that did not fit their
design.

The sense of danger we find in early Puritan accounts of their dealings
with the indigenous inhabitants of New England persisted long after the
founding of the Puritan colonies, for it was rooted in anxieties that
emanated not so much from objective observation or actual experience
as from subjective fears of the subversive potential of intimate contact
with the Other. Although that fear of corruption, of loss of virtue, drove
much of the Euro-American response to the presumed savagery of the
New World's peoples, there were other reactions that are not so easily
categorized. Some of the very qualities in portrayals of savage life that

defenders of Christian civilization deplored and resolved to extirpate could also inspire envy and longing, followed, of course, by guilt. Descriptions of savagery thus aroused some very contradictory reactions, for there were many who found the idea of liberation from the restraints of civilized life not altogether unattractive. While English spokesmen for colonial expansion publicly trembled at the prospect that tolerance of Indian ways could lead to emulation of Indian savagery and thence to loss of civilization and of salvation, contemplation of the liberty and the indulgence savage peoples presumably enjoyed sometimes prompted other feelings as well. If one of those feelings was envy, another was rage. An early example is Robert Gray's warning to the Jamestown colony against toleration of New World "Canaanites." Gray insisted that, if the Indians proved resistant to English efforts to civilize and Christianize them, they must be exterminated. In their natural state they were, Gray declared, "odious" in the eyes of God. He reminded the colonists that "Saul had his kingdome rent from him [and] his posteritie because he spared Agog, that idolatrous king of the Amelichite, whom God would not have spared; so acceptable a service it is to destroy idolaters, whom God hateth." Gray's contemporary William Symonds also called for the slaughter of unregenerate savages, declaring that God "putteth away all the ungodly of the earth like drosse. . . . It is God's ordinance to bring a curse upon them and to kill them as the children of Israel did Balaam." Though New England's Puritans agreed with critics who questioned Gray's and Symonds's premise that heathenism alone justified extermination, they were, as we shall see, quite willing to cast themselves in the role of instruments of "God's wrath" when persuaded that Indian iniquity threatened the security of God's people in the wilderness.[19] Images of Indian savagery were reinforced by complex, sometimes contradictory, motives and emotions. To see the Indian in other terms would have threatened the foundations of an intricate but potentially vulnerable ideological structure.

Let us turn now to specific Puritan perceptions of Native American culture. Edward Winslow's tract "Good Newes from New England" (1624) contains the first detailed English description of the religious practices of the New England indigenous peoples. It is a document that tells us far more about Puritan preconceptions than Indian customs, but as those preconceptions were to play a vital role in shaping later Indian policy, Winslow's account deserves close attention. Winslow repeated Smith's erroneous interpretation of Algonquian initiation rites and claimed that the Indians often murdered their own children in satanic rituals. He was unable to interpret accurately the information provided by his Indian informants and tried to make some sense out of Algonquian mythology by using Judeo-Christian categories to classify Indian gods. Thus, told about a creator-God named Kietan, Winslow assumed that he was Jehovah. Learning to his distress that the Indians only infrequently called upon Kietan, an austere and distant figure, but more often appealed to a lesser deity named Hobbomoch, who sometimes appeared to them incarnated as a snake, Winslow decided that they had forsaken worship of the Creator to follow an evil and satanic spirit. Indeed, Winslow was persuaded that Hobbomoch was probably the devil himself. When he was permitted to witness a shaman's healing ceremony, Winslow's fears were confirmed. After describing the frenzied dancing, shrill musical invocations, and the "priest's" trance, Winslow informed his readers that the shaman cured patients through the power of the devil himself, who sat on the shaman's shoulder throughout the ceremony, manifested as an eagle or a serpent but visible only to his disciples. After further inquiries, Winslow also learned of a class of Indian warriors who allegedly through alliance with the devil attained exceptional prowess and near invulnerability in battle. A satanic presence, Winslow warned, permeated Native American life.[20]

Closer association with their Indian neighbors did not bring the New England Puritans greater understanding of Native American spirituality. Ten years after the publication of Winslow's garbled and distorted observations, William Wood, in *New England's Prospect*, repeated Winslow's claim that Indian "powwows" invoked the devil and used diabolical power to heal the sick. After attending a healing ceremony, Wood reported:

> The manner of their action in their conjuration is thus: the parties that are sick or lame being brought before them, the powwow sitting down, the rest of the Indians giving attentive audience to his imprecations and invocations, and after the violent expression of many a hideous bellowing and groaning, he makes a stop, and then all the auditors with one voice utter a short canto. Which done, the powwow still proceeds in his invocations, sometimes roaring like a bear, other times groaning like a dying horse, foaming at the mouth

like a chased boar, smiting on his naked breast and thighs with such violence as if he were mad. Thus will he continue sometimes half a day, spending his lungs, sweating out his fat, and tormenting his body in this diabolical worship.

Wood believed that, with the devil's aid, the powwow could effect remarkable cures. An Englishman, "a reliable gentleman," had told him of a medicine man who, in his presence, extracted "the stump of small tree . . . past the cure of his ordinary surgery" from the foot of a lame man by wrapping the foot in a beaver cloth and then rapping on the cloth. Wood also gave credence to rumors that the sachem-shaman Passaconaway possessed such diabolical power that he could "make the water burn, the rocks move, the trees dance, metamorphise himself into a flaming man," produce a live snake out of a dead snakeskin, and in the winter create green leaves from ashes.[21]

Belief that Indian religious practitioners were in league with the devil and that the native inhabitants of New England were the devil's slaves persisted throughout the seventeenth century. Echoing Edward Winslow, Thomas Mayhew, missionary to the Indians of Martha's Vineyard in 1652, declared that the "Devil . . . with his angels had his Kingdom among them" and that Indian "pawwwaws" sought "to pacify the Devil through their sacrifice and get deliverance from their evil." The Reverend William Hubbard, writing in 1680, declared Indian religion unworthy of discussion, as it consisted only of "what was diabolical." Several years later, an English visitor, John Josselyn, reported that the Infernal One "scares them with his Apparitions and panick Terrours, by reason whereof they live in a wretched consternation, worshipping the Devil for fear." In 1702 Cotton Mather wrote that "the devil decoyed those miserable savages hither, in hopes that the gospel of the Lord Jesus Christ would never come to destroy or disturb his absolute empire over them."[22]

Roger Williams's partial acceptance of the Puritan stereotype of Native American religion as satanism is particularly telling. A pathbreaking advocate of freedom of conscience, of separation of church and state, and of respect for Indian land rights, views unacceptable to the Puritan ruling oligarchy, Williams was exiled from the Massachusetts Bay Colony in 1636. Fleeing in the dead of winter to escape deportation to England, he settled among the Narragansett Indians of Rhode Island. Williams's sympathy and affection for his Indian neighbors and associates, extraordinary for a seventeenth-century New England Puritan, has often been noted.[23] Making his living as an Indian trader, Williams published in London in 1643 the *Key into the Language of America*, the most perceptive of the Puritan accounts of Native American life and culture. It contains, as we shall note, some important insights. But Williams confessed that he did not inquire too closely into Indian religious rituals, for "after once being in their Houses and beholding what their Worship was, I durst never bee an eye witness, Spectatour or looker on, least I should have been a partaker of Sathans Inventions and Worships, contrary to Ephes. 5.14." Indian priests, Williams declared, were "no other than our English witches."[24]

Williams's characterization of the shaman as a witch was the result of a misapplication of Judeo-Christian concepts to the understanding of Native American spirituality. Shamanic rituals were not diabolical, as Williams assumed, but were generally benevolent in purpose, for the shaman's calling was to comprehend and utilize, for the good of both the individual and the group, the remarkable forces that Algonquians, like other Native Americans, believed permeated the world. Preoccupation with satanism blinded seventeenth-century English observers to the true nature of shamanic practice. As John A. Grim notes, "The shaman's ritual assures the flow of . . . vital energy into the community. The dramatic actions, the emotional chants, the terrifying masks, and the elaborate dances all bring about contact with a spiritual energy that sustains society." Impressed by the shaman's "capacity for evocation rather than domination" of natural forces, Grim and other recent scholars have found "profound beauty" in this ancient manifestation of spirituality.[25]

Operating in a culture which held that an array of animate, inanimate, visible, and invisible entities possessed both souls and power, the shaman was a singularly potent figure. But the power that he possessed can be described as "supernatural," "divine," or "satanic" only by invoking and misapplying European categories. Those categories had little meaning in the New England Algonquian mental world of the early seventeenth century, wherein the "supernatural" was immanent and material, not transcendent and otherworldly, and coexisted on the same plane of reality as the mundane. Indeed, to call the shaman a "priest," as Williams and other Puritan observers sometimes did, is only slightly more accurate than to call him a "witch." He could also be described as a savant, a fortune-teller, or a physician, for shamanism embraced all of those functions. The powers that the shaman received from the spirit world were used in a variety of ways for the benefit of the community. Shamanic practice essentially involved the invocation and manipulation of the spirits and forces whose goodwill was essential to health and prosperity. Shamans were sometimes called upon to use their occult knowledge to ward off evil spirits, a process often misinterpreted as "devil worship" by European observers.

The shaman played a vital role in the life of the Algonquian village. Puritan observers erred in equating him with the marginalized and presumably malicious individuals whom the English and other Europeans stigmatized and persecuted as witches. Fundamental to the European conception of the danger witchcraft posed to the community was *maleficium*, the use of diabolical power to injure or kill. English witches were said to inflict horrendous physical and mental torments on their victims.[26] But while Puritan writers throughout the seventeenth century echoed Williams's facile equation of Indian shamanism with English witchcraft, their specific descriptions of Algonquian sorcery in the early years of contact did not support that comparison, as they usually portrayed the shaman as a healer. The shaman's offense, in their eyes, was that he healed with the devil's aid.

In fact, the shaman's power did not come from an evil spirit but was gained through association with the spirit world. That power, being morally neutral, could potentially be abused by the mercenary and the vicious. Even so, the early New England Puritan sources contain no reports comparable to the accounts of a pervasive fear of shamanic malevolence found in some descriptions of the Iroquois and of other Native American cultures. The claim of a mid-seventeenth-century Puritan missionary, echoed by a recent historian, that Algonquian converts to Christianity sought protection from the malevolence of Indian witches is not supported in either the earlier source materials or the later legal records.[27] Increase Mather's assertion, during the Salem witchcraft hysteria of 1692, that Indian medicine men "in their heathenism, by the hands of Evil angels, murdered their neighbors," represents a belated and rather unsuccessful effort to revise the Puritans' own understanding of shamanic practice, which prior to that time was almost always defined as the use of diabolical power in healing. There was even less foundation to

Cotton Mather's assertion in 1699 that the Salem witchcraft outbreak had "some of its Original among the Indians."[28] Both statements, however, tell us much about underlying assumptions regarding Indian character.

The fundamental error in Puritan accounts of Algonquian religious practice lies in the assumption that the shaman's power, whether employed for good or ill, originated in a pact with the devil. Shamanic power was not inherently evil. The other-than-human beings from whom it originally emanated could not be described accurately as satanic. The native New Englanders, as Roger Williams noted, believed in a variety of gods (at least thirty-seven) and also attributed power to the sun, the moon, certain animals, and to a giant named Wetucks. Williams had great difficulty comprehending and classifying those beings.[29] Contrary to English expectation, the Indians did not conceive of supernatural beings in rigidly dualistic terms. The spirits with whom they shared the world were seldom regarded as purely good or purely evil. Winslow had noted to his bewilderment that even their creator-God Kietan was sometimes capable of malevolent behavior. Only by stretching the analogy and disregarding details can any of the Algonquian deities be equated with the Christian devil.

Seventeenth-century English Puritans, as David Hall has noted, possessed an "understanding of the world [that] was magical in presuming that the forces flowing through it were not bounded by ordinary rules of cause and effect."[30] Superficially, Christian and Algonquian religious beliefs appear to reflect some common assumptions. As one authority notes, "both groups" affirmed that "supernatural power affects everyday experience. Regardless of whether blessings or hardships came their way, individuals in both religions attributed their daily lot to the will of divine beings who directed events according to higher purposes."[31] But this commonality is misleading, because Indian spirituality was not grounded in belief in either the divine providence of an all-powerful creator or the presence in the world of a malevolent fallen angel. This is not to deny that the Indians of New England, as elsewhere, told tales about demons. The point is that their religious practices, contrary to Puritan misperceptions, were not based on the invocation of evil forces. As Hultkrantz observes, "for the Indian the notion of the evil spirit pertains to the world of mythology and not that of practical religion." Native Americans believed that they were able to tap into a sacred power essential to their well-being through the performance of rituals given to them by potent other-than-human beings. As Dowd has noted, "ceremonies, old and new, gave Indian villages access to spirit forces that influenced the growth of crops, while others affected the abundance of game. The people's survival depended on the cooperation of spirit forces that inhabited other quarters of the universe. Their most essential relations with other orders—with plants, animals and the other sex—necessitated appeals to sacred power through proper ritual. Disregard for ritual meant . . . earthly disaster and punishment."[32] Despite the importance of ritual, the shamanic practice at the heart of New England Algonquian religious life remained highly individualistic, emphasizing "personal choice and personal innovations" unfettered by either inherited doctrine or "uniform liturgical rules."[33]

Despite his aversion to Native American religious practices, Roger Williams, unlike most other Puritan commentators, found much to commend in Indian character. Writing from exile among the Narragansetts, Williams praised their "kindnesses. . . . It is a strange truth that a man shall generally finde more free entertainment and refreshing amongst these *Barbarians,* than amongst thousands that call themselves *Christians.* . . . I have knowne them leave their House and Mat to lodge a Friend or stranger / when Jewes and Christians oft have sent Christ Jesus to the Manger. . . . There are no beggars amongst them, nor fatherlesse children unprovided for." Native Americans, Williams reported, were not only kindly and generous but "in quick apprehensions and accurate judgements (to say no more) the most high and soveraign God and Creator, hath not made them inferiour to *Europeans.* . . . Boast not proud *English,* of thy birth & blood / Thy brother *Indian* is of birth as good." Through God's grace, Williams warned, some Englishmen might yet "see, Heaven ope to *Indians* wild, but shut to thee."[34]

Williams, as we have noted, was unable to understand or appreciate the true nature of Indian religiosity. But he did realize that many of their beliefs and practices did not really fit the "devil worshiper" paradigm. He was particularly struck by the Indians' enlightened and humane moral code and by evidence of their belief in the punishment of the wicked in the afterlife. Attempting to unravel his Indian informants' rather confusing comments, Williams concluded that they believed that "good men and women" went after death to the southwest, where they lived in the house of the creator-God himself, but "Murtherers thieves and Lyers their Soules (say they) wander restlesse abroad." (Williams probably projected the Christian concept of the afterlife into his interpretation of Narragansett lore, as the idea of spending eternity in the presence of the Creator is not a characteristic Native American belief.) Modifying the usual equation of shamanic healing practices with devil worship, Williams reported that the shaman, as he "conjures out the sicknesse," appealed to vital forces within the individual, for "they conceive that there are many Gods or divine Powers within the body of a man: In his pulse, his heart, his Lungs, &c." [35]

Williams identified the fundamental concept underlying both Algonquian spirituality and its shamanic expressions, the concept of *manitou,* but failed to comprehend its nature. "There is a generall Custome amongst them," he wrote, "at the apprehension of any Excellency in Men, Women, Birds, Beasts, Fish, &c., to cry out *Manittoo,* that is, it is a God, and thus if they see one man excel others in Wisdome, Valour, strength, Activity, &c. they cry out Mannitoo: A God." He concluded that Indian use of the term *manitou* reflected their intuitive knowledge of the Christian God, the "source of all Excellencies." [36] But Williams's understanding of the term was faulty. Like other English commentators, he could not grasp Native American conceptions of the natural world and thus did not realize that their religious conceptions made no sharp separation between the natural and the supernatural. The dualistic assumptions so basic to the Christian tradition posed a serious obstacle to understanding the Indian world view. The anthropologist Ruth Benedict has explained *manitou* as a property emanating from the "existence of a wonderful power, a voltage with which the universe is believed to be charged." [37] Contrary to the assumptions of Williams and other Puritan observers, the Indians of New England did not conceive of that power as an emanation coming to them directly from either the Creator or the devil. It was rather a force possessed by many other-than-human beings: gods, spirits, some animals. Humans might acquire manitou. Shamans and witches owed their potency to their possession of it. But manitou might also inhere in objects that Europeans regarded as inanimate: certain trees or stones, for example. Items of human manufacture, believed to have originally been the gift of other-than-human beings (wampum, for example), might also possess manitou and thus convey power. [38]

Williams's identification of manitou with "excellencies" flowing from the goodness of God and the more commonplace Puritan identification of shamanic power as satanic thus both missed the mark. Manitou was morally neutral and could be used for good or evil. In one sense of the term, it was not supernatural at all, for in the Algonquian world view there was no clear dividing line between the immanent and the transcendent. However, the power manitou connoted was exceptional and inspired that sense of awe and fear associated with European concepts of the holy. The analogy should not be carried too far, of course, as *manitou* permeated the material world and can probably best be regarded as a tangible force subject to human manipulation.[39]

Puritan piety and Algonquian spirituality both affirmed the power of the holy but conceived of that power in very dissimilar ways. Although in a very general sense the Indian belief in taboos, whose observance was intended to avoid offending potent spirits or disrupting certain intricately balanced forces, might be roughly equated to the Christian fear of the divine retribution visited upon sinners, the concepts of divine providence and original sin were completely alien to the Indian sense of man's relationship to creation. The ideas of infant damnation and eternal punishment of the unregenerate were incomprehensible to Algonquians. The Puritan conviction that divine revelation was now to be found only in holy books and that those who claimed ongoing communication with the spirit world were in league with evil forces violated the fundamental premises underlying Algonquian religious practice. For the Native American, the dreams and the vision quests of individuals, as well as the rituals of the community, were designed to establish an immediate, tangible, and sustaining dialogue with the spirit world. The Puritan conversion experience, requiring both intellectual assent to a body of theological doctrine and an emotional sense of personal worthlessness balanced by a conviction of divine election and redemption, had no counterpart in Native American religious practice.[40]

Even more alien was the Puritan division of the community itself into the Elect and the damned and their insistence that divine grace was accessible only to the few. Native American religiosity was community-oriented and holistic and did not distinguish between saints and sinners in this life, nor did it relegate the unregenerate to eternal torment in the hereafter. As Bowden notes, "Christianity threatened to destroy [the] aboriginal sense of community."[41] It is thus not surprising that, by the most generous estimates, no more than a quarter of the Indian population of southern New England in the seventeenth century made any effort to conform to the intellectual and social demands placed upon would-be Christian converts. In their promotional literature, the founders of the Puritan colonies had frequently expressed confidence that the good example of their Christian neighbors would inspire New England's savages to embrace the Puritan way. The Great Seal of the Massachusetts Bay Colony contained the figure of an Indian brave uttering the words, "Come over and help us." That optimism about Native American receptivity to Christian influence was unfounded. New England's native peoples were not at all eager to renounce their own cultural identity. The "praying villages" established after Puritan New England belatedly sent missionaries to the Indians were inhabited primarily by refugees from tribes fragmented and demoralized by war and disease. The missionary John Eliot recorded the testimony of several former shamans who explained that since the coming of the English they had lost their power to heal, had seen numerous friends and loved ones sicken and die, were often ill themselves, and therefore sought in Christ the protection of a stronger power.[42] But they were hardly typical. Throughout the seventeenth century, members of the larger, more powerful groups such as the Narragansetts and the Mohegans were highly resistant to the appeals of Puritan missionaries.[43]

Committed to a religious ideology that held that God's will decreed that man earn his bread by the sweat of his brow and that mandated the diligent exploitation of the earth's resources, the English who settled in New England in the early seventeenth century were unable to appreciate either the Indian economic system or the social values that system expressed. Living in a land of bountiful wildlife and abundant timber (the latter particularly striking in comparison with the deforestation of the British Isles), the Indians built modest wigwams in small villages utterly devoid of the trappings of wealth or power. They thus impressed the colonists as an unenterprising, indeed improvident, people. The Anglican trader Thomas Morton marveled at the natural endowments of New England but noted in puzzlement that the native New Englanders lived "like to our Beggars in England." Morton found the Indians' lack of concern for material wealth in some ways admirable, but most English observers were persuaded that Indian poverty was the result of a serious character flaw. Indians, wrote William Wood in 1634, were by nature highly intelligent, "having quick wits, understanding apprehensions, strong memories." Indian women "were very industrious." But Indian men, Wood claimed, "would rather starve than work."[44]

Puritan commentators pitied the Indian "squaw." Roger Williams observed that "it is almost incredible what burthens the poore women carry of Corne, of Fish, of Beanes, . . . of Mats, and a childe besides." Christopher Levitt declared: "Their women are their slaves, and do all the work; the men will do nothing but kill beasts, fish, etc." Francis Higginson agreed: "The men for the most part live idly, they doe nothing but hunt and fish: their wives set their corn and do all their other worke." William Wood declared disdainfully that Indian husbands used their wives "as porters to lug home their venison which their laziness exposes to the wolves till they impose it upon their wives shoulders." Not only did the women plant and tend the corn, but they were forced by their mates' irresponsibility to hide it away after harvest, "covering it from the inquisitive search of their gourmandizing husbands who would eat up both their allowed portion and reserved seed if they knew where to find it."[45]

The stereotype of the lazy Indian persisted. Daniel Gookin, the Bay Colony's superintendent of Indian affairs (a man generally considered sympathetic to the Indians), wrote of his charges in 1674 that "they are much addicted to idleness, especially the men, who are disposed to hunting, fishing, and . . . war . . . that little tillage or planting used among them, was principally done by the women. Also in their removals from place to place, which they are inclined to, for their fishing and hunting in the several seasons, the women carry the greatest burthen: they also prepare all the diet."[46]

As is often the case with stereotypes, those characterizations of gender roles in Indian society were not totally false, but they were based upon incomplete and misleading information. Women did indeed do most of the work required to tend, harvest, and store crops. But the characterization of the Indian male as an economic drone will not stand close scrutiny. Despite their reliance on horticulture for much of their food supply, fishing and hunting in the Algonquian societies of southern New England were not recreational activities (as English observers often imagined) but endeavors vital to social well-being. In the not-too-distant past they had provided the only significant sources of nutrients and were still an essential source of both protein and, through utilization of hide and bone, materials for clothing and implements.[47]

In assessing gender roles, it must be borne in mind that in the southern New England economy no use was made of domesticated animals. Hunting and fishing thus remained the only means of providing meat and hides. The persistent English description of those activities as play rather than work tells us much about their ethnocentricism but nothing about Algonquian economics. Moreover, the Puritan sources, read closely, reveal that the lazy-Indian stereotype failed to account for certain heavy tasks customarily performed by Indian males. The colonists recorded that they prepared the fields for cultivation by felling trees and removing stumps. They were solely responsible for the manufacture and maintenance of weapons and implements of wood and stone, and they assisted the women in the making of pottery. The men were also responsible for the construction of dugout canoes, some of which were large oceangoing vessels capable of transporting thirty or forty warriors.[48] The work assigned to Algonquian males as providers of animal protein was both demanding and dangerous. Hunters and fishermen were often absent from their home village for weeks on end and were often in danger of injury or death. Their work demanded "many hours of intense labor under hard conditions." It also required long periods of recuperation.[49]

Roger Williams's associations with the Narragansetts led him to a warm appreciation for their skill and perseverance as hunters and trappers. He noted also that they "take exceeding great paines in their fishing. . . . They lay their naked bodies many a cold night on the cold shoar about a fire of two or three sticks, and oft in the night search their Nets; and sometimes goe and stay longer in frozen water." Declining to join with those who regarded Indian hunters and fishermen as idle social parasites, Williams paid them this tribute: "There is a blessing upon endeavour, even to the wildest *Indians*. . . . The substance of the diligent (either in earthly or heavenly affaires) is precious."[50]

But most of the English colonists in New England nonetheless doubted that Indians were truly diligent. The problem was that Indians did not labor constantly. Accepting as divinely sanctioned the premise that the pursuit of individual wealth, if conducted within the framework of Puritan morality and communal values, was an essential element in a well-ordered commonwealth, English Puritans could not comprehend the social rationale underlying the Indians' apparent lack of interest in wealth. Teaching their own children that God had called them "unto a workhouse, not a playhouse," the Saints found the Indian reluctance to work longer hours than necessary for subsistence a sign not only of lack of enterprise but of lack of virtue as well.

As Neal Salisbury has explained, Algonquian society was held together by a different premise. Indian New England valued not individual wealth but rather social cohesion based upon reciprocity. Competitive economic behavior was scorned and greed considered antisocial. Reciprocity "was maintained through a complex sequence of rituals. These rituals were especially elaborate and critical in southern New England, where the system of family agriculture might otherwise have increased the potential for an unequal distribution of wealth within their group." As those ceremonies had no counterpart in the experience of European observers, their descriptions of them are vague and sometimes confusing. Roger Williams recorded that, among the Narragansetts, the host or hostess of the Nickommo festival presented to one of the guests substantial amounts of goods and wampum. At the harvest festival a dancer gave "money, coats, small breeches, knives," to the "poore" who begged for favors. Indian games and ceremonials "redistributed wealth and otherwise reinforced social cohesion." William Wood recorded that substantial goods changed hands in the course of those contests. Goal markers were often heavily laden with furs and wampum. But Wood, like other Puritan observers, assumed, disapprovingly, that the Indians were simply addicted to gambling and thus did not comprehend the social purpose of those exchanges.[51]

Dutch observers of the customs of the Indians of coastal Connecticut were no more perceptive than the English. They were baffled by a practice among the Pequots described by Nicholaes van Wassenaer as follows: "They have a hole in a hill in which they place a kettle full of all sorts of articles that they either have by them, or can procure, as part of their treasures. Then a snake comes in, then they all depart, and the *Manittou*, that is, the Devil, comes in the night and takes the kettle away, according to the statement of the *Koutsinacka*, or devil hunter, who presides over the ceremony." Van Waessenaer believed he had found evidence of Pequot satanism, but it is more likely that he was describing a redistribution ceremony. A Dutch chronicler of Adriaen Block's voyage up the

Connecticut River in 1614 shed some light on Indian economic attitudes when he reported that, even though the region was rich in fur-bearing animals, its inhabitants took only a few pelts each year. French explorers of the southern Atlantic coast of New England and Cape Cod had made the same discovery. Champlain remarked that "they make no provision of furs except to Clothe themselves."[52] The Indian economy in New England, prior to contact with Europeans, served the subsistence needs of the community and was not directed toward the accumulation of individual wealth.

Despite their inability to comprehend, let alone appreciate, Indian economic values, early European observers did occasionally express approval of some of their accomplishments. In 1524 the first European report from Narragansett Bay praised the natives' skill in the use of stone, clay, wood, and bark, out of which they crafted implements that were not only exceedingly functional but also aesthetically pleasing. Giovanni da Verrazzano wrote that "their arrows are wrought with great beauty," with heads made of "emery, jasper, hard marble." He added that they "construct their boats of single logs, hollowed out with admirable skill, and sufficiently commodious to contain ten or twelve persons; their oars are short, and broad at the end and are managed by rowing by force of the arms alone, with perfect security, and as nimbly as they chose." They were also superb farmers, painstaking in their cultivation of their fields. Verrazzano declared Narragansett corn the best in North America.[53]

The Pilgrims, landing at Cape Cod short of supplies in the late fall of 1620, also had good reason to appreciate the Indians' horticulture. As their chronicler recounted, a shore party, digging in a mound of freshly turned sand, found near the surface a basket full of Indian corn of varied colors. "It held about three or foure Bushels, which was as much as two of us could lift up from the ground, and was very handsomely and cunningly made." After carrying off the corn in order to restock their own depleted larders, the Pilgrim foragers found other underground storehouses containing beans and acorns as well.[54]

Shortly thereafter, settled in Plymouth, the colonists endured a bleak winter in which half of their company perished from hunger or disease. In the spring, however, the Pilgrims learned from their newfound Indian friend and informant Squanto how to plant corn, as the chronicler recalled, "according to the manner of the Indians" and that summer enjoyed bountiful harvests. The Indian farmers of southern New England produced a food surplus for trade with nonhorticultural Indian groups to the north and, in the initial years of contact with English colonists, provided food to the newcomers as well.[55] The banquet table at that first Thanksgiving at Plymouth so often celebrated in American popular history was well stocked with Indian commodities.

The Indian economy in southern New England was based not only on the utilization of the crops grown near their villages but also on maintenance of fishing camps and game reserves. The parklike appearance of the southern New England forests so often remarked upon by European observers was the result of systematic clearing out of underbrush and periodic burning of groundcover that, as William Cronon has noted, "not merely attracted game but helped create much larger populations of it. Indian burning promoted the increase of exactly those species whose abundance so impressed English colonists: elk, deer, beaver, hare, porcupine, turkey, quail, ruffed grouse." Their management of game reserves was thus a form of husbandry.[56]

The Puritans, however, refused to recognize the legitimacy of Indian claims to hunting grounds or to uncultivated land adjacent to beaches, lakes, and streams. Invoking the principle of *vacuum domicilium*, John Winthrop, John Cotton, and other colonial leaders declared that New World lands not actually under cultivation did not rightfully belong to anyone and could, therefore, be occupied by the Puritans under the authority of their royal patent. Winthrop, invoking the authority of the Old Testament, asked rhetorically, "Why may not Christians have liberty to go and dwell among them in their wastelands and woods (leaving them such places as they have manured for their corn) as lawfully as Abraham did among the Sodomites?" Adding a secular, legalistic argument in support of the assertion implicit in that question, Winthrop declared that the "natural right" of hunter-gatherers to use of the land was immediately superseded whenever more advanced peoples asserted their "civil right" to improve the land for the raising of crops and the domestication of livestock.[57] A tract published in 1630 to promote the settlement of the Massachusetts Bay Colony declared that "the Indians are not able to make use of one fourth part of the Land, neither have they any settled places, as Townes to dwell in . . . but change their habitation from place to place."[58] In a similar vein Robert Cushman of Plymouth maintained that since the natives of the region were "not industrious, neither have art, science, skill or faculty to use either the commodities of it" but rather allowed the land to be "marred by want of manuring, gathering, ordering, etc.," the English had a superior claim to ownership. The Reverend John Cotton agreed, declaring that "hee that taketh possession of the [land] and bestoweth culture and husbandry upon it, his Right it is."[59]

The Puritan assertion that the Indians of New England made no productive use of the land seems paradoxical—some would say meretricious—in the light of their own testimony about Indian horticulture. But the differences between Algonquian slash-and-burn methods of cultivation and the more intensive (and environmentally disruptive) English agriculture combined with the Indians' lack of domesticated animals and continued reliance on hunting to justify a distorted image of native savagery and sloth. Roger Williams provoked the wrath of the Puritan authorities by arguing that, since the Indians "hunted all the countrey over, and for the expedition of their hunting voyages . . . burnt up all the underwoods in the countrey," they had lawful title to all of New England. The forests of the New World could best be compared, Williams concluded, to the "great Parkes" of the "Noble men" and to the king's "great Forrests in England. . . . No man might lawfully invade their propriety." His unorthodox attitude toward Indian land rights was a factor in Williams's subsequent banishment from the Massachusetts Bay Colony. Of Williams's argument, John Cotton declared: "We did not conceive that it is a just Title to so vast a Continent, to make no other improvement of millions of Acres on it, but onely to burn it up for past time."[60]

Although forced to proceed cautiously in the early years of settlement, out of fear of provoking a pan-Indian uprising, the Puritans by the 1640s came to deny not only Indian ownership of uncultivated lands but also Indian sovereignty in their own villages. In 1648 the trader William Pynchon, resisting attempts by the Massachusetts Bay Colony's magistrates to bring to trial some Indians suspected of murdering other Indians, denied that the English could claim any legal jurisdiction over Native Americans "until they have fully subjected themselves to your government . . . and until you have bought their land; until this be done, they must be esteemed a free people." As Alden Vaughan has noted,

"Pynchon's reasoning, so ripe with possibilities for more peaceful and equitable Anglo-Indian relations, fell on deaf ears."[61]

English observers in the early seventeenth century were puzzled by the Native American political system. They were soon forced to recognize that their earlier preconceptions about Indian lawlessness and anarchy were mistaken. Noting that their Indian neighbors and trading partners acknowledged certain hereditary claims to sachemships, and that the more prominent sachems were often paid tribute, the English at first concluded that those sachems were "kings" and that the Indians were therefore monarchists operating in a feudal political structure. Thomas Lechford claimed that the Indian kings and their "petie Lords," the "sagamores," exercised "an absolute tyrannie" over their subjects. But more perceptive observers knew that this was not the case. Roger Williams observed that, though the sachems might seem to "have an absolute Monarchie over the people," they actually did not have the power to undertake anything "unto which the people are adverse." In New England, as throughout most of North America, Native American leaders governed by building consensus. Daniel Gookin noted some years later that Indian "kings" had little ability to coerce, as their followers, if upset by "harsh dealing," could easily "go and live under other sachems that can protect them." Thus, Gookin reported, the sachems' "principal endeavor" was to win and hold support by "acting obligingly and lovingly unto their people, lest they should desert them, and thereby [diminish] their strength, power and tribute."[62]

It is now understood that the native inhabitants of New England at the time of contact were organized into a large number of village-based kinship bands, each under the leadership of a "sachem" or "sagamore." In some areas, particularly along the coast, villages were loosely confederated in quasi-tribal organizations. Contact with Europeans accelerated that process. Some dominant sachemships such as the Pequots collected tribute from their weaker neighbors. Although the Puritans characterized the tributary relationship as that of defeated and oppressed peoples to a conqueror, receipt of tribute placed the dominant sachem under obligation to protect his tributaries from external enemies but, given the nonauthoritarian nature of Indian polity, did not seriously affect life within the subordinate villages.[63]

In New England, it appears that the office of sachem was semihereditary and patrilineal. On occasion, women (perhaps the daughters of sachems who died without direct male heirs) succeeded to sachemships. On occasion also, the rights of hereditary succession were not observed, leading to much confusion among scholars endeavoring to understand the Indian political system. The evidence suggests that personal qualities as well as the hereditary rights of candidates were factors in the selection, with less able direct heirs sometimes being displaced in favor of more capable relatives.[64]

Seventeenth-century English reports of Indian groups in New England contained a bewildering variety of tribal names. Most were not in fact tribes or even sachemships, for as Gordon Day has noted, early English settlers were prone to coin a new tribal designation for the inhabitants of "each river, village, or fish camp."[65] The proliferation of imaginary Indian tribes was most pronounced in the Connecticut River valley, a region crucial to our analysis of the origins of the Pequot War. A nineteenth-century historian claimed that "ten distinct tribes" lived within the confines of the town of Windsor alone![66] Early twentieth-century ethnologists discarded most of those so-called tribes but generally listed eight tribal entities on or near the lower west bank of the Connecticut River. Following a convention established by the seventeenth-century Puritan historian William Hubbard, they were referred to as the "River Indians." It is now recognized that those groups can better be understood as bands loosely related to one another through intermarriage and allied politically in loose and transitory alliances among village sachems. The well-articulated and continuous leadership hierarchies characteristic of true tribes were not present in the Connecticut River valley in the early seventeenth century.[67]

We have little reliable information on the interrelationships among the River Indian bands. Dutch sources, as we will note later, claimed that they were led in the early 1620s by a "grand sachem" named Sequin. Secondary accounts of the Connecticut Indians written between the eighteenth and the mid-twentieth centuries must be used very cautiously. New England Indian lore contains, as one scholar has warned, "an inseparable mixture of fact and romantic fiction."[68] A particularly blatant example of romantic fiction is a once very popular characterization of the sachem Wagincut and his Podunk "tribe" as valiant freedom fighters opposing the brutal and rapacious Pequots. Mathias Spiess in 1935 wrote that "there is still an old saying among older folk living around East Hartford and South Windsor, when alluding to brave warriors, 'they fought like a Podunk, to the last man,' for it is said that in one battle the Podunks were outnumbered by their enemy and all had been killed but one. He kept up the fight until he was slain."[69]

That tale cannot be traced to any contemporary source and does not ring true, for the Puritan soldiers who observed Indians in battle during the Pequot War testified that they were not particularly fanatical or bloodthirsty as warriors and were hardly prone to "fight to the last man." Contrary to the stereotype that portrays primitive peoples living in a state of constant warfare, with "every man against every other man" (as Thomas Hobbes put it in 1651), the actual level of violence in most of pre-Columbian America was quite low. Describing New England's Indians, Roger Williams reported that "their warres are far less bloudy, and devouring, then the cruell Warres of Europe." The Indian mode of battle, as Williams described it, appeared to be stylized and ritualistic, "with leaping and dancing, that seldome an arrow hits." When blood was drawn, the warriors more often than not withdrew to tend the wounded. Major battles fought on a "pitcht field," Williams reported, would "seldome" result "in twenty slain." Encounters in wooded areas were even less lethal, as "every Tree is a Bucklar." One recent authority notes that "contact . . . invariably transformed war patterns, very frequently intensified war, and not uncommonly generated war among groups who previously had lived in peace. Many, perhaps most, recorded wars can be directly attributed to the circumstances of western contact." As we shall see, that observation is highly relevant to our examination of the origins of the Pequot War.[70]

It is worth noting in connection with the later vilification of the Pequot sachem Sassacus and his followers that, prior to the Pequot War, Puritan sources portray Wagincut the Podunk sachem who visited Salem and Boston in 1631 in a quest for aid against the Pequots not as a hero or victim but as a manipulative and power-hungry opportunist.[71] Early Puritan sources, by contrast, contain a surprisingly positive description of the character and habits of the Pequots. An English visitor to the Bay Colony in the early 1630s, summarizing Puritan impressions of the Indians of the Northeast, described the Mohawks and the Abenakis as potential threats to the English colonies and characterized the Narragansetts as grasping and mercenary but declared that the Pequots were courteous, affable, and trustworthy, "just and equal in their dealings, not treacherous either to their countrymen or English." [72]

The English assessment of Pequot character changed drastically after the Pequots refused to apprehend and surrender to Puritan justice Indians responsible for the death of Captain John Stone, a disreputable trader killed on the Connecticut River in 1633. The Reverend Philip Vincent, in his account of the Pequot War published in London in 1638, contrasted the "very loving and friendly" behavior of the Indians of the Boston-Plymouth area with the "barbarous and cruel" nature of the Pequots, a "warlike people which have been terrible to their neighbors, and troublesome to the English." Other Puritan writers followed Vincent's lead. The vilification of the Pequots reached its height some forty years after the war, when the Reverend William Hubbard declared that they exceeded all other New England Indians in ferocity. In explanation, Hubbard claimed that the Pequots were not natives of the region but had invaded Connecticut "from the interior of the continent" shortly before the founding of the Pilgrim colony at Plymouth in 1620. Driving away the peaceful local inhabitants, the Pequots, he declared, "by force seized upon one of the goodliest places near the sea, and became a Terror to all their Neighbors." [73]

Despite the lack of corroboration for Hubbard's belated claim in the primary source materials from the 1630s, historians, until quite recently, generally accepted his story and often used the Pequot "invasion" to support the argument that the Pequot War was a defensive war against a vicious aggressor who threatened Indians and Englishmen. Most authorities have held that the Pequots were offshoots of the Mahicans, an Algonquian group located in the upper Hudson valley of New York. Pressure from the Iroquois in the late sixteenth century presumably had forced a number of Mahicans to abandon their homeland and migrate to the southeast, where they displaced some of the indigenous inhabitants of coastal Connecticut. [74]

Since most of the archaeological, linguistic, and documentary evidence now available demonstrates that the Pequots did not invade New England on the eve of English settlement but instead were indigenous to the region, an explanation of the extraordinary persistence of the Pequot invasion myth is in order. Quite simply, historians throughout the nine-

teenth and most of the twentieth centuries were misled by some circum-
stantial evidence that appeared to corroborate Hubbard's tale. Sources
from the 1630s call the band led by the dissident sachem Uncas the
"Mohegan." The resemblance of "Mohegan" to "Mahican" suggested a
return to an original tribal designation. Equally suggestive was the presence of the same term on a map of New England prepared in Holland
after Adriaen Block's exploratory voyage up the Connecticut River. Historians drew the wrong conclusions from those references. Since "Mohi-
can" and "Mohegan" mean nothing more than "people of the river" in
the Algonquian dialects of the region, common use of the term does
not really prove a common origin. But some Pequot-Mohegan folklore
recorded early in the twentieth century by Frank Speck, professor of
anthropology at the University of Pennsylvania, also appeared to confirm Hubbard's claim. Fidelia Fielding, the last native speaker of the
Pequot-Mohegan language, told Speck that her forebears had once lived
in New York. He noted that "knowledge of the Mohawks and the ancient
fear in which the latter were held, is still a live resentment in the Mohegan village." Another elderly Mohegan woman related that, "when a
child of 7 years, my great-great aunt used to take my sister, brother,
cousin, and myself on the hill near where the church now stands, point
to the northwest, and tell us that was the way her folks came, and that we
must never forget it." A third informant recalled that his great-
grandfather had told a story of a migration across a great desert and a
great body of fresh water, and of conflicts with the Mohawk which finally
drove them out of New York. The folk memories Speck recorded persist.
To this day, Mohegan Indians living in Uncasville, Connecticut, believe
that they are descendants of the New York Mahicans.[75]

That testimony notwithstanding, it is now apparent that the tale of a
Pequot invasion of Connecticut on the eve of the founding of Plymouth
was a fabrication intended to give added force to the demonic characterization of the Pequots. The study of comparative New England Algonquian linguistics led Speck to conclude that the stories told to him by his
Mohegan informants could not possibly have had their origin in an
early-seventeenth-century flight from the Hudson valley but were instead probably reflections of an earlier, more widespread Algonquian
migration myth, of which the Delawares' Walum Olum was another
expression. (More recently, however, scholars have questioned the authenticity of the Walum Olum.) Memories of conflicts with Mohawk

intruders into western New England in the historic period combined with older migration stories to create an erroneous folk account of Pequot-Mohegan origins. The crucial point is that scientific comparison of the surviving remnants of the Mohegan dialect in New York and Mohegan-Pequot in Connecticut revealed beyond any reasonable doubt that the two dialects were "not closely related." Speck concluded, from his comparison of Pequot-Mohegan with a number of other Algonquian dialects in New England and elsewhere, that the linguistic evidence indicated that the Pequots were indigenous to the region. Recent linguistic scholarship has confirmed that conclusion. Ives Goddard's comprehensive analysis of phonological innovations in eastern Algonquian languages discloses greater similarity between the speech of the Pequots and the dialects spoken by the Pequots' southern New England neighbors than between Pequot and any Algonquian language spoken outside New England.[76]

The available archaeological data also suggest that the Pequots were not newcomers to southern New England. Ceramic remains in the region are scarce, due to the climate, the high acid content of the soil, and the destruction of sites as a result of postcontact construction.[77] But the comparison of contact-period Pequot-Mohegan potsherds with Mahican ceramics from New York disclosed that Mahican pottery "cannot be ancestral" to Pequot ware. Peculiarities in the ceramic remains attributed to the Pequot-Mohegans are now regarded as the result of postcontact innovations common in the Northeast, not as evidence of an extraregional origin.[78] Ethnohistorical evidence also fails to support the invasion story. In a recent survey of the cultural traits attributed to the various New England groups by seventeenth-century European observers, Dean R. Snow has concluded that the Pequots did not differ from their neighbors in any significant way.[79] Finally, some documentary records of a mid-seventeenth-century legal controversy over land claims indicate that Indian witnesses, regardless of group affiliation or attitude toward the claims, agreed that the Pequots had lived on the Thames River "long before the Pequots were conquered by the English" and had therefore been "immemorably of and entitled to" land in Connecticut. The Mohegan leader Uncas, a descendant of Pequot sachems, dictated a statement in 1679 that traced his genealogical descent through four generations. He claimed that a number of his Pequot ancestors had married into prominent Narragansett and Niantic families. If Uncas's recollection of his ancestry was at all accurate, his Pequot forebears must have lived in the region on reasonably congenial terms with their neighbors for at least a century and a quarter prior to their earliest encounters with the Dutch and the English.[80]

At the time of their first contact with Europeans, the Pequots occupied the coastal area between the Niantic River in Connecticut and the Wecapaug River in western Rhode Island. According to the most reliable modern estimates, in the early 1630s they numbered around 16,000. Their territory was the most densely inhabited in New England. The great epidemic of 1616–19, which killed around 90 percent of the Native American inhabitants of the eastern coast of New England, did not reach either the Pequots or their Niantic and Narragansett neighbors. The smallpox epidemic of 1633, however, did not spare any of the Indians of the region. Pequots suffered a mortality rate estimated at around 80 percent and at the outbreak of the Pequot War in 1636 probably numbered only about 3,000.[81]

Contemporary English reports on the Pequots indicated that they possessed two heavily fortified hilltop villages, at Weinshauks (seat of the grand sachem Sassacus) and Mystic (residence of two of their "principal" sachems). These forts, some believe, may have been constructed in response to difficulties with Europeans, for a Dutch report in 1614 enumerating Indian settlements in the area makes no mention of hilltop forts in Pequot country. In addition to Weinshauks and Mystic, there were an undetermined number of smaller villages, each containing about thirty wigwams, "mostly located along estuaries and marshes." There are also reports of smaller settlements containing only a few residences. Each village cultivated fields of approximately 200 acres.[82]

Reports from Indian informants indicate that there were some twenty-six Pequot sachems but that their power and influence varied. William A. Starna, reviewing what is known about their functions, concludes that Pequot sachems, in common with other Indian leaders in the region, operated "within a sociopolitically reciprocal structure." The Pequot sachem possessed little formal power but maintained his influence "through his own persuasive powers" and through ritual gift giving, which functioned to "fulfill social obligations and gain prestige in the process." The feudal and monarchial models that early English observers attempted to apply to Pequot society were, as Starna notes, "misleading." Pequot society operated on "consensus" and maintained "a village oriented consensual government."[83] The claim, first advanced by Puritan writers and often repeated by scholars, that Pequot culture differed from other Algonquian groups finds no support in the ethnohistorical evidence available to us.

As we have seen, the records of early contact tell us that the English in New England regarded their Indian neighbors as a degenerate and lazy people who worshiped and served the devil. Puritan commentators reporting evidence that contradicted their preconceived images of Indians as savages were usually unable to comprehend the meaning of their disclosure and often explained it away by claiming that God had intervened to curtail their savage behavior. But what of the Indian side of the story? How did they perceive the intruders? The impressions of Englishmen formed by the native New Englanders in the early years of contact are difficult to reconstruct, but the sparse evidence available suggests that the Indians at first saw Europeans as men possessing fearfully powerful manitou. Wood related a story told by an Indian informant who reported that "they took the first ship they saw for a walking island, the mast to be a tree, the sail white clouds, and the discharge of ordnance for lightening and thunder, which did much trouble them, but this thunder being over and this moving island steadied by an anchor, they manned out their canoes to go and find strawberries there." But the ship then fired a broadside in salute, and the Indians in terror retreated to the shore, "not daring to approach till they were sent for."[84]

Closer acquaintance allayed some fears but not others. The European presence remained troubling. About twenty years after the founding of Plymouth, an Indian convert to Christianity recalled a dream he believed he had experienced during the plague that devastated Indian New England a few years prior to the appearance of the Pilgrims. As Thomas Shepard recorded the Indian's testimony, "he did think he saw a great many men come to these parts in cloths, just as the English are now apparelled, and among them, there arose up a man all in black, with a thing in his hand which he sees now was all one English mans book: this black man he said stood upon a higher place then all the rest, and on the one side of him were the English, on the other side a great number of Indians: the man told all the Indians that God was *moosquantum* or angry with them, and that he would kill them for their sinnes." In his dream, the Indian narrator was then assured that he and his family would be spared, apparently because they were predestined to embrace Christianity.[85] Shepard rejoiced at the man's acknowledgment of Indian sin and depravity. But the image of a figure clad in black holding up a book and proclaiming God's punishment of Indians tells us much about postcontact Indian perceptions of their Puritan neighbors. No less cogent is a more mundane observation by Roger Williams, who wrote of his conversations with his Narragansett trading partners in Rhode Island:

> *Oft have I heard these Indians say,*
> *These English will deceive us*
> *Of all that's ours, our land and lives.*
> *In th'end they will bereave us.*
> *So say they, whatever they buy,*
> *(Though small) which shewes they're shie*
> *Of strangers, fearefeull to be catcht*
> *By fraud, deceipt, or lie.*[86]

After a meticulous study of Algonquian foklore, William S. Simmons has concluded that "the Indians of southern New England understood and remembered the unprecedented events of colonial contact by means of indigenous symbolic images. Manitos, floating islands, flying and underwater ships, giant birds, thunder and lightning, sounds of music in the air, a strange white whale, dreams, premonitions and warnings, all give us a feeling for how the Indian apprehended this portentous moment in history."[87] The symbols they passed down in the folklore of first contact were, for the most part, sinister. The Gay Head Indians, for example, made use of the image of a white animal, which carried for them the connotation of misfortune. Gladys Tantequideon recorded their prophecy of the white man's coming: "Mitark, the last hereditary chief, called the people together on Indian Hill at sunset and told them that he was going to die. And while he was talking a white whale arose from the water off Witch Pond." Mitark then explained that the white whale was the sign of the coming of a new people, whose bodies would also be white. He warned, "don't let them have all the land because if you do the Indians will disappear. Then he died and shortly after the white people appeared."[88] Mitark's admonition is probably apocryphal. But, given the events soon to unfold, it is tempting to believe that white whales and other strange manifestations did give warning of things to come.

On New England's Atlantic coast, the English settlements established by Puritans and others were dependent in their early years upon Indian goodwill and Indian trade. It was a dependency that the English from the outset found troublesome and problematic. The Plymouth Colony, founded in 1620 by members of a radical English Separatist congregation previously in exile in Holland, owed its survival to the goodwill of Massasoit and his Pokanoket band. But the assistance and support the Pilgrims received from their Indian neighbors, though often celebrated in later histories, had little effect on their belief that Indians were basically treacherous. To cite but one example of English distrust, the Plymouth leaders insisted that Massasoit's people leave their weapons behind when visiting English settlements and that they not visit unannounced. The Pilgrims, however, always remained fully armed in the presence of Indians. Edward Winslow related that one sachem, skeptical of English intentions, asked, if the newcomers did indeed bear Indians the great love they professed, "how cometh it to pass that when we come . . . you stand upon your guard, with the mouths of your pieces presented to us?" Told such military displays were a sign of respect, the sachem declared that "he liked not such salutations."[89]

Plymouth took to heart Captain John Smith's advice about the necessity of intimidating "savages." In 1623, after hearing rumors that Massachusett tribesmen living near a rival English trading colony at Wessagussett were organizing an anti-English uprising, Miles Standish and a small party of armed men killed eight suspects, decapitated their leader, the sachem Wituwamet, and stuck his head on a post on top of the Plymouth blockhouse as a "warning and terror" to other Indians. The Wessagussett traders, deemed incompetent to deal properly with the Massachusett because "they feared not the Indians, but suffered them to lodge with them," were forced to disband. They were offered sanctuary, which most declined, at Plymouth.[90]

The Anglican trader Thomas Morton reported that the Indians were indeed impressed by Standish's ruthlessness and thereafter called the English "Wotowequenage, which in their language signifies stabbers or Cutthroats." Plymouth's willingness to use extreme measures to guarantee its security against the dangers believed to be lurking in the wilderness led also to the arrest and exile of Morton, who was accused of furnishing guns and powder to Indian men and of fornicating with their women. Governor Bradford complained that Morton and his followers at Merrymount "set up a maypole, inviting the Indian women for their consorts, drinking and dancing about it like so many fairies."[91] Plymouth's leaders were offended by both the Wessagussett men, who had not been able to overawe the local Indians, and by Morton, "whose interracial cavorting threatened to fracture a cultural and moral barrier."[92] Wessagussett's weakness, as they saw it, threatened the physical security of Englishmen in New England, but Morton's behavior posed a spiritual danger to them as well. The fact that both were rivals in the Indian trade reinforced the conviction that neither could be tolerated.

The handful of English settlements established in the 1620s remained sparsely populated throughout the decade. Only with the founding of the Massachusetts Bay Colony by more prosperous nonseparating Congregationalist Puritans in 1630 did eastern New England witness a substantial influx of the people Morton's Indian friends called the "Wotowequenage . . . or Cutthroats." The founders of the Massachusetts Bay Colony had planted their towns and fields in a coastal region largely depopulated by the great plague of 1616–19. It has been estimated that the 3,000 English settlers who poured into the colony between 1630 and 1633 outnumbered the surviving Native Americans in the immediate vicinity by more than fifteen to one. By 1638 the English population exceeded 11,000. After the arrival of the Puritans, the local Indians suffered from periodic recurrences of mortality from diseases of European origin. In early March 1631 John Pond, a young resident of the Bay Colony, wrote to his father in England that "here are but few eingeines [Indians], and a great sort of them died this winter. It was thought it was of the plague." The local inhabitants were little threat to the English. They were impressed not only by the noise and destructiveness of English weaponry but also by the newcomers' immunity to the diseases that ravaged the Indians. Shortly after the founding of Plymouth, Squanto had warned a local sachem that the English "had hid the plague under ground . . . if he should give any offense to the English party, they would let out the plague to destroy the all." The sachem was thereby "kept . . . in great awe." The leaders of the Plymouth and Massachusetts Bay colonies made no such claim, explaining that God alone controlled the plague. But the objective of their policy, and Squanto's, was the same: to keep the local inhabitants "in great awe." The methods employed ranged from conducting military drills near Indian villages to the dispatching of armed men to disperse suspicious Indian gatherings. The Indians of the region proved to be quite "tractable." But as trading partners they were disappointing. John Pond's remark, in his letter to his father, that "whereas we did expect a great store of beaver, here is little or none to be had," is amply confirmed in the records of both colonies. Impelled to seek new sources of peltry and interested also in the acquisition of new lands for cultivation to the west, the English in New England would soon encounter native peoples more numerous and less tractable than the handful of demoralized plague survivors they had so easily intimidated during the early years of their venture.[93]

2

Wampum, Pelts, and Power

The arrival of Europeans in southern New England had a profound impact on Native American communities. Along the Atlantic seaboard the depopulation of scores of villages disrupted established kinship systems and impelled some of the survivors to seek English protection from their stronger and more aggressive neighbors in areas less affected by the plague.[1] The early epidemics stopped at the western shore of Narragansett Bay. The Narragansetts, Pequots, and their neighbors would not experience severe mortality from diseases of European origin until 1633. But as Dutch and English traders penetrated the region, the Indian inhabitants felt the effects of the European presence in other ways. For our purposes, the most important result of that commerce was an intensification of conflict among sachemdoms and an acceleration of political consolidation. The incorporation of New England's Algonquian peoples into Europe's world trade network changed relationships among villages as local sachems in their competition for access to European trade goods sought to extend their influence and assert control over their neighbors.[2] After the mid-1620s, the main contenders for dominance of trade in southern New England were the Pequots and the Narragansetts. The Anglo-Pequot War of 1636–37 in one sense can be regarded as an unexpected and inadvertent consequence of that rivalry, for it was their difficulties with the Dutch and the Narragansetts that impelled the Pequots to enter into a relationship with Boston that proved to be most unfortunate.

The story begins in 1622, when a somewhat disreputable Dutch trader named Jaques Elekes visited a Pequot village at the mouth of the Thames River of Connecticut. Though the terse entry in the sole chronicle that records his visit provides few details, it seems that Elekes was dissatisfied with the initial Pequot response to his blandishments, for he seized their principal sachem and declared that, unless the Pequots offered a substantial ransom, "his head would be cut off." For their sachem's freedom, the Pequots paid "forty fathoms" of a strange commodity, which the chronicler of this episode described as "small beads which they manufacture themselves and prize as jewells." To his delight, Elekes discovered that those "jewells" (which the English would later call "wampum") could be exchanged for furs with the Indians of the interior.[3]

Despite Elekes's brutality, the Pequots soon thereafter agreed to enter into a trading relationship with the Dutch. Pieter Barentsen, a more tactful negotiator said to be fluent in all the dialects of the Hudson valley and Long Island Sound, called regularly at the Pequot harbor.[4] Within a few years after their first contact with the Dutch, the Pequots emerged as the dominant Indian power in the region. By the end of the decade, the Dutch in New Netherland were shipping around 10,000 pelts a year to Holland.[5] A substantial portion of that fur trade was in the hands of the Pequots, who soon after Barentsen's visit took control of traffic on the Connecticut River. In 1626 a Dutch chronicler reported that Pequot war parties had defeated the Wangunk sachem Sequin, leader of a loose alliance of River Indian bands, after "three desperate pitched battles."[6] The Connecticut valley Indians thereafter paid annual tribute to the Pequot grand sachem and received in return a pledge of Pequot protection. By 1630 the Pequot tributary system extended throughout eastern Long Island as well. Although the motives underlying Pequot expansionism cannot be determined with any certainty, it is probably not coincidental that Pequot military action placed them in a superb position to dominate trade with Europeans who visited the region. Through their control of the lower Connecticut River, the Pequots had gained easy access to the fur trade developing in the interior. Wampum from their tributaries on eastern Long Island gave them the means to purchase both pelts and European trade goods in quantity.[7]

Wampum also played an essential role in the economy of New Netherland. The earliest Dutch fur-trading expeditions in the region date from 1611, two years after Henry Hudson's exploratory voyage up the river that now bears his name. In 1614 a group of Dutch merchants established a permanent trading post on Castle Island, a few miles south of the site of the future city of Albany. Ten years later, under the aegis of the newly chartered West India Company, Dutch settlers founded several agricultural villages, including the future capital and principal settlement on Manhattan Island. But the profits of the New Netherland venture fell short of expectation until Isaak de Rasieres, the company's commercial agent at New Amsterdam, reorganized the colony's languishing Indian trade by offering wampum to Indian suppliers of pelts. The company had previously sent its Indian traders iron and copper kettles. They proved to be a drug on the market. Indian fur suppliers refused to pay a premium for the more expensive copper vessels, which were thus not a profitable item. Indian demand for iron kettles in the regions adjacent to the Dutch settlements was soon exhausted. They were far too heavy and cumbersome to carry to the more distant tribes. Rasieres procured wampum in quantity from the Indians of Long Island Sound, paying them with duffels (a cheap, coarse cloth) and metal implements. The wampum was then used as currency in the fur trade with the upriver, inland areas of the Hudson and Connecticut River valleys.[8] Rasieres's strategy succeeded. Not only were the shell beads more easily transported than the iron and copper pots and other implements the Dutch had previously sold to their Indian clients, but the demand for Indian wampum was more reliable than the demand for European trade goods. Peter Stuyvesant later declared that, without wampum, the Dutch could not obtain pelts from the Indians. The Great Seal of the New Netherland colony displayed a beaver encircled by wampum.[9]

The Pequots' determination to maintain control over the exchange of wampum, pelts, and European trade goods in the Connecticut valley led to a series of conflicts that culminated in their defeat by the English in the Anglo-Pequot War of 1636–37. But before we can assess those episodes, we must look more closely at the shell beads Elekes described as "jewells." In the early contact period, New England Indian wampum consisted of small tubular-shaped shells drilled and strung as beads. White wampum was manufactured from the shells of two species of whelks, *Busycon carica* and *Busycon canaliculatum*. The more highly prized purple wampum was produced by excising a colored spot on the hard-shell clam *Mercenaria mercenaria*. The shellfish required for the fabrication of wampum could be found only in the waters south of Cape

Cod. The shores of eastern Long Island were of particular importance as
a source of the raw material of the wampum trade.[10]

Some anthropologists have argued that the manufacture of tubular
wampum was not possible prior to trade with Europeans, as "Indians
were not capable of drilling the finer tubular beads until they had acquired metal tools from the Europeans."[11] But we have both historical
and archaeological documentation of its precontact production and use.
In 1642 Roger Williams, who probably knew more about the New England Indian economy than any other contemporary English observer,
reported that "before ever they had *Awle Blades* from *Europe,* they made
shift to bore this their shell money with stone."[12] Williams's report has
been confirmed by archaeological evidence. Although not numerous,
tubular shell beads have been found in precontact sites in the Southeast
and Midwest. X-ray analysis has confirmed that stone, not metal, drills
were used in their fabrication. The assertions of some anthropologists
notwithstanding, the absence of tubular wampum in precontact sites in
the Northeast does not prove that it was not manufactured and used
there prior to European colonization, for "shell is readily affected by
weathering, and the leaching process which particularly affects the rock
of the eastern United States appears to have destroyed much of the
evidence of shell work" in precontact sites.[13]

The evidence, in European documentary sources, of the use of wampum in Algonquian culture at the time of first contact is unequivocal. At
Jamestown in 1608, Ralph Hamor noted that Powhatan's daughter had
been espoused to "a great *Werowance* for two buckets of Roanoke (a
small kinde of beads) made of oyster shells, which they use and pass one
to another, as we doe money."[14] For the Northeast, we have the testimony of Isaak de Rasieres, who reported that sachems levied fines,
payable in wampum, "for fighting and causing blood to flow." The Dutch
confirmed Hamor's account of the use of wampum as bridal gifts and
added that the man who possessed the greatest supply of "sewan" was
most frequently chosen as sachem.[15] These reports are highly suggestive
of wampum's central role in Native American life, but the equation of
the beads to European jewels or money did not accurately convey its true
nature. In Iroquoian and Algonquian belief, wampum was not merely an
ornament or a means of exchange. As Miller and Hamill explain, "in the
Woodland Indian mythic world, crystal, shell, and reflective metals were
obtained by real human-man beings through reciprocal exchange with

extremely powerful Other World Grandfathers, man-beings of horned or antlered serpent, panther, or dragon forms." The materials obtained from those spirit-beings "assured long life, physical well being and success, especially in the related activities of hunting, fishing, warfare, and courtship. Consequently, these substances were charged with great power."[16] The remarkable demand for wampum as a trade good reflected belief in its miraculous origin and in its continued potency. It is sometimes assumed that wampum owed its popularity to Europeans, who were willing to accept it in exchange for highly coveted European manufactured goods. In fact, the acceptability of wampum in the Indian trade reflected its very special place in traditional Indian culture. As noted earlier, both Dutch and English sources indicate that wampum attracted Indian clients otherwise uninterested in trade.

Under European influence, wampum was soon transformed into a form of currency, used by both English and Indians to pay for trade goods.[17] But in precontact Native American societies it was essentially a means of effecting vital social transactions. It served as the insignia of chiefs and commanded the services of shamans. Wampum consoled the bereaved and celebrated marriages. It was offered in compensation for crimes and could be used to end blood feuds. In diplomacy, wampum exchanges sealed treaties of peace and alliances of war. It also, as Captain Elekes discovered, ransomed captives. Dominant sachems received wampum tribute from subordinate sachems, whom they were then obligated to protect. Wampum thus permeated the most vital aspects of life in Indian New England.[18]

In the precontact period, wampum was scarce, its manufacture with stone implements being slow and laborious. The acquisition from Europeans of metal tools, however, made possible large-scale production. The Dutch purchased wampum in bulk from the Indians of Long Island Sound, shipped it to their trading post at Fort Orange on the Hudson River (near modern Albany), and used it to finance the fur trade with Indians "from as far away as the St. Lawrence, whose French traders had no access to the treasured beads." By 1628 the Narragansetts, the Pequots, and their tributary tribes on Narragansett Bay and Long Island Sound were devoting the winter months to the manufacture, on a large scale, of wampum for the Dutch trade. As wampum became more plentiful, its function within Indian society changed. European technology and trade transformed the beads "from one among many items of exchange to a 'currency' that flowed into the hands of prestigious and ordinary Indians alike." [19]

The small colony of English Separatist Puritans founded at Plymouth in 1620 depended upon Indian trade to obtain the furs needed to pay English creditors and secure vital supplies from overseas. In the early years, Plymouth's commerce with the Indians of the eastern Atlantic seaboard fell short of the colony's needs. Plymouth sent a trading party westward to the Narragansetts in 1623, but, as Governor William Bradford recounted, the venture failed because the Dutch traders in the region were able to supply the Indians with cloth and other highly desirable commodities while the Pilgrims could offer "only a few beads and knives which were not there much esteemed." The Narragansetts informed their Dutch trading partners of the English presence at Plymouth. In 1627 the secretary to Director General Peter Minuit of New Netherland dispatched a message to the Plymouth authorities suggesting that the two colonies enter into trade relations. The Dutch offered to supply the Pilgrims with goods shipped from Holland in exchange "either for beaver or other wares or merchandise that you should be pleased to deal for." In the event that the English had no need of Dutch imports, the traders at Manhattan would be more than willing to pay "ready money" for beaver pelts. Should the Plymouth settlers be interested in that offer, the Dutch would immediately send a trader "to deal with you at such place as you shall appoint." The messenger who carried the invitation to Plymouth was instructed "to stay three or four days for your answer." [20]

Governor Bradford responded promptly. In his reply, he graciously recalled that the Dutch had offered a haven to the Separatists in their years of exile from England, "for which we, and our children after us, are bound to be thankful to your nation, and shall never forget the same, but shall heartily desire your good and prosperity as our own forever." He expressed the hope that Plymouth and New Netherland would soon "have profitable commerce together." Though the English colonists were presently "fully supplied with all the necessaries," next year they might buy Dutch goods "if your rates be reasonable." Bradford asked for a price list. But he included in his letter to the director general a warning and an admonition. The Dutch, he declared, were poaching on English territory. The king of England was the rightful sovereign of all of North America, and his patentees had the right to eject intruders. For their part, the Plymouth settlers would leave the Dutch settlements on the Hudson unmolested, but they did ask that the Dutch cease trading with the Narragansett Indians and their neighbors who lived "(as it were) at our doors." He added that, if the Dutch traders stayed out of Narragansett Bay and the regions directly adjacent to the English settlements, then "we think no other English will go any way to trouble or hinder you." Director General Minuit's response to that suggestion was blunt: "as the English claim authority under the king of England, so we derive ours from the states of Holland, and will defend it."[21]

Later that year, Minuit sent his secretary and commercial agent, Isaak de Rasieres, on a mission to Plymouth. Rasieres, then thirty-one years old, was described by Bradford as "of fair and genteel behavior." At the time of his visit to Plymouth he was the second-most-powerful man in New Netherland. However, opposition from independent traders to his efforts to regulate and rationalize the Indian trade would force Rasieres's return to Holland at the end of the decade. Rasieres's strategy for enhancing the profits of the company's Indian trade in North America, described earlier, required secure access to the wampum-producing Indians of Long Island Sound and Narragansett Bay, as wampum was now the company's basic trade commodity in exchanges with fur suppliers. Rasieres feared English competition. Should the Plymouth traders tap into the rich wampum trade of the southwestern New England coast they would soon "discover the trade in furs" in the Connecticut valley. Once that happened, he warned, "it would be a great trouble for us to maintain [trade in Connecticut], for they already dare to threaten us that if we will not leave off dealing with that people [the Narragansetts and their neighbors], they will be obliged to use other means. If they do that now, while they are yet ignorant of how the case stands, what will they do when they get a notion of it?" Rasieres predicted that, once the English comprehended the wealth of the Connecticut trade, they would drive the Dutch out of the area.[22] His forebodings were prophetic. Dutch loss of access to the wampum resources of the sound in the years following English settlement of Connecticut and Long Island was a major factor in the economic decline of New Netherland.[23]

Rasieres's bark *Nassau* landed at a small English trading station at Aptucet on the north end of Buzzards Bay. Disembarking to the accompaniment of trumpets, Rasieres spotted "a house made of hewn oak planks." He soon learned that it was occupied by "two men, winter and summer, in order to maintain the trade and possession." He was alarmed to discover that the English had also built a shallop at Buzzards Bay that easily could be used to ply the waters of Long Island Sound and thereby gain access to the wampum trade. Aptucet was about twenty miles by land from Plymouth. Reluctant to sail around Cape Cod, whose waters he described as treacherous, the portly Rasieres dispatched a letter to Bradford complaining that he could not walk so far and asking that Plymouth arrange for his transportation. The governor obligingly sent a boat for Rasieres and his party.[24] Upon arriving at Plymouth, the Dutch agent made a careful and calculating assessment of the strength of the Pilgrim Colony. He was impressed by the colony's fortifications and reported that "they are constantly on their guard night and day." Given such vigilance, Rasieres concluded that the Plymouth Colony could not easily be dislodged.[25]

The Dutch visitor was also struck by the severity of the Puritans' moral discipline. "They have made," he wrote, "stringent laws upon the subject of fornication and adultery, which laws they maintain and enforce very strictly indeed, even among the tribes which live amongst them." Rasieres related that the Plymouth authorities were offended by the more relaxed attitude of the Dutch traders, who had no aversion to bedding Indian women and "live so barbarously in these respects, and without punishment." He concluded that there was much to be said for the English Puritan approach to Indian relations, as "the tribes in their neighborhood . . . are better conducted than ours." Assessing the economic resources of the Plymouth Colony, Rasieres reported that "their farms are not as good as ours, because they are more stoney, and consequently not as suitable for the plow." But the waters around Plymouth teemed with fish, and "there are also many birds, such as geese, herons, and cranes, and other small-legged birds, which are in great abundance there in the winter." On balance, Rasieres concluded, the Plymouth colonists "have much better sustenance than ourselves."[26]

Determined to forestall the establishment of English commercial ties with the Indians of Narragansett Bay and the sound, Rasieres decided to assist the Plymouth Colony in its hitherto inauspicious efforts to trade with Maine. He offered to supply wampum for use at the Plymouth trading post on the Kennebec River, where the English had previously tried to buy peltry with corn. The Plymouth traders, unfamiliar with wampum, were skeptical but out of curiosity bought fifty fathoms of the shell beads from Rasieres.[27]

William Bradford later attributed Plymouth's economic survival to Rasieres. The wampum supplied by the Dutch agent made it possible for the first time to extract a substantial profit from the Indian trade. Although Plymouth's Indian trading partners to the north at first regarded wampum as suitable for use only by "the sachems and some special people," and thus initially were not inclined to acquire it in bulk, within two years they "could scarce ever get enough."[28] Rasieres's hope that the English could be diverted or excluded from the wampum trade of Narragansett Bay and Long Island Sound proved naive. To the consternation of their Dutch competitors, English traders were soon buying their wampum directly from the Indians of southwestern New England and using the shell beads to buy furs in Maine.[29]

Anxiety over the activities of English traders in the region impelled the Dutch to take steps to secure their interests in western New England. No longer could they rely on itinerant traders to hold their Indian clients within the Dutch commercial orbit. In 1632 Hans Enchluys was dispatched to the mouth of the Connecticut River, where he purchased from the local Niantic Indians a small but strategically located patch of land which could serve as the site of a fortified trading post. Erecting the arms of the States General of the Netherlands on a post, Enchluys named that new piece of Holland Kievet's Hook in imitation of the cry of a bird often heard along the banks of the Connecticut.[30]

Kievet's Hook was left unoccupied. In 1633 Director General Wouter Van Twiller sent a larger force of men to Connecticut under the command of Jacob Van Curler. Their orders were to buy and fortify more land. Kievet's Hook, though well suited to command the entrance of the river, was too far downstream to serve as a fur-trading depot. Van Curler accordingly selected an expanse of riverfront, a mile in length, located on the west bank of the Connecticut some fifty miles upstream, within the city limits of present-day Hartford. On June 8 he gained title to that plot, which extended one-third of a mile inland, by giving the Pequot sachems who claimed control over the region a present consisting of forty-one feet of trading cloth, some children's toys, six axes, eighteen knives, and a sword blade.[31]

Van Curler also negotiated a commercial agreement with the Pequots concerning freedom of trade. The Pequots bound themselves to respect the peace and allow all Indians, regardless of tribal affiliation, access to the Dutch trading post. In response to a plea from Altarbaenhoet, a River Indian sachem, Van Curler persuaded the Pequots to allow Sequin, their former adversary in the struggle for control of the valley, to take sanctuary near the Dutch trading house. He also informed the Narragansetts of the overall provisions of the treaty with the Pequots. Believing that he had thus taken appropriate steps to placate all interested parties, Van Curler proceeded to erect a trading fort, which he named the House of Good Hope.[32]

As described by a West India Company official six years later, the House of Good Hope stood at the juncture of the Little River and the Connecticut, "upon a plain on the margin of the river." Behind the fort stood "a high woodland." The stockade protecting the trading house included two high platforms upon which were mounted small cannons aimed at the river. Within the compound the Dutch traders kept cattle, poultry, hogs, oxen, and draft horses. "Outside the stockade," the official related, "is the farm, containing a kitchen garden planted with beans, pumpkins, and other vegetables, a large field of maize, and a good-sized orchard of apples, cherries, pears, and peaches. There is no chapel, but there is a burying ground with grave markers of sandstone." Within the stockade stood a tool shed and the trading post itself, a two-story structure twenty-six feet square, probably built of logs with yellow Dutch brick corners.[33]

The peace proclaimed in the Dutch-Pequot Agreement of 1633 was ephemeral. The Pequots were not reconciled to the loss of their trade monopoly in the Connecticut River valley. The House of Good Hope had barely been completed when Pequot warriors killed a group of Indian traders en route to the trading house. The victims were probably Narragansetts. It is less likely that Pequots would have assaulted River Indians, who as tributaries were under their protection. It is more probable that they acted to counter the efforts of a powerful and independent commercial rival to make use of a trade facility constructed on land ceded by the Pequots.

The Dutch reprisal was immediate and severe. When the Pequot principal sachem Tatobem boarded a Dutch vessel to trade, he was seized and held for ransom. The Dutch informed his compatriots that they would never again see their leader if they did not pay a bushel of wampum to his abductors. The Pequots immediately sent the payment demanded for Tatobem's freedom to the House of Good Hope. They received in return his corpse.[34]

In response to that outrage, the Pequots could easily have driven the Dutch from the Connecticut valley. Surprisingly, Tatobem's murder did not prompt an all-out assault on the tiny and vulnerable Dutch outpost. Despite their later reputation as implacable foes of the European presence, the Pequots were obviously not interested in terminating trade with Europeans. Their behavior indicates that their objective was to control that trade, not end it. Their response to the Dutch atrocity was limited in scope. Algonquian custom prescribed individual retribution executed by the victims' relatives to avenge murder. Shortly after Tatobem's death, a band of Pequots, accompanied by some western Niantics, killed the captain and crew of a European ship anchored on the lower Connecticut River.[35]

Unfortunately for the Pequots, their victims were English, not Dutch. They had assaulted a small trading vessel captained by John Stone, a smuggler and sometime privateer of unsavory reputation. Stone, his associate Captain Walter Norton, and all six crewmen perished in the raid. The reports we have of Pequot testimony regarding the circumstances of Stone's murder contain some inconsistencies. It appears that Stone had abducted two Indians near the mouth of the Connecticut River in territory occupied by the western Niantics, close neighbors and tributaries of the Pequots. Pequots who related the circumstances of his death during a visit to Boston in 1634 reported that Stone forced his captives to guide him upriver. After Stone's ship anchored for the night, the captain and two of his men took their Indian prisoners ashore, "their hands still bound," and made camp. An Indian rescue party, tracking Stone, waited until dark, then attacked, killing the captain and his two men while they slept and freeing the prisoners. The Indians then made for Stone's ship, but it "suddenly blew up in the air."[36] In 1636, however, a Pequot spokesman who parleyed with Endecott and his army on the banks of the Thames River told the English that the rescue party had boarded Stone's ship, pretending to be interested in trade. While his compatriots diverted the crew above deck, the new grand sachem Sassacus visited the captain in his cabin. Stone, an alcoholic, soon drank himself into a stupor and collapsed on his bunk. The sachem split Stone's head with a hatchet and threw a blanket over his body. In the brawl that followed, the Indians cornered the ship's crew in the kitchen, seized some loaded muskets, and fired into a supply of gunpowder, which exploded. They then killed the remainder of the dazed crew, looted the cargo, and set the ship ablaze.[37]

The most plausible explanation for the differences in those two versions is that the Pequots and western Niantics pursuing Stone's ship divided into two groups after they saw a landing party with Indian captives in tow go ashore. One group attacked the landing party, freed the prisoners, and mistakenly assumed that one of the men they killed in the dark was the captain. Meanwhile, members of the second group boarded the vessel, killed Stone, and set off the powder magazine before the first group rejoined them. The delegation that visited Boston in 1634 told the story from the perspective of the land party and may have included participants in that action. The envoy who called on Endecott on the Thames River two years later recalled the incident from the perspective of the boarding party.[38]

It must be emphasized that in none of their repeated efforts to explain Stone's death to the Puritan authorities did the Pequot leaders deny their complicity. They insisted, however, that they were unaware at the time that the captain was English, not Dutch. They had the right, they argued, to avenge Tatobem by taking some Dutch lives. Within the framework of Algonquian values, the killing of Captain Stone and his men, apart from the unfortunate matter of mistaken national identity, was an entirely appropriate and legal response to the murder of their grand sachem. Blood vengeance executed by the kinsmen of the murder victim was a prescribed means of restoring balance and harmony after a homicide.[39]

Subsequent events suggest that the Pequots did not regard their reprisal as a declaration of war against Europeans and therefore did not anticipate that it would close the door to the resumption of normal trade relations with the Dutch. Shortly after the assault on Stone and his crew, they distributed their loot, giving a generous share to the Niantics, and then sent a trading party to the House of Good Hope. We do not know exactly what happened when the Pequots arrived at the Dutch fort, but within a short time they were at war with their former trading partners. Bradford related that the Dutch killed a Pequot sachem with a blast of cannon shot. Surprised by that turn of events, the Pequots, as we shall see, then looked to the English for aid, sending a delegation to Boston in 1634.[40]

Why, given their experiences with the Dutch, did the Pequots persist in their efforts to trade with the intruders? Although some evidence suggests that Indian demand for trade goods of alien origin was somewhat unpredictable in the first years of contact, European metal implements, pots, woven fabrics, and firearms soon came to be prized in the Algonquian villages of southern New England both for their practical usefulness and for the prestige and the power they conferred on their owners. We have already mentioned that metal tools made possible the production on a large scale of Indian wampum. It must also be noted that Indians came to believe that the exceptional properties possessed by wampum were also to be found in certain European trade goods. Commentators on Euro-American trade have generally emphasized that use of European goods enhanced the material standard of living of those Indian groups who were able to control access to that trade. The appeal of European commodities to Indian purchasers has thus often been explained in terms of economic utility. But that explanation, while by no means invalid, is incomplete and somewhat simplistic. The documentary record suggests some additional explanations for Native American interest in European trade goods in the early years of contact. Indians did not immediately understand how to incorporate European technology into their economic life and did not always assess the usefulness of trade goods in terms comprehensible to Europeans. Both the historical and the archaeological sources indicate that, "when Europeans first met Indians, the exchange of goods that took place bore almost no relation to the economic process with which we are familiar."[41] Rather than displacing Native American technology, European goods were initially incorporated into Native American culture.

In the years immediately following contact, the greatest demand was for certain nonutilitarian items such as glass beads. Excavation of early postcontact sites and review of contemporary European reports reveal that, although the Indians made some use of steel axes and knives, they did not at first displace stone implements and in many cases were not actually used as practical tools. Thus iron and brass kettles were cut up to make medallions and amulets as well as arrowheads. Indian women often continued to cook in woven baskets. Small iron axes were worn about the neck as talismans, as Indian men continued to clear the fields with tools of wood and stone.

Seventeenth-century European observers, baffled by the apparent Indian misuse of European commodities and by their inordinate fascination with bright and shiny objects, dismissed the whole process as an example of Indian "savagery." In Virginia, to cite one example, Captain John Smith declared the Powhatans "generally covetous of copper, beads, and such like trash."[42] At one time, historians considering reports from the early years of the Indian trade commonly portrayed the natives as childlike primitives beguiled by novel and colorful trinkets. But the myth of the Indian as an underdeveloped child of nature has long been discredited, as is the concept of primitivism as a social form of human immaturity. The unusual appeal of certain "nonutilitarian" European trade goods, such as glass beads, must be explained in other terms.

Some insights into Indian perceptions of European objects at the time of first contact can be gleaned from the reports of the early voyages. In 1584, when Sir Walter Raleigh's reconnaissance probe of North America first encountered the Algonquian Indians of North Carolina, a sachem gave the commanders of the expedition "twenty skinnes" for a "bright tinne dish," which he proposed to wear "about his necke, making signes that it would defende him against his enemies arrows." Two years later, Roanoke Indians told Thomas Hariot that they believed that English compasses, telescopes, magnets, and guns were "the work of gods [rather] then men, or at the leastwise they had bene given and taught us of the gods."[43] Linguistic evidence also suggests Indian belief in the miraculous potency of some European trade goods. In his fieldwork among the Naskapis of Labrador early in the twentieth century, Frank Speck discovered that the words these northern Algonquians had coined to describe various European goods all used the stem *manitou*.[44] The use of that term, which signified the presence of supernatural power, tells us much about some early Algonquian conceptions of the issues at stake in exchanges with Europeans.

In the early years of contact, the allure for New England Indians of European products was in part the result of the belief that they were objects possessing great power, capable of bestowing exceptional potency upon their possessors. Indians believed that European metal and glass, like native wampum, were supernatural in origin. They found vivid colors evocative of certain heightened spiritual states. It has often been noted that "Indians preferred European woven cloth to their own traditional dress of fur and skins because it was equally warm and a good deal lighter."[45] But utility may not have been the most important aspect of its appeal, as Indian customers would often buy cloth of only certain colors. Red, "associated with animation, emotion, intense experience, with fire, heat, and blood," was particularly favored. Blue was also in demand. Native Americans utilized the concept of manitou to confer familiar symbolic meaning on items of European origin and thereby facilitate their ideological incorporation.[46]

Native Americans prized European firearms for their effectiveness in hunting and in war. But their superior functional efficiency was attributed to properties Europeans would not recognize. The noise, smoke, and fire emitted by muskets and cannons suggested the imminence of a particularly powerful manitou. Despite the Puritans' best efforts to ban trade in weapons with the Indians, the Pequots by 1636 had acquired "sixteen guns with powder and shot" and wanted more.[47]

Access to European goods meant access to power. That power emanated both from the functional efficiency of tools and weapons and from the intangible but real psychological advantage such remarkable objects conferred on their possessors. In the ongoing struggle for dominance in the Connecticut River valley waged by the Pequots and their rivals, European trade goods would play a vital role.

By the fall of 1634, Pequot control of the lucrative trade of the Connecticut valley was under serious challenge on several fronts. Their commercial alliance with the Dutch had collapsed in the wake of the killings at the House of Good Hope and the assault on Stone's trading ship. They faced not only the hostility of the Dutch but the enmity of their Indian neighbors to the east. The Pequot-Narragansett War was fought ostensibly over control of a twenty-mile-square tract between the Pawcatuck River and the Wecapaug. But the underlying tensions between these two closely related groups were rooted in rivalries over access to European trade.

The Narragansetts, occupants of territory to the east of the Pequots in what is now Rhode Island, were not a major power in the region prior to the virgin-soil epidemic that ravaged the Atlantic seaboard of New England from 1616 to 1619.[48] They had had little contact with their neighbors on the eastern shores of Narragansett Bay and hence, as Bradford related, "had not been at all touched with this wasting plague."[49] Although up to 90 percent of the inhabitants of the coastal regions perished, the Narragansetts gained in power and prestige. Other, more vulnerable Indian groups came to believe that Narragansett survival was testimony to "the efficacy of their medicine people and the rituals they performed."[50] Soon after the arrival of European traders in the early 1620s, the Narragansetts established close trade ties with the Dutch. Although their relationship with the Plymouth Colony had not been particularly cordial, the Narragansetts also entered into a commercial relationship with traders from the Massachusetts Bay Colony in the early 1630s.[51] William Wood, writing in 1634, reported that the Narragansetts brought beaver, otter, and muskrat pelts to the Bay Colony, "returning back loaded with English commodities, of which they make a double profit by selling them to more remote Indians who are ignorant at what cheap rates they obtain them in comparison with what they make them pay, so making their neighbors' ignorance their enrichment."[52]

Although the Dutch had sought to persuade the Pequots and the Narragansetts to agree to free trade at the House of Good Hope, neither group was interested in sharing. Both sought control, and the Narragansetts saw in the expansion of the Pequot tributary system a threat "to what had been a very profitable role as middlemen."[53] It is therefore not surprising that the establishment of Narragansett trade connections with the Europeans was accompanied by a process of political consolidation. The traditional Narragansett sachemdom had occupied a compact territory on the mainland in what are now Washington and Kent counties in Rhode Island, along with two outlying islands. The Narragansett sachems had maintained close social ties through intermarriage and reciprocal gift giving with a number of other villages in the region, but those villages remained politically autonomous. But the process in the 1620s that led to Pequot control of the Connecticut River valley and eastern Long Island also resulted in a more peaceful consolidation of authority in Narragansett territory. By the early 1630s, the authority of the two Narragansett cosachems was acknowledged by the Maniseans on Block Island, the Cowesets in what is now East Greenwich, the Shawomets and the Pawtuxets to the north of the Cowesets, the eastern Niantics near the Connecticut border, and the Nipmucs to the north. At one time or another, the Narragansetts also sought to dominate the Montauks of Long Island and the Pokanokets near Plymouth.[54]

The Plymouth Colony's alliance with the Pokanoket sachem Massasoit was a source of continued tensions between that colony and the Narragansetts. In April 1632 a Narragansett war party surrounded Plymouth's trading house at Sowanset and tried to seize Massasoit. As rumors of an impending Narragansett attack on Plymouth swept through the colony, Miles Standish mobilized his forces, after appealing successfully to the Massachusetts Bay Colony for a donation of gunpowder. But, as John Winthrop noted in his journal, the "great army" that the Narragansett sachem Canonicus was supposedly leading against Plymouth never materialized, and the Narragansetts besieging Massasoit and his English protectors "retired from Sowams to fight with the Pequins."[55]

In their efforts to disrupt the Pequot tributary system, the Narragansetts were probably involved in a scheme to use the English as a counterweight against the Pequots in the Connecticut River valley. In the spring of 1631, several sachems from Connecticut villages ostensibly within the Pequot orbit visited Plymouth and Boston. Their mission: to persuade the leaders of the two colonies to establish an English settlement in the valley. One of the sachems promised Winthrop that they would pay "yearly eighty skins of beaver" and guarantee a goodly supply of corn if the English would "plant in his country." It would appear that the sachems hoped to regain some of their former power through cultivating the English. Acceptance of annual tribute such as the sachems offered Winthrop, in the Algonquian world, carried with it an obligation to provide protection, so it is likely that the sachems were trying to buy a powerful ally. The Puritan governors were wary. Bradford suspected that the sachems hoped to involve the English in their quarrel with the Pequots. Winthrop concurred, noting in his journal that the leader of the delegation, the Podunk sachem Wagincut, was "a very treacherous man." He declined the sachems' invitation to take two Englishmen with them on their return journey to Connecticut "to see the country." The interpreter who accompanied the delegation was a Massachusett Indian closely associated with the Narragansetts, who no doubt encouraged, if they did not instigate, this effort to undercut the Pequots.[56]

The evidence of Narragansett involvement in internal power struggles within the Pequot sachemdom is unambiguous. The murder by the Dutch of the Pequot grand sachem Tatobem marked the beginning of a period of political turmoil. As Neal Salisbury has noted, "while Tatobem had alienated many of the Pequot allies, his son and successor, Sassacus, was unable to hold together even those who were nominally Pequot."[57] A number of Pequot sachems renounced their allegiance to the grand sachem and placed their villages under Narragansett protection. Among the defectors were Wequash, an unsuccessful contender for the grand sachemdom, and Soso (sometimes called Sassawwaw), sachem of a Pequot village on the west bank of the Pawcatuck River. After serving as a Narragansett warrior in the skirmishes of the early 1630s, Soso pretended to reclaim his allegiance to the Pequots. Participating in a Pequot war party that fought against the Narragansetts sometime in 1636, Soso turned on his compatriots and killed and beheaded the Pequot war captain. He then returned to the Narragansett fold. Roger Williams, writing in 1637, described the former Pequot sachem as Miantonomi's "special darling, a kind of general of his forces."[58]

The most serious threat to the Pequot grand sachem came from the defection of the Mohegans. The precise relationship of that "tribe" to the Pequots remains unclear. Until recently, historians generally portrayed the Mohegans as Pequots who, under the leadership of Uncas, seceded and, with the help of the Narragansetts and the English, organized a new political entity. Recent research, however, suggests that the Mohegans were never part of the Pequot sachemdom per se but were instead a distinct and separate kinship group loosely tied to the Pequots through intermarriage and through a tributary relationship with the Pequot principal sachem.[59] Their autonomy is suggested by a dispute over hunting rights in game preserves north of the main Pequot villages. In their efforts to deny Sassacus access to those preserves, Mohegan sachems asserted an entitlement based on kinship not subject to the customary prerogatives of the grand sachem.[60] Additional evidence of Mohegan identity is found on a Dutch map based on the reports of the Block expedition of 1614. The map assigns to the Mohegans a territory and an identity separate from the Pequots nearby.[61]

Evidence of a distinct Mohegan identity notwithstanding, we cannot understand Mohegan-Pequot relations by applying a model that presumes long-term "tribal" stability and continuity or that imagines hard-and-fast national boundaries dividing Pequots from Mohegans, Niantics, and Narragansetts. The loyalties and alliances of the Algonquian villages of this region were rather fluid. The barriers between "tribes" were far more permeable than those that separated European states. The evidence indicates not only that "Pequot, Mohegan and Narragansett royalty constantly intermarried in clearly political alliances" but that Indians of lower status moved freely from one community to another. Moreover, as Burton observes, "whether the Pequot and Mohegan were one people may well be a moot point: their leaders clearly were."[62]

Uncas, the man who would emerge in the mid-1630s as the leader of an autonomous and powerful Mohegan "tribe" was a physically imposing, strong-willed, and ambitious politician aptly described as "a master of seventeenth century *realpolitik*."[63] If we believe the genealogy he prepared for the English late in his life, Uncas had a claim by birth to both Mohegan and Pequot sachemships. A descendant of two Pequot grand sachems, Nukquut-do-woas and Wopigwooit, Uncas had married a daughter of another grand sachem, Tatobem. Willful and ambitious, he had quarreled with his father-in-law and had spent a period of time in exile among the Narragansetts. Begging and obtaining Tatobem's forgiveness, Uncas was allowed to return to his village in Mohegan country near the present site of Norwich, Connecticut.

After Tatobem's murder, Uncas made a bid to succeed him as Pequot grand sachem. Although candidates for that office needed to be members of one of a limited number of prominent families, referred to by the English as "the royal blood," the grand sachemship was not, strictly speaking, hereditary. The struggle over the succession was sometimes acrimonious, and this occasion was one of those times. Uncas was not elected. Wequash's candidacy also failed. Tatobem's son Sassacus was chosen.[64]

Uncas refused to accept that outcome and mounted a campaign to depose Sassacus. His efforts failed, and once again Uncas fled to the Narragansetts. He did not long remain in exile. Many years later, Indian informants told an English court that Uncas "humbled himself to the Pequot sachem, and desired that he might have liberty to live in his own country again." Sassacus granted his petition on condition that Uncas now solemnly swear that he would remain loyal. Uncas agreed but soon broke his oath. His renewed campaign against Sassacus won few adherents, and once again Uncas was forced to flee for his life. Welcomed by the Narragansetts, Uncas soon sent word of his repentance to Sassacus. The grand sachem once again accepted Uncas's renewed pledge of loyalty to the Pequots and allowed him to return to his village. He was soon at work fomenting a new insurrection against Sassacus. Incredibly, the Indian witnesses related that Uncas rebelled, suffered defeat and exile, obtained pardon, and returned to the Pequot fold some five times in all.[65]

Despite his ambition Uncas, at the beginning, according to Indian testimony, had "but little land and very few men," not even enough to form a hunting party.[66] What explains his emergence as leader of the Mohegans? Narragansett support and later English patronage were of course crucial. But even more important was Uncas's skill in exploiting the disaffection of Pequot tributaries. Sassacus's response to the Mohegan challenge to his claim to their hunting grounds was to drive their leaders into exile. The Narragansetts, predictably, gave them refuge. Uncas, who was related by blood to the exiled Mohegans, used the incident to win support in the Mohegan villages for his own aspirations. He was no less adroit in winning over some of the River Indian bands to the west of Mohegan territory. Finally, through careful cultivation of Anglo-Pequot animosities, Uncas would help precipitate a war that would enable him to achieve his goal and take the place of the Pequot grand sachem.

In summary, Pequot leadership in the early 1630s was beleaguered. The image of the Pequots as a domineering, aggressive force threatening the very existence of the English colonies in New England was the product of Puritan mythmaking. By the time of their first official dealings with the Massachusetts Bay Colony, Pequot power was in decline.

3

Pequots and Puritans: The Origins of the Conflict

 It is ironic, given the subsequent history of Anglo-Pequot relations, that Sassacus and his followers in the fall of 1634 turned to Boston for assistance in dealing with their Indian adversaries. The Pequot leaders did not anticipate the coming crisis with the English. The antagonisms that would lead in a few years' time to the most destructive war Indian New England had ever witnessed originated in a misunderstanding over retribution for the death of Captain John Stone. Neither side understood or accepted the meaning that the Stone episode held for the other. English suspicions about the Pequots' motives, first aroused in 1634 by their refusal to surrender Stone's killers to English justice, were exacerbated two years later by rumors of an impending Pequot attack on English settlers and traders in the Connecticut valley. Yet a close reading of the record of early Pequot-Puritan interaction suggests that Puritan anxieties were misplaced.

In John Winthrop's journal entries for October 1634, we find the first record of Pequot contact with the officials of the Massachusetts Bay Colony. Winthrop tells us that a Pequot envoy called that month and announced that the Pequots desired the friendship of the English. The visitor, Winthrop wrote, "brought two bundles of sticks, whereby he signified how much beaver and otter skins he would give us for that end," and held out the promise of "a great store of wampum" as well. He had "brought a small present with him," which he gave his hosts as a token of goodwill. The magistrates gave him in return a "moose coat of as good value." However, after they learned that their visitor was not a sachem, they sent him on his way, with instructions to tell the Pequot grand sachem Sassacus that he would need to send envoys of higher rank if he wanted to enter into formal negotiations with the Bay Colony.[1]

Soon thereafter, two Pequot sachems arrived at Boston, bearing wampum and peltry. They asked the Puritan magistrates to use some of the wampum to negotiate on their behalf an end to the Pequot-Narragansett War. Two days after their arrival, rumors reached Boston of a Narragansett war party, said to number 300 warriors, lying in wait "to kill the Pekod ambassadors." The Bay Colony authorities quickly mustered a small armed force at Roxbury, which then marched to the Narragansett encampment at Cohann. Upon arrival, they asked the Narragansetts to accept English assistance in mediating their dispute with the Pequots. The English troops found the reports of a Narragansett attack force greatly exaggerated. "There were," Winthrop recorded, "no more but two of their Sachems, and about twenty more, who had been on hunting thereabouts, and came to lodge with the Indians at Cohann, as their manner is." Accepting the Pequot wampum, the Narragansetts agreed to grant the Pequot envoys safe passage. As Winthrop explained, the Pequots were too proud to make a direct offer to buy off the Narragansetts but "were willing we should" and were willing to pay the English for their aid. The Narragansetts for their part took the proffered gift and "departed well satisfied."[2]

At Boston, the English signed a treaty with the Pequots, with Sassacus's envoys making their marks, a bow and arrow and a hand, on the document. The text of that treaty has not survived, but the information that can be found in the contemporary source materials enables us to draw some conclusions about its terms. From Winthrop's journal and from his correspondence it is clear that the Pequots asked for, and received, a trade agreement. "They desired us," Winthrop wrote, "to send a pinnace with cloth" and promised that "we should have all their trade." The Pequots also offered the Puritans handsome land concessions in order to encourage English settlement in Connecticut. Weakened by internal dissension, threatened by both the Dutch and the Narragansetts, the Pequots were no longer able to control the Connecticut River valley. Winthrop noted in his journal that the Pequots "could not trade safely any where." Desperately grasping for a means to regain some advantage, the Pequots, as Winthrop recorded, "offered us also all their right at Connecticut" and promised assistance to the English "if we would settle a plantation there." Just as the River Indian sachems three years earlier had sought to regain their hold on the valley by attaching themselves to the English, so the Pequots now hoped to maintain their precarious access to the rich trade of the Connecticut by means of an alliance with the Bay Colony Puritans.[3]

The agreement reached at Boston fell short of Pequot hopes and aspirations, for Winthrop recorded that the magistrates declined to pledge themselves to "defend them." Winthrop and his associates well understood that it would not be in their interest to intervene on behalf of the Pequots in any future Indian trade war, as the Narragansetts not only were more powerful but were also closer to the English settlements. The Pequots thus failed to find a European military ally in Boston.[4]

As noted earlier, the Pequot envoys did obtain a trade agreement. But the English asked a high price for their trade and friendship. The Boston magistrates declared the gift offered by the Pequots inadequate. They informed their visitors that they would expect to receive 400 fathoms of wampum, forty beaver skins, and thirty otter skins. The value of the goods specified as a condition for ratifying the treaty was equivalent to half of the total tax income of the colony in 1634 and would have imposed a very substantial burden on Sassacus and his followers. The Puritans had demanded, as Francis Jennings notes, "much more than the Pequot ambassadors had been authorized to offer, and it failed of ratification in their council at home."[5]

The other major Puritan requirement for peace and trade with the Pequots was even more troublesome. Bay Colony officials informed the envoys that "because they had killed some Englishmen, viz., Captain Stone, etc., they must first deliver up those who were guilty of his death." The Pequots responded that Captain Stone had been killed in reprisal for the murder by the Dutch of their grand sachem. His assailants, the envoys explained, had not known that he was English rather than Dutch. The captain, they added, had acted in a provocative manner by abducting two Indians at the mouth of the Connecticut River. All but two of the participants in the attack "were dead of the pox." They declared that, "if they were worthy of death, they would move their sachem to have them delivered, (for they had no commission to do it)," but cautioned that given Stone's bad behavior they could not be certain that the sachem would agree to take action against Stone's killers. Winthrop confided to his journal that the magistrates were initially satisfied with the Pequots' explanation of the circumstances of Stone's death and were not inclined to press the matter. The Pequot account, Winthrop wrote, "was related with such confidence and gravity, as, having no means to contradict, we were inclined to believe it." In a letter to Bradford at Plymouth, Winthrop reported that the Pequots had explained that they had killed Stone "in a just quarrel."[6]

In light of the foregoing, the subsequent Puritan claim that their war against the Pequots was necessitated and justified by Pequot refusal to apprehend and surrender the murderers of John Stone and his crew at first glance seems less than credible. The Stone affair requires close scrutiny, for historians have been hard-pressed to explain the Bay Colony's growing intransigence on the issue of retribution for the captain's death. To some, it has offered a particularly blatant example of Puritan cant and hypocrisy, for Boston had no reason to mourn Stone's passing, had every reason to believe that he had indeed abused the Indians, and at first seemed rather pleased by the news of his murder.

John Stone was a member of an influential and wealthy London family. A licensed privateer who had once scourged the Caribbean, he had most recently pursued a career as a smuggler. Stone was, as New England's Puritans described him, a drunkard, lecher, braggart, bully, and blasphemer. Adding to his unsavory reputation were rumors that he had resorted to cannibalism while shipwrecked during one of his privateering expeditions. But the captain was also a very skillful entrepreneur whose savoir faire had won the admiration of English, Spanish, Portuguese, and Dutch officials from Brazil to New Netherland. Some of those admirers had aided and abetted his smuggling activities. Stone counted among his intimate friends both the governor of Virginia, Sir John Harvey, and the director general of New Netherland, Wouter Van Twiller.[7]

On his last voyage, in the spring of 1632, carrying a cargo of cattle and salt from Virginia to Boston, Stone became embroiled in an altercation on Manhattan Island with some members of the crew of Plymouth's trading bark. Enraged by some remarks he took to be insulting, Stone resolved to steal the Plymouth ship and its cargo. As Plymouth's governor later told the story, Stone got his friend Van Twiller "drunk so as he could scarce say a right word" and then secured his mumbled permission to board the Plymouth bark while its captain and the colony's commercial agent were still ashore. Leaving the sodden Dutch official, Stone seized the ship and forced its startled crew at gunpoint to "weigh anchor, set sail, and carry her away towards Virginia." However, some Dutch seamen who "had been often at Plymouth and kindly entertained there" witnessed Stone's piracy and determined not to "suffer our friends to be thus abused and have their goods carried away before our faces, whilst our governor is drunk." They accordingly pursued Stone and forced him to return the bark. Its own captain then took command, sailed back to Plymouth, and reported the episode to the authorities there.[8]

When Stone landed with his cargo at Boston soon thereafter, Plymouth promptly "sent Capt. Miles Standish to prosecute against him for piracy." Troubled by Standish's account of the incident at New Amsterdam, the Bay Colony officials at first were inclined to bind Stone over to the Admiralty Court in England. But they feared Stone's influence in London, and on further reflection Governor Winthrop and his advisors decided that it would be politic to let the matter drop. They advised Plymouth not to prosecute the case, on grounds that the master of Plymouth's trading bark, who also happened to be a member of the colony's governing council, had earlier given in to pressure from Stone and Van Twiller and had signed a statement in which he promised to take no action. Plymouth grudgingly agreed. When Captain Stone and his crew visited Plymouth, although he received "friendly and civil entertainment" (according to Bradford), he nonetheless had to be restrained from stabbing his host.[9]

Despite their efforts to placate a man whose influence they feared, the Bay Colony officials were soon pushed beyond the limits of their forbearance by the choleric captain. After his return to the Bay Colony, Stone got several of the good citizens of Boston roaring drunk and soon thereafter was discovered in bed "with one Barcroft's wife." Utterly unrepentant and openly contemptuous of the Bay Colony's hidebound morality, the captain was called before the governor and ordered to stand trial on charges of drunkenness and adultery. Winthrop confided to his journal his doubt that the adultery charge could be made to stick, as Stone was "in drink" when he bedded Mrs. Barcroft and was probably temporarily incapable of consummating the act. Stone, ignoring his indictment, prepared to set sail, but "a warrant was sent out to stay his pinnace." He responded by abusing Roger Ludlow, a member of the Massachusetts governing council. Enraged, Winthrop had Stone clapped in irons but thought better of it and had the irons removed a few hours later. Kept under heavy guard, Stone was brought before the court. As Winthrop anticipated, the charge of adultery was dismissed. Stone was, however, convicted of drunkenness and fined a hundred pounds (a very substantial amount in 1634). The fine was suspended, and Captain Stone was then "ordered upon pain of death to come here no more." Mrs. Barcroft "was bound to her good behavior." [10]

As the Puritan Colony's magistrates waited anxiously to discover what trouble Stone would create for them once he reached London, word arrived via Plymouth that he had been killed by Indians on the Connecticut River. The tenor of their response to that news was well captured by a young settler, Roger Clap, who wrote: "Thus did God destroy him that proudly threatened to ruin us, by complaining against us when he came to England. Thus God destroyed him, and delivered us at that time also." Clap was under the impression that the Indians had roasted Stone alive but expressed no regret that he had met with so cruel a fate. The Massachusetts council considered the matter very briefly but decided to take no action other than informing the governor of Virginia and thereby offering him an opportunity to do something to avenge his friend if he were so inclined. At Plymouth, Bradford hinted that Stone, given his bad character, had probably abused the Indians and was therefore responsible for his own death. In 1633 Puritan New England clearly had no intention of going to war over Captain John Stone. [11]

But a year later the Bay Colony authorities made the avenging of Stone and his crew a major objective in their negotiations with the Pequots. Puritan writers later pointed to Pequot refusal to comply with English demands that they apprehend and surrender Stone's murderers as evidence of a Pequot conspiracy against all Englishmen. The attack on Stone's ship was generally cited as the principal cause of war in Puritan justifications of their subsequent assault on the Pequots. The documentary evidence relating to the Bay Colony's decision to make retribution for Stone an essential condition for peaceful coexistence with the Pequots is sparse and cryptic, but Winthrop's journal and his correspondence contain a very interesting disclosure. After noting twice that the magistrates were "inclined to believe" the Pequots' explanation of Stone's death, Winthrop then recorded, both in his journal and in his correspondence, that the civil authorities referred the question to the clergy. After "taking the advice of our ministers and seeking the Lord in it," the magistrates decided that friendship with the Pequots would be possible only if they agreed to "deliver up to us those men who were guilty of Stone's death." [12] The treaty presented to the Pequots in 1634 therefore included a provision requiring the apprehension and surrender of Stone's assailants. Given Winthrop's comments, it is reasonable to conclude that, although the civil authorities suspected that Stone had provoked the Indians, the ministers had advised against any compromise, and the magistrates had therefore decided not to forgive the Pequots' mistake.

To understand that decision, we must bear in mind that fear of Indian malevolence was pervasive in Puritan New England. Puritan letters, diaries, and journals reflect a constant expectation that the "savages," as one of John Winthrop's correspondents put it in 1633, would prove "dilligent to sute an opportunytye to their Natures." Anxiety led to a determination never to show weakness in the face of Indian provocation. Grounded in a fundamental distrust of "savages," the Indian policy followed by Plymouth and Boston in the early years of settlement did not preclude the use of terror, where necessary, to intimidate the "hirelings of Satan." As we noted previously, the Plymouth Colony, in an incident in 1623 that foreshadowed the Bay Colony's campaign against the Pequots, had sent an armed force under Miles Standish to massacre a group of Massachusett Indians suspected, on the testimony of some of their Indian enemies, of conspiring to murder Englishmen. [13] The conviction that God's people in the wilderness must deal sternly with "savages" who threatened Christians explains both the clergy's insistence that the magistrates demand that Pequots, as a sign of their goodwill, surrender the murderers of Stone and his crew and the magistrates' ready agreement to that condition.

The suspicion persisted throughout the seventeenth century and beyond that Indians were in league with a satanic power that threatened not only physical survival but the basic spiritual foundations of the Puritan commonwealth. As Segal and Stineback have noted, Indians who remained "proud and insolent" after contact with the Saints were particularly suspect, for "savages" who were not agents of the devil were expected to accept willingly English authority. By their refusal to comply with the Bay Colony's demand for wampum and for Stone's murderers, the Pequots had placed themselves among those "proud and insolent" Indians whom the Puritans feared as a threat to their security.[14]

We can only conjecture about Pequot reactions to the English demands. Although the Puritans, and some historians, charged the Pequots with bad faith in not paying the full price for friendship discussed with the envoys in 1634, the record clearly indicates that the treaty drawn up in Boston was never ratified by the Pequot ruling sachems. It is reasonable to assume that the sachems, informed that the Bay Colony was willing to offer only a trade agreement, not a protective alliance, saw no justification for the payment of a substantial tribute to the Bay Colony. Since the payment of wampum in Algonquian custom was a means of atoning for murders, it is also quite likely that the sachems assumed that the wampum they did send to Boston had removed any serious resentment the English might harbor over the death of Stone and his crew, and therefore they did not take seriously the demands for the apprehension and surrender of the participants in the raid. This was a grave miscalculation.

The physical separation of Puritan and Pequot territory prevented an immediate confrontation. But English migration into Connecticut in 1635 prompted renewed efforts to secure Pequot agreement to Puritan demands and also led to new misunderstandings. We must digress from our account of Anglo-Pequot relations at this point in order to trace the complex and convoluted origins of the English settlements in Connecticut. The Connecticut River valley, offered by the Pequots to the Bay Colony in the negotiations at Boston in 1634, had already attracted the attention of several groups of potential English settlers. The Plymouth Colony was interested in the acquisition of land for a new trading post that would provide access to the rich fur trade in southwestern New England. The Indian traders of the Bay Colony, of whom Winthrop was the most prominent, were also well aware of the rich stores of wampum and peltry to be had in Connecticut. Thomas Hooker's congregation at Newtown, dissatisfied with their land allocations in Massachusetts, clamored to improve their lot by relocating in the Connecticut valley, as did prominent residents of Watertown, Roxbury, and Dorchester. A group of Puritan aristocrats in England hoped to establish their own colony in New England and claimed to be in possession of a patent giving them title to Connecticut. And there were individuals unaffiliated with any of the quasi-official Puritan ventures listed above who coveted the trade and the land that lay beyond the western boundaries of English settlement.

Let us consider first the history of Plymouth's interest in Connecticut. Shortly after the visit in 1631 of the River Indian delegation that had solicited English settlement in Connecticut, Plymouth had quietly sent a reconnaissance party, led by Edward Winslow, to the valley. Winslow's probe confirmed the Indians' description of the region as a "fine place" to live. But Plymouth needed trade, not land. Possessed of an ample supply of Indian trade goods, but not of Indian clients, the colony had to expand its fur trade in order to satisfy English creditors. Plymouth's explorers were thus disappointed to learn, upon their arrival in Connecticut, that the Indians there had few pelts to offer in trade. They claimed that the English had arrived at the wrong time of the year. Plymouth's leaders found that excuse less than convincing and suspected that the real reason for the shortage was that the River Indians had not conducted their annual hunt for "fear of their enemies." It is more likely that the proceeds had already been delivered to the Dutch, via the Pequots, for the River Indians at that time were Pequot tributaries.[15]

Rumors of a lucrative fur trade in the Connecticut valley persisted. The Plymouth authorities remained interested in the region, for they needed a trade outlet closer to home. Their Maine posts were hard to supply and defend. In 1632 the Plymouth trading post at Kennebec was looted by a band of French raiders. Later in the same year, the French struck again, this time destroying a trading fort at Machias owned by Thomas Allerton, the controversial agent of Plymouth's creditors in England. Two of Allerton's men were killed, three were taken captive, and all of his goods were seized. In 1635 the French seized Plymouth's trading post in Maine. The commander of the French expedition, Captain D'Auny, promised to pay for the goods he took, at a depreciated price he set himself, but never made good on his pledge. He seized the post itself outright, without even the promise of compensation, "saying that they which build on another man's ground do forfeit the same." Outraged, Plymouth appealed to the Massachusetts Bay Colony for help in recapturing the post. Boston expressed sympathy but declined to provide any tangible aid.[16]

Disappointed by that parsimonious response, the Plymouth colonists turned to a ship captain named Girlings, master of a 300-ton armed vessel named *The Great Hope*. Girlings agreed, for a fee of 700 pounds of beaver skins, to drive the French from Maine. Plymouth's small trading bark, loaded with the promised beaver skins and manned by Captain Miles Standish and twenty Plymouth soldiers, piloted Girlings to the contested trading post. Standish advised that the French be invited to a parley, deeming it likely that, once they realized that they were badly outnumbered, they would surrender without a fight. But Girlings proved "so rash and heady as he would take no advice." While still far from shore, he opened fire "like a madman." The French, safely ensconced behind earthen breastworks, were out of his range. From his bark, Standish bellowed at Girlings to hold his fire and stand in, but by the time the befuddled ship captain realized his error, he had used up most of his gunpowder. He cried that he needed to break off the engagement and return to port to get more powder. Standish, afraid that he really intended to seize Plymouth's bark and the beaver pelts it carried, gave Girlings all of his powder, then hastily sailed back to Plymouth after enjoining Girlings to resume his attack on the French. "But," wrote Bradford, "Girlings never assaulted the place more, seeing himself disappointed, but went his way."[17]

Plymouth warned the Bay Colony that the French were "now likely to fortify themselves more strongly, and become ill neighbors to the English." Boston promised some help and suggested that the two colonies confer on the French menace. But nothing came of the proposed collaboration, as Massachusetts insisted that Plymouth pay most of the expenses. William Bradford later charged that the Boston Puritans were secretly trafficking with the enemy. "Some of their merchants," he wrote, "shortly after sent to trade with them and furnished them both with provisions and powder and shot" and thus "have been cheerful supporters of the French." Governor Winthrop flatly denied the accusation, writing Bradford, "You are misinformed. . . . we neither sent nor Incouraged ours to trade with them." On the margin of that letter, Bradford wrote that Winthrop was lying.[18]

An earlier incident had also raised doubts in Plymouth about both the security of their northern holdings and their relationship with the Massachusetts Bay Colony. In 1634 John Alden, assistant governor of Plymouth, was arrested and charged with murder during a visit to Boston. Alden had been at Plymouth's trading post at Kennebec when a rival English trader named Hocking had attempted to monopolize commerce with the local Indians by anchoring his bark upriver to "intercept the trade that should come down to them." When Hocking ignored requests that he move on, Plymouth's agent at Kennebec, John Howland, sent two men by canoe to cut the cables of his ship. Finding himself adrift, Hocking fired at the canoe, killing one of Plymouth's men, Moses Talbot, instantly. Talbot's compatriot returned fire, hitting Hocking, "who fell down dead and never spake a word."[19]

Unfortunately for Plymouth, Hocking was an agent of the influential Puritan nobleman Lord Saye and Sele. Governor Winthrop, upon hearing of the incident, complained to Plymouth that Hocking's "murder has brought us all and the Gospel under the common reproach of cutting one another's throats for beaver." When Plymouth's trading bark put in at Boston, Alden was seized, imprisoned, and indicted. Plymouth's Governor Thomas Prence promptly dispatched Miles Standish to explain the circumstances of Hocking's death and thereby secure Alden's release. But to Plymouth's exasperation, the Bay Colony magistrates insisted on conducting a formal investigation of the affair. They summoned Standish as a witness and sent to Plymouth a demand that their patent to Kennebec and other relevant papers be made available for their scrutiny.[20]

The Plymouth leaders were outraged at Boston's presumption and denied that the Bay Colony had any right to meddle in the Maine trade. But Governor Winthrop responded with a warning about possible English retaliation from London for Hocking's murder and suggested that an investigation of the case by a special court representing both colonies would best safeguard their common interests. Reluctantly Plymouth agreed. The court of inquiry found the deceased Mr. Hocking responsible for provoking his own demise. Winthrop wrote in his journal that the Plymouth traders "acknowledged, that they did hold themselves under guilt of the breach of the sixth commandment," and therefore resolved in the future not "to hazard [a] man's life for such a cause." Edward Winslow from Plymouth was dispatched to England with the court's finding. For their part, the Massachusetts authorities wrote both the Council for New England and Lord Saye and Sele on Plymouth's behalf. Though not dissatisfied with the final outcome, Plymouth nonetheless found Boston's conduct overbearing and offensive.[21]

Given the various problems that had plagued its commercial enterprises in northern New England, it is thus not surprising that Plymouth led the way in the English occupation of Connecticut. In writing of that venture several years later, Bradford made no effort to conceal his bitterness toward the Massachusetts Bay Colony. Boston, he complained, had gladly allowed Plymouth to take all the risks in opening up the Connecticut valley to English traders and settlers. But as soon as profits began to be made, Plymouth was "little better than thrust out" by its greedy neighbors from the Bay Colony. Plymouth had originally sought to collaborate with Boston in the development of the Connecticut trade, having been led to believe that, although the Massachusetts Colony could not afford to bear the full cost of establishing a trading fort on the river, it was quite "willing to embrace" an enterprise in which both colonies would "put in equal stock together."[22]

On July 12, 1633, Plymouth officials journeyed to Boston to spend a week conferring with their Bay Colony counterparts about matters of common concern. The main item on the agenda, Winthrop noted in his journal, was the establishment of a trading post on the Connecticut River "to prevent the Dutch, who were about to build one." In their conversations with the Plymouth delegates, the Massachusetts magistrates threw cold water on the proposition. Connecticut, they declared, was not fit for habitation by Englishmen, being populated by "three or four thousand" hostile Indians who could easily overpower a small English outpost. They maintained further that their reconnaissance reports had revealed that the Connecticut River, the only artery to the interior of the valley, was virtually unnavigable, as a huge sandbar at its mouth barred passage to all but the smallest vessels throughout the year. For seven months annually, the channel was totally impassable "by reason of the ice . . . and the violent stream." (Those reports were exaggerated.) In his journal, Winthrop noted that, given the inhospitable nature of the country, "we thought fit not to meddle with it."[23]

Winthrop's account of conversations with Plymouth contained an important omission. William Bradford's record indicates that the Bay Colony officials had also protested that their newly settled colony simply did not have enough trade goods to contribute even half a share of the cost of the venture. In response to that objection, Plymouth offered to bear all of the cost in the first year, provided that Massachusetts Bay agreed to repay one-half of that investment at some future date and also make a commitment to contribute at least half of the resources needed to sustain the operation in its second year. Despite those generous terms,

Massachusetts declined Plymouth's offer. Undaunted, the Plymouth emissaries declared that they intended to proceed with their plans for a trading post on the Connecticut River and expressed the hope that the Bay Colony would not take offense if they now occupied Connecticut unilaterally. Governor Winthrop offered assurances that his colony had no reason to oppose Plymouth's venture.[24]

We must not take that cordial exchange at face value. The Bay Colony also needed a western trade outlet. Access to beaver pelts was essential to the procurement of supplies from England. The sparsely populated Indian lands surrounding the bay lacked river access to the interior and yielded little peltry. Massachusetts needed to find a route to the rich beaver meadows of northern and western New England. The colony's leaders actually had no intention of yielding the trade of the Connecticut River valley to anyone. Quite simply, Winthrop lied when he disavowed interest in Connecticut.

Unbeknownst to Plymouth, Boston's leaders promptly took steps to secure the region for themselves. A few weeks after Bradford and his colleagues returned to Plymouth, Winthrop dispatched his newly launched bark, *The Blessing of the Bay,* on a trading mission to Long Island and New Amsterdam. Landing at Manhattan Island to trade for beaver pelts, Winthrop's men "were very kindly entertained by the Dutch." But under the governor's instructions, the captain of *The Blessing of the Bay* called on Director General Van Twiller to lodge a protest against Dutch trading activities in Connecticut. As Winthrop recorded, the captain showed Van Twiller "their commission, which was to signify to them [the Dutch], that the King of England had granted the river and country of Connecticut to his own subjects." Since the "commission" in question could only have been the charter of the Massachusetts Bay Colony, Winthrop in effect was claiming for Massachusetts a region he had earlier, informally, ceded to Plymouth. Van Twiller, enjoined by the Bay Colony Puritans "to forbear to build there," was circumspect in his reply, sending Winthrop a letter which the recipient characterized as "very courteous and respectful." The director general suggested that since the Dutch government "had granted the same parts to the West India Company" the colonists should refer the matter to the king of England and his Dutch counterpart for settlement.[25]

The Blessing of the Bay carefully explored the Connecticut coast and Long Island Sound. The voyage confirmed earlier reports regarding the

Connecticut River, the captain relating to Winthrop that it was "barred at the entrance . . . they could not find one fathom of water." The Indians on nearby Long Island appeared to be "a very treacherous people" whose prowess in war should not be discounted, as "they have many canoes so great as one will carry eighty men." They were also wealthy, possessing great quantities of high-quality wampum. The trading potential of the region was thus substantial. In Boston, Winthrop and his colleagues pondered that report and weighed the benefits and risks of expansion into Connecticut.[26]

In late August 1633, Massachusetts sent a trading expedition to Connecticut under the command of John ("Mad Jack") Oldham, a colorful and controversial trader who had been exiled from Plymouth some years earlier for complicity in the Reverend Mr. Lyford's efforts to undermine that colony's government. Now a respected citizen of the Massachusetts Bay Colony, Oldham had been instrumental in opening up trade relations with the Narragansetts. During this first visit to the Connecticut River valley, he acquired some samples of black lead, as well as a quantity of hemp, which Winthrop noted was both abundant and of high quality. Lodging at various Indian villages, Oldham followed a route later named "the Old Connecticut trail," which ran from Watertown through Waltham and Wayland to Farmington, and then southwest to the Connecticut River by way of Oxford. On his return to Boston, Oldham estimated the distance as 160 English miles.[27]

Intrigued by Oldham's report, the Bay Colony authorities placed the sixty-ton pinnace *Rebecca,* which had been launched at Medford the previous November, at his disposal for use in development of the Connecticut trade. Winthrop's journal entries in October 1633 reflected speculation in Boston that control of the Connecticut River might well be the key to gaining access to the fur trade of upper New York. The Connecticut, Winthrop believed, "runs so far northward" that it could provide a vital route to "the Great Lake of the Iroquois." "From that lake, and the hideous swamps about it," he wrote, "come most of the beaver which is traded between Virginia and Canada." Whereas Massachusetts' local trade with the Indians in 1632–33 yielded only 622 pelts, the Iroquois trade alone brought the Dutch "yearly . . . about ten thousand skins." Winthrop's geography was of course faulty. His interest in the Connecticut River as a pathway to the Iroquois trade may have been prompted by Thomas Morton, the Anglican trader expelled by Plymouth for selling guns to Indians. In *The New English Canaan,* published in London in 1634, Morton suggested that the English should occupy the shores of the "Great Lake" via the Connecticut River and thereby no longer "suffer the Dutch ... to possess themselves of that so pleasant and commodious country."[28]

Boston's interest in Connecticut notwithstanding, Plymouth established the first English outpost in the valley. After learning that the Dutch had built "a slight fort" on the Connecticut River, they promptly ordered Lieutenant William Holmes, second in command to Miles Standish, to sail for Connecticut. Before embarking, the Plymouth traders prefabricated "a small frame of a house" which they stored in the hold of their bark, along with enough boards and nails "to cover and finish it." Anticipating difficulty with both the Dutch and the Pequots, they went prepared to fortify their post on the Connecticut River. To gain a foothold in Connecticut, Plymouth had dealt with River Indian sachems hostile to the Pequots. Aboard the Plymouth bark was Natawante, a River Indian sachem and persistent visitor to the English colonies who hoped through English entrance into the valley to regain his former power. As Bradford noted, Plymouth had finally determined that Natawante was to be "brought home and restored [as] the right sachem of the place." From their newly installed sachem, Plymouth purchased a tract of land about a mile above the Dutch post at Hartford.[29]

Having used Natawante to contest the Dutch claims of occupancy by right of agreement with the Pequots, Plymouth expected that the latter would be "much offended" and anticipated a Pequot attack. But, whatever their feelings about Plymouth's collusion with the River Indian sachem, the Pequots did not in fact oppose the English presence. Instead, as noted in the previous chapter, they sent a deputation to Boston in the following year to seek an alliance. The Pequots wanted to resume their trade with the Europeans. For that reason, they did not attempt to expel either the English or the Dutch traders from the Connecticut valley. Plymouth's trading post on the Connecticut River and the Dutch House of Good Hope were both extremely vulnerable. Neither was attacked.[30]

Holmes's orders were to erect and fortify a post upriver from Good Hope and then intercept downriver traffic bound for the Dutch traders. His small bark crossed the bar at the mouth of the Connecticut River in early September 1633. As they passed the House of Good Hope, the

Englishmen were hailed from the shore by the Dutch, who demanded to know their mission. On learning that they were bound upriver to trade, the Dutch warned Holmes and his party to turn back, threatening to blow their ship out of the water with their post's two cannons if they went any farther. Defiantly Holmes pressed on, and, despite their bluster, the Dutch held their fire. Disembarking a mile above their rival, the Plymouth traders landed their provisions, hastily erected their house, threw up a palisade around their new trading post, and sent the bark home to Plymouth.[31]

Dutch resistance to Plymouth's presence on the river was halfhearted. The traders at the House of Good Hope dispatched a messenger to New Amsterdam (now Manhattan Island) to complain about the intrusion and seek aid in ejecting the intruders. Van Twiller responded by sending to Connecticut "a band of about seventy men, in warlike manner, with colors displayed." But despite their martial swagger, the Dutch troops turned out to be less than "warlike." After they arrived at the Plymouth encampment and looked over the fortifications, they quickly lost heart, realizing that an attack "would cost blood." They parleyed with the Plymouth traders "and returned in peace." In his account of the incident, Bradford asserted that Plymouth had done "the Dutch no wrong," as they had not evicted the traders at the House of Good Hope or squatted on their land "but went to a place above them," which the Dutch did not own. But the Dutch could hardly agree with that assessment. The Plymouth post was strategically located to cut off their trade with the upriver fur suppliers. However, they were not willing to use force against the intruders.[32]

With great satisfaction, William Bradford ended his account of the year 1633 by recording that "it pleased the Lord to enable them this year to send home a great quantity of beaver besides paying all their charges and debts at home, which good return did much encourage their friends in England." He also noted that, despite that sign of God's favor to his Elect, an epidemic of unknown nature in 1633 had claimed twenty English lives at Plymouth and severely affected the Indians near the settlement. Bradford regarded the sickness as a tribulation sent by the Almighty to test the faith of his people. He rejoiced that "sadness and mourning" had "caused them to humble themselves, and seek the Lord." Expressing the Puritans' fascination with the physical signs of God's imminent judgment, Bradford recounted that in "the spring before, and especially all the month of May, there was such a quantity of great sort of flies like for bigness to wasps or bumblebees, which came out of holes in the ground and replenished all the woods, and ate the green things, and made such a constant yelling noise as made all the woods ring of them, and ready to deaf the hearers. They have not by the English been heard or seen before, or since. But the Indians told them that sickness would follow, and so it did in June, July, August, and the chief heat of summer." [33]

The "great sort of flies" were the seventeen-year locusts *(Cicada septemdecim)* and were unrelated, as we now know, to the sickness. But as the locusts left, the epidemic ended in Plymouth, leaving the English to ponder its beneficent effect as a reminder of the awful power and majesty of God. God's affliction of the Saints at Plymouth had been gentle, but disease soon struck the Indians of the Connecticut valley, and the Dutch traders there, with the full force of an inexplicable and terrible judgment. Bradford solemnly recounted "some strange and remarkable passages" which could be construed as evidence that the Almighty had used disease as a means of advancing the cause of the Plymouth traders in Connecticut. Shortly after the erection of the Plymouth trading post, the Dutch, unable to drive the English from the valley, tried to outflank them. Three or four traders from the House of Good Hope early that winter moved upstream some miles above the English position and took up residence with an unidentified group described as a "stout people" greatly feared by the Indians of the valley. In their palisaded village, inhabited by about a thousand Indians, the Dutch urged their hosts to boycott the English and assist in maintaining the House of Good Hope's trade monopoly. But, Bradford recounted, "their enterprise failed, for it pleased God to visit these Indians with a great sickness." Of the thousand who welcomed the Dutch, less than fifty survived the winter, and many of the dead in the following spring thaw "did rot above ground for want of burial." The Dutch traders, though immune to the disease, almost perished of starvation in the afflicted village. Trapped for many weeks by "ice and snow" which made travel impossible, "almost spent with hunger and cold," they finally straggled into the Plymouth post in early February. Taken in by their rivals, the Dutch men were nursed back to health, then allowed to return to the House of Good Hope.[34]

A few weeks later the Indians who lived near the English and Dutch posts on the Connecticut were also struck. As Bradford recounted,

> those Indians that lived about their trading house there, fell sick of the smallpox and died most miserably; for a sorer disease cannot befall them, they fear it more than the plague. For usually they that have this disease have them in abundance, and for want of bedding and linen and other helps they fall into a lamentable condition as they lay on their hard mats, the pox breaking and mattering and running one into another, their skin cleaving by reason thereof to the mats they lie on. When they turn them, a whole side will flay off at once as it were, and they will be all of a gore blood, most fearful to behold. And then being very sore, what with cold and other distempers, they die like rotten sheep.

The English traders did what they could to minister to the sick, "daily fetched them wood and water and made them fires, got them victuals whilst they lived; and buried them when they died. For very few of them escaped, notwithstanding they did what they could for them to the hazard of themselves. The chief sachem himself now died and almost all of his friends and kindred." Bradford added that, "by the marvelous goodness and providence of God, not one of the English was so much as sick or in the least measure tainted with this disease." Winthrop's journal entry of January 20, 1634, recorded that three of his compatriots who had journeyed by land to Connecticut the past November had gotten lost and endured "much misery." The smallpox epidemic had spread "as far as any Indian plantation was known to the west," with 700 deaths reported by the Narragansetts alone. For that reason, "they could have no trade." [35]

In the fall of 1634, John Oldham made another overland journey to the Connecticut valley, establishing a small trading post at the site of the future town of Wethersfield, where his party wintered in crude log huts and planted a small crop of winter wheat. A handful of restive and land-hungry inhabitants of Watertown, defying a General Court edict directing them to remain in the Bay Colony, accompanied the traders to the valley. Winthrop, though opposed to the dispersion of the colony's population, encouraged the work of the Connecticut traders. Oldham's expeditions were intended to secure for the Massachusetts Bay Colony control of the Connecticut fur trade. As Francis Jennings has observed, the Bay Colony leaders' real reason for declining to enter into a partnership with Plymouth in Connecticut had nothing to do with the presumed cost or risk. "They hoped to make it Massachusetts' exclusive possession."[36]

The fertile land watered by the Connecticut River attracted Massachusetts settlers dissatisfied with their land holdings in the Bay Colony. Impressed by reports of the bounty of the Connecticut River valley, where meadows were said to be far more fertile than the stony soil of the bay, residents of Dorchester, Watertown, Roxbury, and Newtown looked westward. In Dorchester, the proposal to occupy Connecticut was supported by Roger Ludlow, deputy governor of the Massachusetts Bay Colony. But the greatest impetus came from the ministers at Newtown, Thomas Hooker and Emanuel Stone, and from their eminent parishioner, John Haynes, a future governor of the Bay Colony. On May 14, 1634, the Newtown congregation had informed the General Court of their dissatisfaction with their land allocation at Newtown and sought permission "to look either for enlargement or removal." The court raised no objections at that time.[37]

In the summer of 1634, several residents of Newtown accompanied *The Blessing of the Bay* on its voyage to New Amsterdam. En route, they looked over the Connecticut country, intending, Winthrop noted, "to remove their town thither." A year later, Roger Ludlow led a group of settlers from Dorchester to the site of the Plymouth trading post on the Connecticut River. The Plymouth agent in charge, Jonathan Brewster (son of Elder John Brewster), was astonished at the sudden influx of people and angered by their conduct. In his dispatch to Plymouth, dated July 6, 1635, he reported that "the Massachusetts men are coming almost daily, some by water, and some by land." The newcomers proceeded to squat on the large meadowland adjoining the post, which Plymouth had bought from the River Indian sachems. They had refused to discuss their plans with him, Brewster complained, but from the idle talk of "their servants . . . I perceive their minds." They planned to take over the meadowland. Brewster assured the Plymouth authorities that "I shall do what I can to withstand them. I hope they will hear reason, as that we were here first and entered with much difficulty and danger both in regard of the Dutch and the Indians, and bought the land, to your great charge already disbursed, and have since held here a chargeable possession and kept the Dutch from further encroaching, which would else long before this day have possessed all, and kept out all others, etc. I hope that these and such-like arguments will stop them." [38]

Despite his annoyance at the attitude of the newcomers, Brewster complied with instructions and provided them with badly needed assistance. "It was your will that we should use their persons and messengers kindly," he wrote to Plymouth, "and so we have done and do daily, to your great charge; for the first company had well nigh starved, had it not been for this house, for want of victuals; I being forced to supply twelve men for nine days together. And those which came last, I entertained the best we could, helping both them and the others with canoes and guides." Brewster also stored their trade goods and assisted them in an unsuccessful effort to buy land from the Dutch. But, as Charles McLean Andrews noted, "for these friendly offices he was ill-requited. The Dorchester people ignored the Plymouth title to the meadow north of the rivulet and proceeded to lay out their home lots and build their houses along the high ground above and west of the great river." [39]

It took two years of intercolonial bickering to settle the dispute. Plymouth charged the Dorchester emigrants with theft of their land. The accused replied: "Look that you abuse not God's providence in such allegations!" The land in question, they maintained, was unoccupied, and "being the Lord's waste, and for present altogether void of inhabitants," they had every right "with God's good leave to take and use it, without just offense to any man." Plymouth responded indignantly to that claim by declaring that, if the great meadow "was the Lord's waste," it was Plymouth, not Massachusetts, that first "found it so" and thus could claim it by right of discovery. But in fact Plymouth had "bought it of the right owners, and maintained a chargeable possession of it all this while." The Dorchester men, Plymouth insisted, were well aware of that fact, and their claim that they believed the meadowland was simply "the Lord's waste" was false and hypocritical. The Dorchester settlers, now organized as the town of Windsor, finally agreed, very grudgingly and under the pressure of a visit from Plymouth's Governor Thomas Prence, to make a nominal payment for the property they had so unceremoniously seized. The settlement deprived the Plymouth traders in Connecticut of about 94 percent of the territory originally purchased from the River Indian sachems. [40]

Plymouth remained embittered by the loss. William Bradford noted that in the fall of 1635 "two shallops going to Connecticut with goods

from Massachusetts of such as removed hither to plant" were shipwrecked off Plymouth. "The boats' men were lost and the goods were
driven all along the shore, and strewn up and down at high water mark."
Soon thereafter, another Bay Colony vessel bound for Connecticut was
lost at Scussett. Some at Plymouth, Bradford recounted, regarded those
incidents as God's punishment of the Bay Colony "for their intrusion, to
the wrong of others," into Connecticut. He added, "but I dare not be
bold with God's judgments in this kind." [41]

Plymouth was not alone in regarding the Dorchester men as interlopers
and squatters. In 1632 Robert Rich, second earl of Warwick, and several
other prominent lords and gentlemen of Puritan persuasion laid claim,
through a patent submitted to the Council for New England, to a vast
but vaguely defined expanse of land beginning at Narragansett Bay and
extending to the Pacific Ocean. There is reason to doubt that the council
ever ratified "the Warwick patent." The patent purportedly granted the
lords and gentlemen a place of refuge in the New World and, authentic
or not, provided the basis for extensive land claims. [42] In 1635 one of the
presumed beneficiaries of the patent, Sir Richard Saltonstall, resolved to
establish a plantation in Connecticut. To that end, Saltonstall privately
outfitted and dispatched to New England a ship carrying an advance
party led by Francis Stiles, a master carpenter from London, and including Stiles's two brothers and eighteen indentured servants. The party
landed briefly at Boston, then proceeded to the Connecticut River valley.
Arriving at the meadow, which Saltonstall had specified as the site for his
plantation, the Stiles brothers found the best land already taken by
Ludlow and his associates. Receiving an inhospitable reception from
both the Dorchester emigrants and the Plymouth traders, Stiles and his
people were confined to a narrow tract of land at the south end of the
great meadow, which was clearly not adequate to support Saltonstall's
proposed venture. Learning of Stiles's frustration, Saltonstall charged
that he had been victimized by Bay Colony treachery, as Ludlow, learning
of his plans, had taken advantage of Stiles's delay at Boston to send men
into the Connecticut valley to "greedily snatch up all the best ground on
the river." [43]

The Saltonstall-Stiles expedition was a small-scale venture. Several
months prior to his abortive effort to establish his own plantation at
Windsor under the Warwick patent, Saltonstall had also joined with

several other Warwick patentees, all of them noblemen or gentlemen of Puritan persuasion, in a more ambitious plan to establish an independent colony at the mouth of the Connecticut River which would provide a refuge and home should the course of events place Puritans in England in jeopardy. On July 7, 1635, the patentees led by Lord Saye and Sele appointed John Winthrop, Jr., son of the Bay Colony's principal leader, as "Gouenour of the river Connecticut in New England and of the Harbors and places adjoininge." The younger Winthrop, then twenty-nine years old, had been sent to England the previous year to recruit immigrants for Massachusetts. His agreement with Lord Saye and Sele and associates specified that Winthrop would recruit a company of "fifty men at the least for makinge of fortifications and buildinge of houses." He was to construct "within the fort" at the mouth of the river houses appropriate for "men of qualitie," should any or all of the patentees choose to reside in their colony in New England. The agreement also charged the governor of the colony with responsibility for assuring that at least 1,000 to 1,500 acres would be reserved for the fort and for the residences of the notables. As to the other settlers, all were to locate, for their protection, "either at the harbour or neare the mouth of the river."[44]

John Winthrop, Jr., returned to Boston aboard the *Abigail* on October 6, 1635. His father noted in his journal that he came armed "with comission from the Lord Say, Lord Brook and divers other great persons in England, to begin a plantation in Connecticut, and to be governor there. They sent also men and ammunition, and 2000 pounds in money, to begin a fortification at the mouth of the river." Hearing rumors of an impending Dutch expedition to reoccupy Kievet's Hook at the same site, the younger Winthrop on November 3 dispatched an advance party of "about twenty men, with all needful provision, to take possession of the mouth of the Connecticut and begin some building." Edward Gibbon, a former associate of Thomas Morton of Merrymount now reconciled to the New England way, was placed in temporary command. The party encountered no Dutchmen but did find the Dutch coat of arms nailed to a post. They tore it down.[45]

John Winthrop, Jr., was also worried about the encroachments from Plymouth and Massachusetts Bay upon the lands claimed by his employers. Connecticut, he declared, was not under the jurisdiction of either colony but was the rightful domain of the holders of the Warwick patent. All other Englishmen who hoped to reside in Connecticut would need to obtain their title from the new colony of which he was now the governor. One of Winthrop's traveling companions on the *Abigail* lent his not inconsiderable influence to the cause. Sir Henry Vane, son of King Charles I's chamberlain, bluntly informed the Boston magistrates that the squatters in Connecticut must either "give place" or take steps to see to it that "sufficient room" were "found for these lords and their companions."[46]

Given his father's high office, Boston's rulers thought it wise to cultivate the young man. Shortly after his arrival in New England, twenty-three-year-old Sir Henry Vane was elected governor of the Massachusetts Bay Colony. He was not imposing in appearance. One historian writes that, "if Vane was not actually cross-eyed, his lopsided face made him appear so; his overlarge chin, accentuated by his plumpness, made him seem like a petulant child about to break into a tantrum; and he wore a habitual harried expression as though evil spirits were pursuing him." But Vane, brought up at court, was gracious in manner, sincere in his commitment to the Puritan cause, "grave, pleasing, accomplished." The Bay Colony quickly accepted him as "a gift from above." But Winthrop and his fellow magistrates were soon astounded and appalled by their new governor's sympathy for the schismatic Anne Hutchinson and the so-called antinomians who supported her and were greatly relieved by his early and permanent departure for England. A few years later Vane emerged as one of the more able leaders of the revolutionary Long Parliament. A man of independent views, with the courage of his convictions, Vane was imprisoned by both Cromwell and Charles II. He was beheaded during the reign of the latter.[47]

Winthrop's journal that fall also recorded the arrival in Boston Harbor of "a small Norsey bark, of twenty five tons, sent by Lord Say, etc. with one Gardiner, an expert engineer . . . and provisions of all sorts, to begin a fort at the mouth of the Connecticut." Lion Gardener, a Scotsman and Puritan, had fought as a youth against the Spaniards with an English volunteer force in the Netherlands under the command of Sir Horace Vere. He stayed on in Holland, winning appointment as a lieutenant of engineers on the staff of the prince of Orange. Having twelve years experience with the Dutch as a master of fortifications, Gardener was ideally suited to supervise the building of a refuge for Puritan noblemen in the American wilderness. Contacted in Rotterdam in 1635 by two Puritan divines, Hugh Peter and John Davenport, Gardener accepted their offer and resigned his Dutch commission. His Dutch wife, whom he married shortly after agreeing to go to New England, accompanied him aboard the bark *Batchellor*. Landing at Boston on November 28, Gardener was briefed by John Winthrop, Jr., on the Dutch threat to their plan to plant a colony at the mouth of the Connecticut River. But an early and severe winter delayed Gardener's departure. The Connecticut River had frozen solid on November 15. A supply ship, the *Rebecca*, returning from the settlement at Windsor was trapped in ice twenty miles upriver, freed by "a small rain falling," then grounded in the treacherous sand at the mouth of the river. Several crew members starved to death. As the *Rebecca* lay grounded, a Dutch sloop appeared "to take possession of the mouth of the river." Gibbon and his men, defending the makeshift English settlement with two artillery pieces, "would not suffer them to land."[48]

On assuming his command in Connecticut, Lieutenant Gardener constructed a very respectable fort. The placement of the two cannons on "Fort Hill," a ten-foot-high mound within the palisade, enabled Gardener to command the treacherous, sand-clogged channel at the river's mouth. Within the fort grounds were a small freshwater pond and ample space for both a garden and an orchard. Although the residences suitable for "men of qualitie" envisioned in the patentees' instructions never materialized, Gardener did erect a substantial wooden "great hall" subdivided into apartments, as well as a barracks and small storehouse. The settlement was named "Saybrook" in honor of two prominent patentees, Lord Saye and Sele and Lord Brook.[49]

Conditions at Saybrook were harsh. Gardener's highly placed employers failed to make good on their lavish promises to supply men and material. About seven months after the landing of the first garrison, the inhabitants of the fort drew up a petition of grievances, wherein they complained that they had been deprived of both spiritual and material sustenance. "We have lived a great while without the means of grace and salvation," the petitioners declared, "we being ignorant and scarse know anything of the way and hav great need of teaching." They reminded the sponsors of the colony that they had come to New England in order to enjoy the Gospel "in a more frequent and gloriouse way then we had in our natiue countrie" and demanded that they send a minister. As one historian has noted, this complaint, "unusual even in Puritan New England . . . was an obvious tribute to the screening to which the Puritan patentees had subjected their personnel." The men of Saybrook also complained about the neglect of their physical well-being. They no longer had bread or beer but subsisted on a grim and demoralizing diet of pease porridge. They also lacked adequate clothing to cope with the harsh winter. The material shortages proved to be temporary, but many years were to pass before Saybrook enjoyed the regular ministrations of a preacher. Only one of the Warwick patentees, George Fenwick, ever took up residence at Saybrook, and the promised influx of English commoners of Puritan persuasion never materialized. Fenwick stayed only a brief time and in 1645 deeded Saybrook to the colony of Connecticut.[50]

The governor of the river colony did not take up residence at Saybrook until early April 1636. The delay was occasioned not only by the severity of the winter but also by Winthrop's determination to resolve the jurisdictional dispute with the settlers from Massachusetts who were now occupying parts of the Connecticut valley. The Saybrook associates expected their governor to defend their interests against all intruders in Connecticut. Sir Richard Saltonstall wrote to complain of "the abuse and injurie done me by Mr. Ludlow and others of Dorchester." Not only had Ludlow and his friends refused to yield Warwick patent land to Francis Stiles and his party, but they had referred to Sir Richard himself "with many unbeseeming words." Saltonstall demanded that Lieutenant Gardener be sent upriver with an armed party to enforce his claim by ejecting Ludlow's people. But the river governor was in no position to use force. The tiny Saybrook garrison was soon outnumbered, as reports of the fertility of the Connecticut meadowlands attracted scores of Bay Colony settlers dissatisfied with the rocky and ungenerous soil of Massachusetts. The most prominent of those who abandoned the bay for Connecticut were the members of the Reverend Thomas Hooker's congregation at Newtown. The elder Winthrop had noted in his journal on May 15, 1634, that Hooker's flock had complained about the inadequacy of their land, "especially meadow," and had asked the court for permission "to look out either for enlargement, or removal." They were encouraged to look over sites in northeastern Massachusetts and Maine but found them wanting. Residents of Newtown visited Connecticut and found those lands most appealing. They promptly sought permission to remove to the Connecticut River valley.[51]

The Newtown residents' request had led to an acrimonious debate within the Massachusetts Bay Colony General Court in the late summer of 1634. Although Governor Thomas Dudley was sympathetic to their desire to settle in Connecticut, former Governor Winthrop and other prominent magistrates argued that "we ought not to give them leave to depart . . . being that we were now weak and in danger to be assaulted . . . the departure of Mr. Hooker would not only draw many from us, but would also divert other friends who would come to us." In addition, by approving Newtown's petition, Winthrop and his associates warned that "we should expose them to evident peril, both from the Dutch (who made claim to the same river, and had already built a fort there) and from the Indians, and also from our own state at home, who would not endure that they should sit down without a patent in any place which our king lays claim unto." Moreover, their departure would reflect badly on the Puritan community at the bay since "the removing of a candle-stick is a great judgment, which is to be avoided." Winthrop argued that Newtown's petitioners should satisfy their needs by accepting offers from neighboring towns for "enlargement," or by moving to "Merrimack, or any other place within our patent." In response to those arguments, Hooker responded that there was simply not enough good land in Massachusetts to meet his people's needs. They could neither pasture their cattle nor properly "maintain their ministers" and were thus impelled to move westward by "the fruitfulness and commodiousness of Connecticut." Hooker also argued that they must act promptly to counter "the danger of having it possessed by others, Dutch or English."[52]

The General Court approved Newtown's petition by a vote of fifteen in favor, ten opposed. However, a majority of the assistants, including Winthrop (who was serving that year as deputy governor), refused to approve the removal request. They argued that under the colony's charter no vote of the court was binding unless six assistants concurred. "Upon this," Winthrop recorded in his journal, "grew a great difference between the governor and the assistants, and the deputies." The deputies refused to recognize the assistants' claim of veto power over the actions of the General Court, leading Winthrop to worry about "how dangerous it might be to the commonwealth" if "the greater number" gained power. Deadlocked over the constitutional issue, "the whole court agreed to keep a day of humiliation to the Lord, which accordingly was done in all the congregations, the 18th day of the month, and the 24th the court met again." It was then decided that the clergy should address the court on the nature of government. Hooker declined the assignment, and the Reverend John Cotton thereupon preached a sermon to the deputies on the need to maintain the authority of magistrates in general and the veto power of the assistants in particular. The Lord, as Winthrop saw it, blessed Cotton's efforts, as "the affairs of the court went on cheerfully, and although all were not satisfied about the negative voice to be left to the magistrates, yet no man moved aught about it." Given the deputies' disinclination to press the matter, Hooker and his congregation temporarily abandoned their plan to move to Connecticut and accepted additional lands in Massachusetts offered by Boston and Watertown. John Haynes was elected governor of the Massachusetts Bay Colony on May 6, 1635. Some conjectured that the magistrates selected Haynes "partly with the intent of detaching him from the enterprise."[53]

But Newtown remained dissatisfied, and soon residents of several other villages in the Bay Colony—Watertown, Roxbury, and Dorchester—also clamored for access to the rich lands believed to lie in the Connecticut valley. Winthrop and his allies, though fearful that the removal of Saints from the godly commonwealth at the bay to the howling wilderness in the west would loosen the bond of both church and state and thus undermine the Holy Experiment, reluctantly concluded that continued opposition would prove inexpedient. Accordingly, with the concurrence of the assistants, the General Court in May and June of 1635 granted the inhabitants of several towns permission to emigrate, "provided they continue under this government." Shortly thereafter, settlers from Dorchester, as noted earlier, settled near Plymouth's trading post on the Connecticut River, founding the town of Windsor. A handful of emigrants from Watertown established a crude settlement near the site of the future town of Wethersfield. A larger party of about sixty colonists set out for Connecticut in October, driving a herd of cattle over the narrow Indian trails. The onset of severe cold in late November disrupted their plans. While most dug in as best they could to weather the storms that followed one another in quick succession, twelve of the would-be Connecticut planters straggled back to Boston, where they reported that the Connecticut River had already frozen solid, thus blocking the way to the resupply of their associates by water. Winthrop noted in his journal that "they had been ten days upon their journey, and had lost one of their company, drowned in the ice by the way, and had all but starved, but that, by God's providence, they lighted upon an Indian wigwam."[54]

In March of the following year, the General Court set up a commission of eight members with limited power to govern the settlements in Connecticut. The commission, appointed for one year, was authorized to regulate trade, allocate land, and, if necessary, call a general court and raise a militia for defense of their villages. On May 31, 1636, Winthrop wrote in his journal, "Mr. Hooker, pastor of the church at Newtown, and most of his congregation, went to Connecticut. His wife was carried in a horse litter; and they drove one hundred and sixty cattle, and fed of their milk by the way." Hooker and his people founded Hartford.[55]

Back in Boston, the magistrates remained uneasy about the possibility of the corruption and degeneration of Englishmen in the wilderness. In 1635 they had passed a statute requiring that all houses be built within a half-mile walk to a meetinghouse. The following year, they adopted resolutions that forbade the founding of new towns or the gathering of new churches without their explicit permission. Those laws proved to be unenforceable.[56]

The occupation of Connecticut by settlers from the Bay Colony, in addition to antagonizing both the Dutch and the Plymouth traders, violated the presumed rights of the Saybrook associates. John Winthrop, Jr., lacking the means to prevent that occupation, endeavored to negotiate a settlement that would protect the interests of his employers. As one historian has noted, "the problems were not easy to solve and the discussions were conducted with the greatest secrecy." But "as the grantees wanted settlers and the emigrants wanted security and a legal title," there was sufficient commonality of interest to point the way to a settlement. The upriver settlers agreed to recognize Winthrop as governor of all of Connecticut, and Winthrop in turn gave his consent to their settlement on Warwick patent lands. Under his instructions from the patentees, the governor at Saybrook could not agree to either the extension of Massachusetts Bay Colony jurisdiction over the valley or the establishment of a rival colony in Connecticut. To resolve that impasse, the negotiators agreed to a rather ingenious legal contrivance wherein "the Massachusetts General Court was accepted by both parties as qualified to give proper constitutional character to the proposed plantation and was invited to serve, not officially as a principle, but as a go-between or friendly broker, in the task of putting into authoritative form the agreement arrived at." The eight-member governing commission, appointed by the General Court on March 3, 1636, and alluded to previously, was the outgrowth of that agreement.[57]

It was a clever solution, but, as Francis Jennings has noted, Connecticut in 1636 "presented the curious spectacle of a substantial colony upriver, pretending to have a governor, and a fortified governor downstream, pretending to have a colony." In actual fact, the governor at Saybrook had no real authority over the burgeoning upriver towns. Lord Saye and Sele, accepting reality, wrote to the elder Winthrop to express "a great deale of satisfaction" with the work of his son but added wryly that "those up the river have carried largely for themselves" and might one day come to regret their selfish conduct.[58]

The younger Winthrop took up residence at Saybrook shortly after the conclusion of the negotiations leading to the Connecticut settlement. He soon wrote to his father to complain that supplies intended for Saybrook had been stolen en route and that his trading ship, the *Batcheller,* had been "pillaged" at Salem so "pitifully that she hath neyther blockes nor braces nor running ropes." Maintaining the ship proved burdensome, so Winthrop asked his father to find a buyer. In May 1636, George Fenwick, one of the Warwick patentees, arrived unexpectedly in Boston. Informed of Saybrook's discouragement over the lack of supplies, he wrote to John Winthrop, Jr., to urge him to make do for the time being "in as frugall a way as can stande with securinge the place." Fenwick promised the young Winthrop that the next ship from England would bring "a good quantitie" of provisions, "with spades and some such other things as you wrot for." But the elder Winthrop received a very different impression and, after a conversation with Fenwick, wrote his son to warn that the patentees appeared to be losing interest in the project. Lieutenant Gardener shared Winthrop's disillusionment. He had been promised that the fort would be manned by 300 sturdy Puritans from England, "whereof 200 should attend fortification, 50 to till the ground, and 50 to build houses." They never materialized, and in his old age Gardener, in a letter to two of the men who served under him at Saybrook, reminisced that he had had to try to learn carpentry in order to help build the fort. "You know," he wrote, "I could never use all the tools."[59]

While Saybrook languished, settlers from the Massachusetts Bay Colony flocked to the upriver settlements at Hartford, Windsor, Wethersfield, and Springfield. The river governor tried to use his influence to protect Plymouth's interests in the area, as well as the patentees', but to no avail. In a letter to John Winthrop, Jr., Edward Winslow, disgusted at the grasping attitude of the Massachusetts men who seized Plymouth's land in the valley, wrote that they "deserve no favor. . . . 'tis pitty religion should be a cloake for such spirits." But to complain to the river governor was pointless. As his biographer notes, the outcome of the land disputes on the river made it "painfully evident that Winthrop's writ ran no further than a cannon shot from Saybrook." The towns upriver ignored his wishes regarding respect for Plymouth's rights in the valley. They nonetheless asked for use of the facilities at Saybrook and for permission to build warehouses at the river's mouth to accommodate their trade. The Bay Colony governor, Sir Henry Vane, advised Winthrop to grant those requests. He had no choice but to comply.[60]

Soon after his arrival at Saybrook, John Winthrop, Jr., was also troubled by rumors of an impending Pequot attack. The Pequots had made no provision to pay the full wampum tribute mandated in the agreement at Boston in 1634, nor did they comply with English demands that they apprehend and deliver to Puritan justice the murderers of Captain John Stone and his crew. When John Oldham pressed them on those matters, the Pequots replied that the tribal elders had not ratified the treaty. Oldham, on returning from a trade mission to the Pequots in 1635, declared them a "very false people." English suspicions and anxieties about Pequot motives were exacerbated by reports from "friendly" Indians who warned of Pequot plans to destroy the English settlements in Connecticut. The documentary evidence available to us points to Uncas as the main, and perhaps the only, source of these rumors. His reports were of doubtful reliability. William Pynchon, a shrewd Indian trader who had established a post at Springfield on the upper Connecticut River, advised his friends at Saybrook to discount assertions that the Pequots were responsible for the recent deaths of two English traders on Long Island.[61]

Plymouth's Indian agent at Windsor was more credulous. On June 18 Jonathan Brewster wrote to Saybrook to report that he had learned from Uncas that Sassacus, the Pequot grand sachem, had called a council of war which had lasted "one day, and most part of one Night." The purpose of the conclave, Uncas claimed, was to plot an attack on Plymouth's trading bark. Uncas added that soon thereafter some eighty Pequot warriors were dispatched to the river to plunder the vessel, which was then in "habour weakely manned." However, as Brewster recounted, "it pleased the over Ruleing power of God to hinder [the Pequots] for as soone as these bloody executioners arose out of ambush with their canoes, the[y] deserned her vnder sayle with a fayre winde returning Home." The Pequot design against the bark was not, Brewster warned, an isolated incident. The Pequots had stalked the vessel two years before, having boasted to other Indians on that occasion that, "if our Barke had but stayed 6 houres longer in their Harbour," they would have attacked it. Uncas also reported that the murder of Stone three years before had been carefully planned in a Pequot council of war and that Sassacus himself had led the operation. Despite Pequot claims not to know the whereabouts of Stone's killers, one of them was their own chief sachem, and three others were living openly in the principal Pequot village. Moreover, the Pequots were so alarmed by rumors of an impending English attack on them that they were now plotting a preventive war and "out of desperate madnesse doe threaten shortly to sett both upon Indians and Englishmen jointly." Accepting Uncas's tale at face value, Brewster declared Pequot treachery "intolerable." As he reflected further on the matter, the Plymouth agent completely lost his composure and wrote twice on the same day to warn John Winthrop, Jr., of Pequot perfidy. In his second letter, he repeated the story of the conspiracies to attack the bark and declared that Sassacus's people "continewes still in their blody mynds toward the English." Persuaded that the Pequots were indeed about to attack both the English and their Indian friends in the valley, Brewster appealed to Winthrop to order that all English ships traveling upriver be armed.[62]

Did the Pequots actually intend to attack in 1636? Despite Uncas's story, there were no verified incidents of Pequot aggression against the English after their visit to Boston in 1634. They took no advantage of the many opportunities they had to strike at English trading parties and settlers on the isolated trails leading into the Connecticut valley, nor did they actually interfere with the commerce on the river. Pequot complicity in the killings on Long Island has often been assumed but never demonstrated. Pynchon's skepticism about their guilt seems well founded, given their record in Connecticut. Jonathan Brewster no doubt believed that the hand of the Almighty on two occasions had thwarted Pequot plans by inspiring the crew of his bark to sail away before the Indians could strike, but we must ask why Pequots allowed small, vulnerable groups of Puritans to enter and reside undisturbed in Connecticut if they were actually hostile to the English presence there. If one discounts rumors and stories spread by nervous Englishmen and by Indians hostile to Sassacus, it would appear that the Pequots had honored fully their promise concerning English occupation of Connecticut. But their failure to comply with the more extreme provisions of the 1634 "treaty" aroused deep suspicions in the minds of men persuaded that recalcitrant Indians were the devil's agents.

The rumors about Pequot malevolence alarmed the authorities at Boston. In early July, John Winthrop, Jr., was informed by Governor Vane that he had been commissioned by the Bay Colony to investigate Pequot conduct and to secure both the surrender of the murderers of Stone and the full wampum payment discussed in 1634. Winthrop's instructions specified that he was to begin by asking the Pequot's "Principall Sachem . . . in a friendly manner" for a "solemne Meeting" to discuss "matters of importance." If Sassacus did not grant that request promptly, Winthrop was to return the wampum and furs received from the Pequots in 1634 and abrogate the Anglo-Pequot treaty of friendship by declaring that "we hold ourselves free from any peace with them as a People guilty of English blood." Should the meeting occur, he not only was to renew the demand for Stone's murderers and for wampum but was to advise the Pequots that the Bay Colony could not accept their excuse that the tribal elders had not ratified the treaty but would regard the repetition of such a claim as proof of Pequot bad faith. (Since the Puritans, as Winthrop's journal reveals, were well aware that the 1634 envoys had no authority to make a binding treaty, that stance can only be taken as an expression of contempt for Pequot sovereignty.) Winthrop was also directed to confront the Pequots with the charge that they had killed two English traders on Long Island and had plotted an attack on Plymouth's trading bark. He was to listen carefully to their reply, assess its veracity, and report back to Boston. Finally, the Pequots were to be warned that, if they should persist in their refusal to surrender the murderers of Stone or were unable to prove themselves innocent of the deaths on Long Island, the English would take revenge upon them. In effect, Winthrop's instructions were to threaten war if he could not secure Pequot submission.[63]

The river governor was to be assisted in his negotiations with the Pequots by the patentee George Fenwick, the Reverend Hugh Peter (Winthrop's father-in-law), the trader John Oldham, and Thomas Stanton, a gifted young translator fluent in the southern New England Algonquian dialects. Fenwick and his party carried to Saybrook "some otter skin coats, and Beaver, and skeins of wampum" that the Pequots had presented to the Boston magistrates in 1634. In the very likely event of Pequot refusal to capitulate to all of the Bay Colony's demands, they were to underscore the termination of friendly relations by returning that present.

At Saybrook, Lieutenant Gardener was appalled by the proposed proceedings with the Pequots. He exclaimed to the commissioners from Boston, "I know you will keep yourselves safe . . . in the Bay, but myself, with these few you will leave at the stake to be roasted, or for hunger to be starved . . . we being so few in the River, and have scarce holes to put our heads in." He reminded the delegation that, when he had been asked by the Massachusetts magistrates to advise on the fortification of Salem, "I told them that Nature had done more than half the work already, and I thought no foreign potent enemy would do them any hurt, but one that was near. They asked me who that was, and I said it was Capt. Hunger that threatened them most, for (said I) War is like a threefooted stool, want one foot and down come all: and these three feet are men, victuals, and munition." Saybrook, Gardener declared, was "famished . . . in peace." It could not be defended in war without substantial reinforcements. He demanded that the magistrates in Boston be asked if they had forgotten his advice, and he pled with the delegation to leave the Pequots alone "till we get more strength here about us." They must consider that there were only twenty-four people at the fort, "men, women, boys and girls, and not food for more than two months, unless we saved our corn field, which could not possibly be if they came to war, for it is two miles from our home." Gardener later claimed that Winthrop, Fenwick, and Peter promised him that "they would do their utmost to endeavor to persuade the Massachusetts authorities to desist from war a year or two, till we could be better provided for it." That promise was not kept. "The Pequit sachem," he recalled bitterly, "was sent for, and the present returned, but full sore against my will." Having thus placed Gardener and his garrison in jeopardy by provoking the Pequots, John Winthrop, Jr., left Saybrook for good, disregarding his promise to return promptly to his duties there. The Saybrook associates in England accordingly declined to pay his full salary.[64]

We have little information about the conference with the Pequots held at Saybrook in July 1636. It is not known whether Sassacus attended. It is known that, in addition to unnamed Pequot representatives, Sassious, sachem of the western Niantics, who lived on the east bank of the river across from Saybrook, was present. Sassious's people paid tribute to the Pequots and, as noted earlier, were probably involved with them in the killing of John Stone. Sassious, intimidated by talk of avenging Stone and his crew, sought to place himself and his people under the protection of the English and accordingly presented John Winthrop, Jr., with a generous grant of land. After the beginning of hostilities, the Pequots, perhaps suspicious of Sassious, asked Lieutenant Gardener if the English would wage war on the western Niantics as well as the Pequots. Gardener replied that the Saybrook garrison "knew not the Indians one from another, and therefore would trade with none." John Winthrop, Jr., having left the scene, was unable to intervene on behalf of the western Niantics, who subsequently fought on the side of the Pequots. After the war, however, he nonetheless laid claim to the land deeded to him by Sassious at Saybrook.[65]

With the all-too-prompt embarkation of the younger Winthrop and his fellow negotiators for Boston, Lieutenant Gardener was left to cope with whatever consequences might follow the ultimatum to the Pequots. Several days after Winthrop's departure, an Indian named Commithus appeared at the gates of Fort Saybrook. In fluent English, he explained that he had once lived at Plymouth but had joined the Pequots and now came bearing a message from Sassacus. The grand sachem, despite the ultimatum, wanted trade with Saybrook. Moreover, he had taken into his care two stray English horses. If the English would send a trading party, he would return the strays. Seeking out Stephen Winthrop, younger brother of the recently departed river governor and manager of William Pynchon's warehouse near the fort, Commithus urged the trader to take some of the trade cloth and other goods stored there and visit the Pequots. Sassacus, he promised, would buy the goods and give his men the horses.[66]

Gardener was troubled by that invitation. He was eager to stall for time, to take any step that would restore at least temporarily amicable relations with the Pequots. But, mindful of rumors of Pequot plans to attack the English, he feared a trap. He finally reluctantly agreed to send Stephen Winthrop, Thomas Hurlbut, Sergeant Tilly, and three other men to the Pequots. He carefully instructed the party to "ride in the middle of the river, and not to go ashore until they had done all their trade." They were to permit only one canoe at a time to approach the shallop, with no more than four Indians aboard each canoe. The traders were to remain armed at all times, "with their guns by them, and swords by their sides." They were not to remain in Pequot country for more than one day and were to leave the river before dark. In the event that the Pequot sachem did return the horses, they were, Gardener directed, "to take them in at a clear piece of land at the mouth of the River, two of them [to] go ashore to help the horses in, and the rest [to] stand ready with their arms in their hands . . . to defend them from the Pequits, for I durst not trust them."

After their return, Gardener was distressed to learn that his men had "forgotten what I charged them." As they sailed into their harbor, the Pequots did not seem hostile. They were, however, reluctant to board the shallop in the manner the English specified. No doubt they remembered both Tatobem's death aboard a Dutch ship and the recent English threats to take revenge for John Stone. Two of the Englishmen therefore went ashore. One, Sergeant Tilly, started "to boil a kettle," perhaps intending to prepare a meal. The second, Thomas Hurlbut, brashly walked into "the Sachem's wigwam, not far from the shore, inquiring for the horses." All but one of the Indians inside, startled by the sudden appearance of an armed Englishman, bolted. Only "Wincumbone, the great Pequit Sachem's wife," remained. She, as Hurlbut later told Gardener, "made signs that we should be gone" and by gesture seemed to suggest that the Pequots planned to "cut off his head." Alarmed, Hurlbut drew his sword and bounded out of the wigwam. He yelled to Tilly, who quickly grabbed his weapon, emptied the kettle, stuck it on his head, and ran for the ship. Pequots then poured out of wigwams and, running to the riverbank, called to the English to come ashore again. But the traders instead "immediately set sail and came home." Lieutenant Gardener, told of the squaw's ominous gesture, assumed the worst and concluded that the Pequots "plotted our destruction." [67]

Would Stephen Winthrop and his compatriots have been massacred had they not fled from the Pequot village? Probably not. Hurlbut probably misinterpreted the sachem's wife's gesture. As he was armed with a sword and suddenly appeared unannounced in a crowded wigwam, she may have been warning him not to resort to violence, or predicting the Pequot response if he took *her* life. Or she may have been joking about the braves' fears that Hurlbut would cut off *their* heads with his sword. We will never know for certain just what she meant. But one very important key is provided in Gardener's account of the aftermath, which contains no hint of any actual attack on the departing Englishmen. No stones, arrows, or spears were hurled at the crew members as they hauled up the anchor and set sail. Instead, the Pequots begged them to come ashore. Perhaps they were only biding their time, hoping to catch the English off guard. But given their behavior in the wigwam, that seems unlikely. Why, if they intended to kill Hurlbut, did the Indians flee rather than killing him then and there? Hurlbut was extremely vulnerable in the close quarters of the wigwam. All things considered, it appears that the Pequots were interested in trade but were intimidated by the heavily armed Englishmen. Given the tensions between the two peoples, their reluctance to board the English ship two by two is quite understandable.

Soon thereafter, death at the hands of Indians did come to an English trader, but the killers were not Pequots. Following the Saybrook conference, John Oldham had returned to his trading post upriver at Wethersfield. In late July, Oldham visited Saybrook again, sold a few items to Lieutenant Gardener, and set sail for Block Island accompanied by two Narragansett Indians and two English boys. On July 20 John Gallop, on a trade mission to Long Island in a small bark of twenty tons manned by a crew of three, was suddenly driven by a "change of the wind" toward Block Island. Near the island, he spied a pinnace at anchor, which he recognized as Oldham's. Gallop hailed the little ship but "had no answer." Drawing closer, he saw that "the deck was full of Indians, fourteen in all." Nearby, a canoe was heading toward the island, laden with Indians and trade goods. Suddenly, the Indians aboard the pinnace "let slip and set sail, being two miles from the shore." But they handled the ship awkwardly, catching the offshore wind and tide and lurching toward the mainland. As he watched, Gallop suddenly "suspected that they had killed Oldham." He gave chase and, though armed with only two muskets, two pistols, and some duck shot, began firing at the Indians who stood on Oldham's deck, "ready armed with guns, pikes and swords." Frightened by the duck shot pelting the deck, the Indians dove into the hatches. Gallop then stood off but caught "a good gale" and rammed the pinnace on its quarter, almost capsizing it, "which so frightened the Indians" that "six of them leaped overboard and were drowned." Lacking the manpower to board Oldham's ship, Gallop stood off again, planted his anchor into its stern, caught the wind, and crashed again into the pinnace. The anchor held firmly in the bow, and "so sticking fast to her," Gallop raked the deck with duck shot. He then broke loose and stood off again. "Four or five more of the Indians," to escape the gunfire, "leaped into the sea, and were likewise drowned."

Since there were now only four Indians left on board, Gallop and his companions boarded Oldham's vessel. One Indian emerged from a hatch and surrendered. He was tied up and thrown into the hold. Then another surrendered. Gallop, fearing that "given their skill to untie themselves" the two captive Indians, if placed together in the hold, would break loose, threw his new prisoner "bound into the sea." Gallop and his men then searched the ship. They found the body of John Oldham hidden "under an old seine, stark naked, his head cleft to the brains, and his hands and legs cut as if they had been cutting them off." The corpse was still warm. After burying Oldham at sea, Gallop found two other Indians hiding below deck in a small room. They were armed with swords and could not be dislodged. Gallop then unloaded what remained of Oldham's cargo, took his sails, and tried to tow his ship. "But night coming on, and the wind rising, they were forced to turn her off, and the wind carried her to the Narragansett shore." [68]

Who killed John Oldham? Some writers blame the Pequots. But the Pequots were not in control of Block Island. The Block Island Indians may once have paid tribute to the Pequots, but in 1636 they were allied to the eastern Niantics, who in turn were affiliated with the Narragansetts. Not long after Gallop's gruesome discovery, two Indians who had worked for the murdered trader journeyed to Boston, accompanied by a Narragansett envoy. They bore a letter from Roger Williams conveying assurances from principal sachem Canonicus that the Narragansetts were deeply grieved by Oldham's death and would take appropriate steps to avenge it. He reported that Miantonomi, the other principal sachem, had already left for Block Island at the head of a force of "seventeen canoes with two hundred men" to punish the Block Islanders. But the Bay Colony officials were suspicious and refused to accept at face value the Narragansett claim that they had not condoned Oldham's murder. They closely interrogated the prisoner brought back by Gallop. He told a very different story, claiming that "all the Sachems of the Narragansett, except Canonicus and Miantunnomok [Miantonomi], were the contrivers of Mr. Oldham's death." Asked the reason for the murder, the prisoner responded that the Narragansetts were angry at Oldham because of his involvement in the Bay Colony's efforts to trade with the Pequots. His death, in this version, was thus an episode in the ongoing conflict between Pequots and Narragansetts for control of trade with Europeans.[69]

The captive also alleged that the two Narragansett Indians who sailed with Oldham were part of the conspiracy and had participated in the fatal assault on Oldham. The magistrates were enraged by that revelation but refrained from seizing the two presumed villains "because they were sent as messengers from Canonicus" and were therefore entitled to diplomatic immunity. Deeply troubled by the prisoner's tale, Governor Vane on July 26 wrote to Williams to ask him to present Canonicus with a demand for the immediate return of the two English boys who had accompanied Oldham on his last voyage and who, according to the prisoner, had been spared. He added that the sachem should be told in no uncertain terms that he was indeed expected "to take revenge upon the islanders." Vane added a warning to Williams. Since Block Island was within the Narragansett sphere of influence, the episode might well portend war with that tribe. Williams, who lived in their territory, should be prepared "to look to himself." The next day, the governor wrote to Canonicus directly. He informed the sachem that he suspected his Indian envoys of complicity in Oldham's murder, that he had refrained from arresting them because they were on a diplomatic mission, but that he now expected the Narragansetts to send them back to Boston for investigation. After receiving Vane's two messages, Miantonomi asked the eastern Niantics to release the two English boys. A few days later they were delivered to Boston. The Narragansetts also sent word that they had recovered and would return "near one hundred fathoms of wampum and other goods of Mr. Oldham's." However, they ignored the request that Oldham's Narragansett crew members be turned over to the English.[70]

Meanwhile, Roger Williams grew suspicious of Narragansett protestations of innocence. His own inquiries, he informed Sir Henry Vane, confirmed the prisoner's claim that prominent Narragansett leaders had plotted Oldham's murder. He had learned that three of the seven Indians drowned when Gallop interrupted the looting of Oldham's shallop were Narragansett sachems. Another was in the pay of the head sachem of the eastern Niantics. In response to that report, the Bay Colony informed the Narragansetts that, while it did not hold either Canonicus or Mianto-nomi responsible, it was convinced that "six under-sachems were guilty" of Oldham's death. Thus, in addition to returning Oldham's trade goods, the Narragansetts must surrender to the English all of those who played a role in the attack on his ship.[71]

Although the Bay Colony authorities at the time believed that Oldham was murdered by Narragansetts and their tributaries, later writers, eager to justify the subsequent Puritan assault on the Pequots, insisted that Pequots were somehow implicated. The contemporary chroniclers of the war blamed Oldham's death on either the islanders or the Narragansetts. Gardener reported that the Narragansetts sold goods taken from Old-ham's ship to the Dutch traders at Good Hope. They also took several gold pieces which Gardener had seen in Oldham's possession shortly before his death, punched holes in them, and wore them "about their necks for jewels." Believing the Narragansetts responsible for the cap-tain's murder, Gardener could not understand why Puritan retribution had fallen on the Pequots but spared the real culprits. However, the Narragansett sachem Miantonomi, seeking to deflect English wrath, sug-gested that Oldham's assailants had taken refuge with the Pequots. His blatantly manipulative effort to spread blame to a group clearly not involved in the incident may not have convinced Gardener, but it was seized upon by later writers intent on justifying the Pequot War. Some years later the Reverend William Hubbard, in his history of New En-gland's Indian wars, declared that in addition to killing John Stone the Pequots "treacherously and cruelly . . . in the like manner slew one Mr. Oldham . . . at Block Island, a place not far from the Mouth of their harbor." Hubbard a few pages later conceded that the inhabitants of Block Island were not in fact Pequots but claimed that since some of "those that murthered him fled presently to the *Pequods,* by whom they were sheltered," the Pequots were therefore also "Guilty themselves of his Blood."[72]

Hubbard's ingenious effort to implicate the Pequots has been echoed

over the years by pro-Puritan historians. But those who accept his logic
have ignored one very important fact. There is neither evidence nor
likelihood that Oldham's killers took refuge among the Pequots. The
contemporary sources indicate instead that they were sheltered by
the eastern Niantics, who were tributary to the Narragansetts, not the
Pequots. Miantonomi paid that tribe some six fathoms of wampum to
execute a sachem named Anduah who was said to be the leader of the
party that attacked Oldham's shallop. He later asked Roger Williams to
obtain reimbursement for him from the Bay Colony. Miantonomi was
apparently never repaid but his blood money bought the Narragansetts
peace with the English, who then turned their attention back to the
Pequots and the unresolved problem of avenging Stone.[73]

While the identity of Oldham's killers is thus fairly well established,
their motives remain obscure. John Underhill, commander of the Massachusetts Bay Colony force that assisted Connecticut troops in the burning of Pequots at Fort Mystic a year later, believed that simple greed
inspired the attack on Oldham. The Block Islanders killed him, Underhill
wrote, "to the end that they might clothe their bloody flesh in his lawful
garments." The claim that the Narragansetts' lesser sachems ordered
Oldham's death because of resentment of his dealings with the Pequots is
more plausible, but it is supported by little more than the testimony of a
single lowly and frightened Indian prisoner. He may not have known, or
told, the whole story. It is possible that the episode was the outgrowth of
tensions within the Narragansett leadership over relations with the English that dated back to their first contact with Plymouth a decade earlier.
The attack on Oldham may well have been engineered by anti-English
sachems hoping to force a change in policy. That supposition is supported by indications that John Oldham may have been held responsible
for the smallpox epidemic that had recently struck the tribe. The elderly
sachem Canonicus later accused the English of deliberately sending the
plague against them.[74] It is also possible that Oldham's death was ordered
in reprisal for some unrecorded provocation. Given the paucity of evidence, we can only speculate.

Shortly after news of the death of Captain Oldham reached Boston, Bay
Colony officials also learned of the Pequots' refusal to comply with their
renewed demand that the terms of the treaty of 1634 be honored by
payment of wampum and by surrender of the murderers of Stone. The

magistrates interpreted both Oldham's murder and Pequot recalcitrance as evidence of Indian conspiracy. The Reverend Philip Vincent related that, as New England's leaders assessed reports from the frontier, they were reminded of Opechacanough's massacre of English settlers in Virginia in 1622. That sad event, Vincent explained, provided clear proof that "savages" must never be trusted. The magistrates were determined not to repeat the Virginians' mistake. Rather than waiting for an Indian attack, the Puritans therefore sought to assure "their peace by killing the barbarians" who threatened their security. They believed that a preemptive strike would guarantee their safety, as the Indians would be "terrified" into submission by the example of a "severe execution of a just sentence" against those of their fellows who had murdered Englishmen.[75]

With that premise in mind, the governor and council of the Massachusetts Bay Colony consulted with the colony's clergy "about doing justice upon the Indians for the death of Mr. Oldham." Assured that the Lord would smile upon a punitive raid, the Bay Colony accordingly dispatched a force of ninety men, under the command of John Endecott, to Block Island. Endecott's orders were to take possession of the island by force, kill all of its adult male inhabitants, and enslave their women and children. After punishing the Block Islanders, Endecott was to sail to the Pequot village near the mouth of what is now the Thames River, demand the surrender of "the murderers of Capt. Stone and other English," exact from the Pequots a payment of damages to the colony of a thousand fathoms of wampum, and take some Pequot children as hostages to assure the tribe's future good behavior. If the Pequots refused to supply those children for shipment to Boston, they were to be taken "by force."[76]

The man appointed to lead this expedition was ill suited for the task of negotiating with the Pequots, being by nature of impatient and sometimes violent temperament. Forty-eight years old at the time of the Block Island raid, Endecott, a native of England's West Country, had been in New England since 1628, having first settled among the Old Planters near the site of the future town of Salem. While serving as interim governor of the Puritan settlement founded there, Endecott's self-righteous and abrasive manner had led to conflicts with the non-Puritan Englishmen already residing in the region. In 1631, presiding as a judge in a Salem court, Endecott had earned further notoriety by striking a defendant. One of the more fanatical of the Bay Colony's founding fathers, Endecott's uncompromising commitment to Puritan principles impelled him in the early 1630s to demand that the cross be cut from royal flags displayed in New England. Later in life, Endecott prosecuted Quakers and other religious dissenters with a zeal that made a mockery of the judicial process. He was, despite or perhaps because of his relentless intolerance, highly esteemed as a leader of the Puritan Commonwealth. At the time of his appointment to the command of the Block Island punitive expedition, Endecott was serving as one of the assistants to the governor. He would later be elected both deputy governor and governor of the Massachusetts Bay Colony. The Puritan historian Edward Johnson celebrated Endecott as "the honored and much desired servant of Christ."[77]

Endecott's ninety soldiers were all volunteers. They served under the command of two captains, John Underhill and Nathaniel Turner, who were assisted by two ensigns named Davenport and Jenyson. Captain Underhill was somewhat defensive about the command arrangements, writing after the war that "the world" should "not wonder at the great number of commanders to so few men." Indian battle tactics, he explained, usually involved attack or ambush by small parties of warriors. Hence, the English had no choice but "to subdivide our divisions to answer theirs." As a final answer to any who might still be inclined to quibble about the Block Island campaign's top-heavy command structure, Underhill reminded his readers that the Old Testament spoke of "captains of hundreds, and captains of thousands, and captains of fifteen, and captains of tens."[78]

Accompanied by two Indian guides, Endecott's little army embarked in three pinnaces on August 22, 1636. Reaching Block Island just before dusk, the ships encountered a high surf raised by a gale blowing out of the northeast. The landing proved both difficult and hazardous. Riding uneasily at anchor, the English troops, as Underhill related, "espied an Indian walking by the shore in a desolate manner, as though he had secured intelligence of our coming." Since he was the only human being in sight, some of Underhill's men conjectured that the rest of the Indians, on hearing of the planned reprisal for Oldham's murder, had abandoned the island. Others, however, suspected that the warriors were hidden behind the embankment near the shore. They were right. As Underhill tells us, "fifty or sixty able fighting men, men straight as arrows, very tall, and of active bodies . . . their arrows notched," awaited the English landing party. As the men in the first detachment to hit the beach struggled through the pounding surf toward shore, the Block Islanders let fly a heavy barrage of arrows. It was, Underhill recalled, "as though they had meant to have an end to us in a moment." In the rolling sea, the shallops were so unstable that the soldiers who had not yet disembarked could not stand up to fire their muskets at the bowmen. Nor could they land their vessels. They therefore jumped overboard, waded through the shallow but turbulent waters to the beach, and once on firm ground, began firing at the Indians. As bullets flew over their heads, the warriors quickly withdrew.

Their arrows had done little damage to the invaders. Only one Englishman had been hit, struck in the neck by a shaft that pierced his collar and "entered his flesh to a good depth." But the man's collar, stiff as an "oaken board," had shielded him from mortal injury. Captain Underhill had been hit by arrows twice but emerged unscathed. The first cut through his coat sleeve. The second bounced off his helmet. He later reflected that, "if God had not moved the heart of my wife to persuade me to carry it along with me, (which I was unwilling to do) I had been slain." [79]

In the gathering darkness, Endecott's army moved a short distance inland and quickly made camp for the night. Sentinels were posted in anticipation of an Indian attack, which never came. Exploring the island by daylight, the English found it "full of small hills, and all overgrown with brushwood of oak, no good timber on it." The underbrush was so thick that the soldiers had to march single file along the rough and narrow Indian trails. They later determined that the island, "ten miles long and four broad," contained two Indian villages about three miles apart, each with "about sixty wigwams, some very large," surrounded by more than 200 acres of corn, "some gathered and laid on heaps, and the rest standing." [80] The English, as we shall see, found both villages deserted.

On their first day on the island, Endecott's men saw little action. "The Indians," Captain Underhill complained, "retreated into swamps.... we could not find them ... they kept themselves in obscurity." Only twice that day did the invaders make contact with their intended victims. Captain Turner spotted a few Indians at the edge of a swamp, fired at them, and was then hit by an arrow which struck his armor with such force that he felt like "he had been pushed with a pike." The armor saved his life, but the Indians escaped. In the other engagement of the day, an Indian guide with the English forces fired at, and presumably killed, an islander who called out to urge him to desert the English. Although they spent the day in the "burning and spoiling of the island," putting corn-fields and wigwams to the torch, Endecott's troops were not able to kill and enslave Indians as ordered. The Block Islanders were virtually invisible.[81]

Pondering their failure over the campfire that evening, the Puritan commanders decided to send out a midnight patrol to locate the Indians. Assuming, mistakenly, that the inhabitants would not sleep in the thicket but would rather seek shelter for the night in wigwams the English had not yet located, John Underhill accordingly led ten of his men down a narrow trail, which ended about two miles from the Puritan encamp-ment in a large clearing containing "much corn, many wigwams, and great heaps of mats." Underhill, convinced that he had found the missing "savages," considered setting the village on fire while its inhabitants slept. He decided, however, that an attack in force at dawn would yield more Indian casualties. He marched his party back to the English camp, mus-tered his full company of forty men, and, at first light, fell upon the village. It was deserted. The troops found only a few dogs. Enraged, the Puritan soldiers slaughtered the hapless Indian canines and then set fire to the village and surrounding fields. Later in the day, the army came upon a second village, also deserted. There the wigwams, much larger than the others, were filled with the fruits of the summer's harvest just past, "great heaps of pleasant corn readily shelled." The English threw piles of Indian mats on top of the corn and set both on fire. The soldiers saved for souvenirs some "well wrought mats" and some "delightful baskets" but cast the rest of the Indians' worldly goods into the confla-gration.[82]

Leaving the blazing village, Endecott and his men crashed through narrow and overgrown footpaths in search of the Block Islanders. The natives remained elusive. Finally, in frustration, Endecott admitted de-feat, reembarked his forces at the close of the second day of the cam-paign, and sailed away from Block Island. Having fired at some fleeing Indians, Captain Underhill later estimated that his troops had probably "slain some fourteen, and maimed others." But that claim was clearly exaggerated. The Narragansetts later informed the Bay Colony that only one Block Islander had died during the raid. John Winthrop, after listening carefully to the stories of the soldiers, concluded that the Block Island raiders "could not tell what men they had killed," as they admitted that they saw no Indian corpses, only a few natives "wounded and carried away by their fellows." Although not confirmed by contemporary accounts of the Block Island raid, later records suggest that at least one Block Islander may have been captured and enslaved. Although Endecott's clumsy efforts to carry out his orders and put Block Island to the sword had been ineffectual, his burning of the Indian villages and their harvests nonetheless made a deep impression. The Block Island Indians thereafter sought English protection through an annual wampum payment to Boston.[83]

Departing Block Island, Endecott's expeditionary force sailed for Saybrook at the mouth of the Connecticut River. The fort's commander, Lieutenant Gardener, learning of the plan to confront the nearby Pequots with new demands for wampum and hostages, had a fresh reason for outrage. "You come hither to raise these wasps around my ears," he stormed at Endecott, "and then you will take wing and flee away." Since his cornfield was located some distance outside the palisade, a Pequot siege, Gardener protested, would mean the loss of his harvest and certain starvation for his men at Saybrook. But Endecott refused to heed his plea that the encounter with the Pequots be postponed. In anger and desperation, Gardener then asked that Endecott's army at least confiscate some of the Pequot harvest, "now gathered with them and dry, and ready to put into their barns," and use it to provision the fort at Saybrook. He offered to hire the boat of a Dutch trader then anchored at Saybrook to transport the corn and promised to share the loot with Boston. But Endecott and his officers balked at Gardener's proposition. Gardener then declared that he would provide bags for the grain and, as Endecott continued to protest, ordered six of his men to follow the Dutchman in the fort's pinnace. Grudgingly, the Bay Colony commanders finally agreed to the plan. Gardener then gave the raiders his instructions. As soon as they came to the cornfield outside the main Pequot village on the river, eight men were to stand guard while the other four quickly filled their bags with corn and loaded them into the pinnace.[84]

The departure of Endecott's army was delayed by bad weather. After four uneasy days at Saybrook, the English fleet, augmented by the Saybrook pinnace and the hired Dutch trading ship, finally set sail for the short voyage to the Pequot River (now the Thames). Western Niantics and Pequots, hailing the English from the shore, at first hoped that they had come to trade. In a passage that raises questions about later claims that the Pequots provoked the conflict, Underhill recalled that "the Indians spying us came running in multitudes along the water side crying, 'What cheer, Englishmen, what cheer, what do you come for?' They not thinking we intended war, went on cheerfully until they came to Pequeat river." The English aboard the ships remained silent. As their greetings met with no response, the Indians' mood changed. Sensing "that we would make no answer," Underhill recorded, the Indians then "cried, 'What, Englishmen, what cheer, are you hoggery, and will you cram us?' That is, are you angry, will you kill us, and do you come to fight?" They received no reply.[85]

That evening, as the fleet lay at anchor at the mouth of the Pequot River, the Pequots and their western Niantic allies kept anxious watch, having "made fire on both sides of the river, fearing we would land in the night." Throughout the hours before dawn, the Indians called to one another "to gather their forces together, fearing the English were come to war against them." Their cries, eerie and unsettling to English ears, were so loud, Underhill recalled, that "we could scarce rest." At daybreak, a Pequot elder, described as "a grave senior, man of good understanding, portly carriage, grave and majestical in his expressions," boarded one of the English ships at anchor in the river and asked for an explanation of their visit. With some severity, the Puritan officers informed him that "the governors of the Bay sent us to demand the heads of those persons that had slain Captain Norton and Captain Stone and the rest of their company." The Pequots needed to understand that it was not the English custom "to suffer murderers to live." They must thus either "give us the heads of the murderers" or face war.[86]

To their surprise, the Pequot envoy, "witty and ingenious," responded to that ultimatum with a confession. The Pequots, he conceded, had indeed killed Stone and his company. In fact, their grand sachem Sassacus had personally dispatched the captain. As the English listened in horror, the envoy described the death of Stone in vivid detail. As his ship lay at anchor on the Connecticut River, Sassacus had snuck into Stone's cabin, found him in a drunken stupor, and "having a little hatchet under his garment, therewith knocked him in the head." As his listeners struggled to retain their composure, the Pequot hastened to explain that the killing of Stone was not really the sort of thing that would justify a war, as it had been intended as an act of just retribution to settle a deep and intolerable grievance. By braining Stone, Sassacus had intended to avenge the death of his own father who, not long before, had been kidnapped by the Dutch, who had then betrayed all decent custom by putting the former grand sachem to death *after* his kinsmen had paid the substantial ransom demanded for his life. With great emotion, the Pequot envoy demanded that the English consider the implications of that outrage. Who, he cried, "could blame us for avenging so cruel a murder?" As the English started to protest, he added that the Pequots could not possibly have known that Stone and his compatriots were not accessories to the murder of Tatobem, "for we distinguish not between the Dutch and the English, but took them to be one nation, and therefore we do not conceive that we wronged you, for they slew our king: and thinking these captains to be of the same nation and people of those that slew him, made us set upon this course of revenge." [87]

The envoy's strategy in dealing with the English ultimatum was quite shrewd. By revealing that the Pequot's own chief sachem had personally murdered Stone and then explaining the deed as an honorable but misguided act of lawful retribution, the Pequots turned the English demand for the heads of Stone's killers into an unreasonable request which clearly they could not meet without loss of honor. The envoy no doubt hoped that the English would respond by offering to accept some lesser recompense for Stone.

But that ploy failed. The English commanders were impressed by the envoy's cleverness, but they found his story implausible and responded by bluntly charging that he had lied to them. Certainly, they argued, Pequots could easily tell an Englishman from a Dutchman, as they "had sufficient experience of both nations." "You have slain the King of England's subjects," they shouted, "we have come to demand an account of their blood." But the Pequot elder again insisted that "we know no difference between the Dutch and the English, they are both strangers to us, we took them all to be one; therefore, we crave pardon, we have not willfully wronged the English." With mounting anger, the Puritan commanders again rejected that excuse and appeal, declaring that if they were not given immediately "the heads of those persons that have slain ours" they would attack. The Pequot envoy controlled his anger and alarm and responded evenly, declaring, as Underhill recalled, "Under-

standing the ground of your coming, I will entreat you to give me liberty
to go ashore, and I shall inform the body of the people what your intent
and resolution is, and if you will stay on board, I will bring you a sudden
answer."[88]

The ambassador was allowed to disembark, but Endecott, suspicious
of his intentions, disregarded his request that he await the Pequot response aboard ship and immediately landed his forces, clad in armor and
in full battle array. The envoy, alarmed, rushed back to the English and
asked that they advance no farther but wait in a small hollow near the
river. But the English saw that between that point and the main Pequot
encampment there stood a small hill which the Indians could man "to
our prejudice." In order to seize the advantage, Endecott marched his
troops to the higher ground. Soon after they had taken possession of the
hill, the Pequot envoy reappeared. This time he informed the English
that there was no one in the area who could respond to their demand, as
both the high-ranking sachems had gone to Long Island.[89]

Once again, the Puritan commanders called the Pequot envoy a liar.
Sassacus, they declared, was in fact at home in his village nearby. If he
did not call upon the English at once, they would "beat up the drum,
and march through the country, and spoil your corn." The envoy then
promised to make another effort to locate Sassacus. The army, standing
uncomfortably in full armor under the blazing sun, waited in silence.
Captain Underhill later praised their forbearance, claiming that he and
his men "used as much patience as ever men might, considering the
gross abuse they offered us, holding us above an hour in vain hopes."
Finally, the Pequots sent word that a lesser sachem named Mornmeno-
tech had been located and would visit them presently. But another hour
elapsed before an Indian came to ask the English to wait a little longer, as
the Pequot leaders were about to conduct an inquiry to identify and
apprehend Stone's murderers.[90]

While pondering that message, the English soldiers suddenly realized
that there were no women or children among the Pequots assembled
nearby, and, looking closer, they saw several men busily burying corn
and household goods. Concluding that the Pequots had no real intention
of complying with the English ultimatum but were rather preparing for
war, Endecott determined to strike the first blow. As they planned their
attack, the English were suddenly visited by a new envoy, who told them
that if they would lay down all of their arms, march thirty paces forward

toward the Pequots' position, a sachem would come forward to parley with them. Endecott and his officers immediately suspected treachery and, as Underhill wrote, "rather chose to beat up the drum and bid them to battle." The English, fully armed, marched forward, battle flags flying, "but none would come near us." The Pequots uttered cries which the English took as expressions of mockery for their gullibility. Enraged, they opened fire at the Indians, who fled. Marching into the village, Endecott and his men set fire to the wigwams and the corn harvest and dug up and destroyed the goods that the Pequots had buried. "Thus," Underhill recalled, "we spent the day burning and spoiling the country."[91]

Before returning to Saybrook, Endecott tried to visit vengeance on the Pequots' western Niantic allies. But, as the chronicler of the campaign noted, "no Indians would come near us, but ran from us, as deer from dogs." Frustrated by the western Niantics' prudence, the troops "burnt and spoiled what we could light on." After a brief stay at Fort Saybrook, Endecott and his men reembarked and returned to Boston. The sole English casualty of the Pequot raid was "one man wounded in the leg." In his report, Underhill was uncertain about Pequot losses but felt that "certain numbers" had been "slain and many wounded." Winthrop later recorded that the Narragansetts claimed that thirteen Pequots had been killed by the English raiders.[92]

Lieutenant Gardener at Saybrook was not impressed by Endecott's performance as an Indian fighter. "The Bay-men," he wrote, "killed not a man." The members of his company who had accompanied Endecott in order to seize Pequot grain told him that the only Pequot casualty had been slain by Cutshamekin, one of Endecott's Indian guides. Gardener charged that the Bay Colony commanders had broken their promise to assist in gathering provisions for Fort Saybrook. While Endecott's troopers put heaps of Indian corn to the torch, Gardener's men had been forced to scramble desperately to collect a small quantity. In his account of this episode, he noted that it had been agreed at Saybrook before the attack on the Pequots that, since his two ships were the most vulnerable, they would be the first to be evacuated. Endecott did not keep his word. The Saybrook men were still loading corn when the Bay Colony army trooped aboard their three ships and sailed away. The small provisioning party from Saybrook was thus left alone, unprotected and surrounded by angry Pequots. The men clambered aboard their two small boats and tried to set sail, but a shift in the wind blocked their passage downriver.

Still lacking an adequate supply of corn, they therefore imprudently went ashore again to confiscate some more of the Pequot harvest. As they made their way back to the river, the Indians attacked.[93]

The Pequots had been concealed in the nearby woods, but, as the Saybrook party related later, "came forth, about ten at a time," and shot arrows at the English corn gatherers. Quickly, the Saybrook men fell into a single-file line. A few fired muskets at the Pequots as they emerged from the undergrowth. The others, swords unsheathed, stood ready to repel a frontal attack, which never came. The encounter lasted through most of the afternoon. Finally, the Pequots withdrew, and the English rushed back to their ships. The wind having shifted, they made their way home to Saybrook.[94]

At Boston, John Winthrop, informed of Lieutenant Gardener's anger at the abandonment of his men, dismissed the incident, noting in his journal that the Pequot arrows were shot at too steep an angle to do any real harm. Despite the fact that only one of the Saybrook men wore armor, the Pequot attack did them little injury. The men easily ducked the arrows as they fell, then picked them up off the ground so that they could not be reused. The only casualty, Winthrop claimed, was the armored man who, being less mobile than the others, sustained a leg wound. English musket fire killed several Pequots and wounded a number of others. But Gardener, predictably, saw the incident in a very different light. Through the malfeasance of Endecott and the cowardice of the Bay Colony men, he declared angrily, "my men were pursued by the Indians . . . and two of them came home wounded."[95]

The Saybrook commander was not alone in his exasperation. The governor of the Plymouth Colony soon thereafter wrote to Winthrop to complain, as Winthrop recorded, "that we had occasioned a war, etc., by provoking the Pequods." Stung by that accusation, Winthrop replied that Plymouth should blame the Pequots, not the Bay Colony. God had clearly "deprived" the Pequots of "common reason"; otherwise, they would have complied long before with the request that they surrender the murderers of Captain Stone and his men. Endecott's recent action, Winthrop proclaimed, was entirely justified, "as we went not to make war upon them, but to do justice." Endecott's army had killed thirteen Pequots and burned sixty wigwams, a fair and reasonable retribution for their killing of "four or five" Englishmen. Winthrop apologized only for the failure to kill more Pequots, explaining that "they fled from us, and we could not follow them in our own armour, neither had any to guide us in their country." He concluded his explanation of the rationale for the Endecott raid by expressing the hope that the Pequots had finally learned their lesson as "they saw that they could not save themselves nor their corn and houses from so few of ours."[96]

Plymouth's traders on the Connecticut River and other settlers vulnerable to Pequot reprisals did not share Winthrop's sanguine view of the matter. The river towns of Connecticut were no less exasperated than Saybrook or Plymouth at Boston's heavy-handed provocation of an Indian war. In April they wrote to the Bay Colony to protest that their lives had been placed in jeopardy by Endecott's raid.[97]

As we have now come to the point in our narrative when Pequot belligerence is no longer a rumor but will soon assume a frightening reality, it is appropriate that we should pause and reflect on the events that led to that sad outcome. The record of Pequot-English interaction in the crucial years between Stone's death and Endecott's raid offers little if any evidence to support the image of the Pequots as savage killers threatening the lives of English settlers in the Connecticut wilderness. That image was the product of Puritan mythmaking, not of real occurrences on the New England frontier. It should now be recognized as such. Careful scrutiny of the record of their dealings with the English prior to the outbreak of war in 1636 indicates that the sinister portrayal of the Pequots that once dominated New England historiography can be sustained only by an act of chronological inversion, only by confusion of cause and effect, for Pequot acts of war followed, rather than preceded, English aggression. To label the Pequots the aggressors is to misread the record of their behavior in the years prior to the outbreak of the war. The Pequots were hardly pacifists, but their aggressive actions were aimed at Indian rivals, not Europeans, and were motivated in large measure by the desire to control access to European trade. Had they been more aware of the dangers to their own security posed by the English Puritan belief in a divine mandate to subdue the "wilderness" and reduce its presumably savage people to "civility," the Pequots might well have been inspired to resist Puritan incursions into Connecticut by all means possible. But we have no reason to believe that they possessed any such insight.

Instead, we find evidence that the Pequots were puzzled and uncertain about English intentions until Endecott's raid forced war upon them.

Their efforts to resume trade with the Dutch after the murders of Tatobem and Stone, their subsequent appeal to Boston, their attempt to
continue trading with Saybrook even after the English abrogation of the
1634 agreement, all indicate that the Pequots hoped to maintain friendship and trade with Europeans. Their evasive responses to repeated
requests that they apprehend and surrender to Puritan justice Stone's
killers suggest that the Pequots simply did not grasp the fact that the
English could not be persuaded to accept the Stone incident as a misplaced act of legal retribution or to regard the wampum and pelts already
delivered to Boston as adequate recompense for his death. Their behavior immediately before Endecott's raid suggests that they were only
vaguely aware that their recalcitrance might provoke an all-out war with
the English. Although there are some indications that they had heard
rumors of English war plans, the Pequots did not fully appreciate the
danger until Endecott presented the Bay Colony's final demands and
then mounted an attack before receiving a reply. As we shall see in
the next chapter, Pequot actions thereafter partially fulfilled the savage
prophecy and have given Puritan apologists their evidence of Pequot
malevolence: specifically, their siege at Fort Saybrook, their torture and
killing of prisoners taken during that siege, their assaults on commerce
on the Connecticut River, their attack on Wethersfield, and their efforts
to enlist the Narragansetts in an anti-English alliance. However, in some
crucial respects, the Pequot reputation for ferocity does not stand close
scrutiny. To anticipate the story yet to be told, we shall find that their
warriors were so lacking in the capacity to butcher their enemies wholesale that one English commander was moved to exclaim in disgust that
they could fight seven years and not kill seven men. We must ponder also
Pequot requests that women and children be spared during the conflict
and the Puritan refusal to honor those requests, for the exchanges on
that sensitive matter suggest that the Pequot concept of the rules of war
was less savage than their adversary's.

The record of Anglo-Pequot negotiations indicates that English intransigence, not Pequot belligerence, barred the way to an accommodation. Puritan insistence that the Pequots apprehend and surrender
participants in the Stone raid set a condition that the Pequots simply
could not meet without loss of honor. The Bay Colony's position on that
issue reflected the Puritan magistrates' determination to set terms for
dealing with intercultural conflict that would secure total English control

of the process. The issue was one of power, not justice, for the magistrates had no illusions about Captain John Stone. The Massachusetts Bay Colony authorities displayed a consistent lack of respect for Pequot sovereignty. The ultimatum at Saybrook in July 1636, the return of the Pequot presents at the conclusion of that conference, and the subsequent decision to demand that the Pequots pay a substantial indemnity and send some of their children to Boston to serve as hostages all offer telling evidence of the English determination to humble, if not humiliate, the Pequots. The reasons for the Puritans' belligerence remain controversial. But one thing is clear. They bear primary responsibility for the war that ensued.

4

The Pequots Humbled

 Puritan historians of the Pequot War were fond of portraying the Saints as a beleagured people surrounded by hostile savages. The victory over the Pequots, in their pages, was attributed entirely to the intervention of the Almighty, who had delivered his people from the clutches of a cruel and powerful adversary. But the correspondence of Puritan officials and the eyewitness accounts written by their military commanders make it clear that the English were supported by Indian allies far more numerous in number than the Pequots. Later writers generally have grossly overestimated Pequot strength. Though Puritan mythmakers represented the Pequots as a deadly threat to the survival of Christ's church in the wilderness, the Pequots in fact were by far the more vulnerable party, for by 1636 they had few Indian allies. As one recent student of Native American politics in seventeenth-century New England notes, the Puritans "by siding against the Pequots aligned themselves with a powerful network of Indian allies that was already in the process of isolating and breaking up the Pequot Confederation."[1] English intervention in the Pequot-Mohegan-Narragansett power struggle paved the way not only for the acquisition of substantial tracts of land in Connecticut but also for the establishment of a lucrative tributary network dominated by Boston. It led ultimately to the successful assertion of English political hegemony throughout southern New England. Uncas and the Mohegans would flourish under English patronage, but most of the Indian groups that had so eagerly solicited English aid in their quarrel with the Pequots would soon discover that they had acquired a very dangerous ally.

In preparing for the impending war with the Pequots, the Bay Colony officials in 1636 were hampered by their lack of a good intelligence network. They were too reliant upon self-seeking and manipulative Indian informants such as Uncas. Since few Englishmen spoke or understood the Algonquian dialects, they were often unable to corroborate rumors and correct misinformation. The magistrates' reliance on a Separatist clergyman whom they had earlier expelled from the Bay Colony for his radical opinions on personal liberty and Indian land rights is indicative of their desperate need for contacts in the Indian villages west of Cape Cod. Roger Williams had taken refuge among the Narragansetts and now made his living as an Indian trader. Through his correspondence with John Winthrop, Williams provided badly needed, though sometimes inaccurate, information on the activities of the Narragansetts and the Pequots. He would soon undertake a crucial and sensitive diplomatic mission for the government that had sent him into exile.

Shortly before the departure of Endecott's expedition, Williams learned from Indian informants that the Pequots planned to rely on their shamans to protect themselves against the English and were thus not intimidated by threats from Boston. "The Pequts heare of your preparations, etc.," he wrote Winthrop, "and Comfort themselves in this that a witch amongst them will sinck the pinnaces, by diving under water and making holes, etc." The Pequots, Williams continued, expected by defeating the Puritans through witchcraft to "enrich themselves with a store of guns," but there was reason to hope that "through the mercie of the Lord . . . the Devill and his Lying Sorcerers shall be Confounded."[2]

Several weeks later, Williams reported that not only had the Endecott raid failed to accomplish any of its objectives but that the Pequots and the western Niantics, enraged by that episode, were now determined to "live and die togeather, and not yeald one up."[3] Soon thereafter, Winthrop received word from Williams of a far more ominous development. Pequot envoys were now endeavoring to persuade the Narragansetts "that the English were minded to destroy all Indians." A Pequot-Narragansett alliance would have placed in jeopardy not only the tiny Puritan settlements in Connecticut but the parent colonies as well. Contemporary observers agreed with Williams that, their recent squabble with the Pequots over control of the European trade notwithstanding, Narragansett participation in an anti-English coalition was a distinct and frightening possibility. John Mason, commander of the Connecticut forces in the Pequot War, noted the extensive intermarriage between the Narragansetts and the Pequots and concluded that only "God . . . by a more than ordinary providence" had forestalled a general Indian uprising in southern New England in the wake of Endecott's raid.[4] Mason and others may have overstated the danger. Neal Salisbury suggests that the Narragansetts had little to gain "from abandoning the English in favor of their declining, detested enemies."[5] But it does not follow that an Anglo-Narragansett alliance was a foregone conclusion. Some anti-English Narragansett leaders opposed any assistance to the Puritans in their quarrel with the Pequots. Winthrop and his associates were aware of their opposition and suspected, perhaps correctly, that the same sachems were implicated in the murder of Captain John Oldham. Given the Puritans' general distrust of Indians, their anxieties about Pequot-Narragansett collusion are understandable.

The Bay Colony magistrates were so alarmed by the Pequot mission to the Narragansetts that they swallowed their pride and appealed to the outcast Williams to do all that he could to win the Narragansetts to the English side. Many years later, Williams recalled how "upon letters recd. from the Govr. and Councell at Boston, requesting me to use my utmost and Speediest Endeavors to breake and hinder the league labored for by Pequts . . . the lord helped me immediately to put my Life into my hands, and, Scarce acquainting my wife, to ship myselfe, all alone, in a poore canow, and to Cut through (a stormie wind, 30 miles in great seas, every minute in hazard of Life), to the Sachems howse." Williams recalled that "dayes and nights my Busines forced me to lodge and mix with the bloudie Pequt Embassadors, whose Hands and Arms, (me thogt,) reaked with the bloud of my countrimen, murther'd and massacred by them on Connecticut River, and from whome I could not but nightly looke for their bloudy Knives at my owne throat allso." Through his earnest entreaties to his Narragansett friends, Williams was able, as he said, "to breake to pieces the Pequts' negociation and Designe, and to make, promote, and finish, by many travells and Charges the English league with the Naheggonsike [Narragansetts] and Monhiggins against the Pequts." In recognition of that invaluable service, John Winthrop proposed to the governing council of the Massachusetts Bay Colony that Roger Williams be "recalld from Banishmnt." The council refused to approve that proposal and made no acknowledgment of Williams's help.[6]

Williams's diplomatic mission to the Narragansetts might well have failed had it been entrusted to less capable hands. Despite their interest in trade, some of the Narragansetts had harbored deep resentments against the English ever since the formation of the Plymouth-Wampanoag alliance a decade earlier. Their principal sachem, Canonicus, now old and infirm, had delegated most of the tasks of leadership to his high-strung, physically imposing nephew Miantonomi but still retained much influence among the lesser sachems. While Miantonomi was receptive to English flattery and appeared eager to win their favor, Canonicus was suspicious of all Europeans and had insisted that the Narragansetts maintain a policy of aloof independence. Williams related that on his arrival the old sachem, in a "sour" frame of mind, "accused the English and myself for sending the plague amongst them" and added that they had tried "to kill him especially." Persuaded that Canonicus had been misled by anti-English elements within the tribe, Williams endeavored to set his mind at rest. "The plague and other sicknesses," he explained to Canonicus, had not been sent to them by the English but came from God, who had struck down Englishmen for the same reason that he afflicted the Indians: "his divine displeasure" with sins such as "lying, stealing, idleness, and uncleanness." Canonicus was delighted to hear that the Almighty was also angry with Europeans. That news, Williams reported to Winthrop, "sweetened his spirit." But the old sachem nonetheless remained wary. Williams related that he had "far better dealings" with Miantonomi, who followed Williams back to his trading post and "kept his barbarous court lately at my house. . . . . he takes some pleasure to visit me."[7]

Roger Williams's efforts to enlist the Narragansetts in an anti-Pequot alliance were not immediately successful, but he did secure Narragansett neutrality. The Pequot envoys returned home empty-handed. After Williams's departure, Indian enemies of the Pequots continued his work among the Narragansetts. Cutshamekin, a Massachusett sachem who had served as an interpreter to Endecott's raiding party and in the process had lifted a Pequot scalp and sent it to Canonicus, was particularly effective in stirring up long-standing Narragansett animosity toward the Pequots. Two of Sassacus's Pequot enemies, Wequash and

Wuttlackquiakommin, now living in a Narragansett village, also played a role in paving the way for Narragansett aid in the campaign against the Pequots.[8]

Later that fall, the Massachusetts Bay Colony sent a formal delegation to negotiate a military alliance. One of the members of that diplomatic party, Edward Johnson, later wrote of the anxious urgency of their mission. Were they to fail, he recorded, the Bay Colony's 4,000 inhabitants might soon be assailed by 30,000 hostile Narragansett and eastern Niantic warriors. (Unaware of the full impact of the recent outbreak of epidemic disease among the Narragansetts, Johnson overestimated their strength.) He made no mention of Roger Williams's crucial work in securing the Puritan colony's safety, and his uncharitable omission was to be repeated by every New England chronicler of Indian wars for over a century thereafter. Johnson did note the hospitable reception the Narragansetts extended to the Boston delegation. They were, he wrote, "entertain'd royally." The boiled chestnuts the Indians served as the equivalent of white bread Johnson found "very sweet," and their puddings "made of beaten corne . . . with black berryes, somewhat like currents" were excellent. He provided no details on the other items on the menu but recorded that the Narragansetts, "having thus nobly feasted them [the English envoys], afterward gave them Audience, in a State house, round, about fifty foot wide, made of long poles stuck in the ground, like your Summer Houses in England, and covered round about, and on the Top with Mats, save in a small place in the middle of the Roofe, to give light, and let out the Smoke."

Looking about the Narragansett "State house" as the formal negotiations began, Johnson caught sight of Canonicus, old and infirm, reclining on a mat, surrounded by the "nobility," who sat "with their legs doubled up, their knees touching their chins." As the English spoke, the assembled sachems "with much sober gravity . . . attend the interpreters' speech." Expecting to find himself in the midst of unruly and lawless barbarians, Johnson recalled that "it was a matter of much wonderment to the English, to see how solidly and wisely these savage people did consider the weighty undertaking of a War, especially Old Canonicus, who was very discrete in his answers."

Miantonomi, despite his pro-English inclinations, was also wary of involvement in the impending Anglo-Pequot conflict. In the first round of negotiations with the English he prefaced his remarks by stressing that he wanted peace with the English. Comparing the power of the two people, he noted pointedly that the English were greatly outnumbered by the Narragansetts and "were but strangers to the woods, swamps, and advantageous places of the wilderness." But he conceded that English weapons of war were superior, "especially their guns, which were of great terror to his people." Moreover, Miantonomi understood that the Puritans "came of a more populous Nation by far than all the Indians were, could they be joyn'd together." Even so, "with mature deliberation," he preferred not to antagonize the Pequots, given their "cruell disposition and aptness to make war" and the Narragansetts' own preference for peace. So Miantonomi declared that "hee deemes it most conducing to his owne and his peoples safety to direct his course in a middle way, holding amity with both." The Massachusetts delegation returned home with nothing more than that pledge of neutrality.[9] Roger Williams continued to urge the Narragansetts to join in an alliance with the English against the Pequots.

Through Williams's efforts, Miantonomi was persuaded to accept an invitation to visit the Bay Colony in late October 1636. As Winthrop recorded in his journal, the Narragansett sachem arrived "with two of Canonicus's sons, and another sachem, and near twenty sanaps." Escorted by twenty English musketeers who had met them at Roxbury, the Narragansett delegation "came to Boston about noon. The governor had called together most of the magistrates and the ministers to give countenance to our proceedings, and to advise with them about the terms of peace. It was dinner time, and the sachems and the council dined by themselves in the room where the governor dined, and their sanaps went to the inn." After dinner, Miantonomi delivered a speech wherein he assured the Boston authorities "that they had always loved the English and desired firm peace with us: That they would continue in war with the Pequods and their confederates until they were subdued, and desired that we should do so: They would deliver our enemies to us, or kill them." Miantonomi then stated a Narragansett grievance, demanding, as Winthrop recorded, "that if any of theirs should kill our cattle, we would not kill them" but accept payment for damages. With that understanding, Miantonomi declared, "they would now make a firm peace, and two months hence they would send us a present."

The Bay Colony authorities listened to Miantonomi's speech impassively; then Governor Vane "told them, they should have answer the next morning." The following day, the Narragansett delegation was presented with a treaty which bound them in a defensive and offensive alliance against the Pequots. By its terms, they were required to deny haven to Pequots, to put to death or deliver to English justice any Indians guilty of killing Englishmen, and to return runaway English servants who sought refuge in Narragansett country. The treaty obligated the English "to give them notice when we go against the Pequods." Upon receipt of such notice, the Narragansetts were to furnish guides. It was agreed that neither party would "make peace with the Pequods without the others consent." Another provision called for "free trade" between the English and the Narragansetts but also, ostensibly for their protection, stipulated that Narragansetts were not "to come near our plantations during the wars with the Pequods, without some Englishmen or known Indians." Miantonomi and the members of his entourage placed their marks on the treaty but complained that they did not really understand some of its provisions. The magistrates therefore "agreed to send a copy to Mr. Williams, who could best interpret it for them."[10] Through Williams's good offices, the Narragansetts received the reassurance they required, and the frontiers of the Massachusetts Bay Colony and Plymouth remained secure.

The English in Connecticut remained in jeopardy. Soon after Endecott's confrontation with the Pequots, Lieutenant Gardener, short of provisions for the long winter's siege that he now regarded as a certainty, led a party of men on foot to Saybrook's cornfield two miles from the stockade. After harvesting the crop, Gardener secured it in a small "strong house" he had built in the field "for the defense of the corn." He left behind five men armed with "long guns" and arranged for the fort's shallop to pick up the men and the harvest the following day. But as soon as Gardener departed, three of the five guards, believing that there were no Indians nearby, disregarded their orders and went duck hunting. Wandering about a mile from the strong house, they walked through tall grass that concealed a hundred Pequots. The Indians let them pass, then, as they returned laden with water fowl, "suddenly came out of the covert, and set upon them." One man, armed with a sword, hacked his way through the ambush and ran back to his comrades in the strong house. The other two, burdened with muskets useless in close combat, were taken captive and tortured as their companions huddling in the house listened in terror to their screams. Finally, the shallop from the fort appeared and anchored at the riverbank, and the three survivors ran to safety. The Indians then set fire to the strong house and, following the shallop, soon put to the torch hay stacks and outbuildings "within a bow shot of the fort itself. They slaughtered a cow outside the pallisade, and for some days thereafter other cattle wandered back to the fort with arrows stuck in their hides." [11]

On the day the Pequots ambushed the cornfield guards, Matthew Mitchell, a trader from Wethersfield upriver, pressed Gardener to lend him a shallop so that he and a few of his men could harvest corn at Six Mile Island. At first Gardener refused, arguing that Mitchell did not have enough men to do the job safely. In addition to the four men he had engaged to bail hay, he would need another to stand guard in the field, Gardener warned, and "two more at the foot of the Rock, with their guns, to keep the Indians from running down on them." Mitchell, however, persisted, and Gardener relented and lent him his shallop. He cautioned Mitchell that his party should "scour the meadow" with dogs to safeguard against a Pequot ambush. Mitchell's men ignored Gardener's warning. Upon arriving at the island, they immediately set to bailing hay. Gardener recorded that "the Indians presently rose out of the long grass, and killed three." The fourth member of the party was taken captive. The Pequots "roasted him alive." [12]

A few weeks later, Gardener received word that John Winthrop, Jr., had decided not to return to Saybrook. On November 6 the lieutenant wrote to the river governor to protest Saybrook's abandonment. Even though they were now under siege, Gardener and his men had received none of the provisions promised the preceding summer. Weekly, ships went up the Connecticut River carrying supplies to the settlers at Windsor, Hartford, and Wethersfield, "but none for us." Gardener reminded the younger Winthrop of his warning about the danger of provoking the Pequots without reinforcing Saybrook. Despite his understandable resentment over the Bay Colony's high-handed conduct of Indian affairs, he had kept the garrison at the river's mouth in "a warlike condition" so "there shall be noe cause to complayne of our Fidelitie." However, if some help did not arrive soon, Gardener hinted that he might need to evacuate the fort. "If I see that there be not such care for us that our lives may be preserved, then I must be forced to shift as the lord shall direct." He pointedly remarked that a Dutch trader upriver was willing and able to supply his garrison with "some corne and rye but we have no thinges to pay him for it." Short of manpower, he had recently taken in a Dutch tailor and a Dutch shipwright, both accompanied by their wives. "I sett them both to worke, but have neather money nor victualls to pay them. . . . I pray let us not want money or victualls."

To this letter of complaint, Gardener added a quick postscript. A supply vessel had just come to Saybrook "in dark night beyond expectation." Gardener apologized for his impatience but went on to warn the younger Winthrop that all vessels plying the Connecticut River in the future must be armed and their crews instructed to stay on board except when visiting the English settlements. Hostile Indians numbering several hundred, Gardener explained, lined both banks of the river. They had some muskets, taken from dead Englishmen or purchased from unscrupulous traders.[13]

The river trader Joseph Tilly saw no point to Gardener's demand that unarmed ships stay out of the Connecticut River. A Bay Colony resident, Tilly several months earlier had established a small depot at Saybrook to serve the needs of the Windsor settlement upriver. Arriving in Saybrook shortly after a Pequot raid in April 1637, he took exception to "a paper nailed up over the gate" which ordered all ships to stand inspection by Gardener "that I might see whether they were armed and manned sufficiently." Gardener's notice also declared that no ship should land at any point between Fort Saybrook and the English settlement at Wethersfield. Gardener explained to Tilly that he had issued those orders after Mitchell's men were killed at Six Mile Island, but, as Gardener recalled, Tilly "gave me ill language for my presumption." Gardener then told Tilly to take a look at his ruined warehouse, burned in the recent Pequot raid. Tilly responded by accusing Gardener of destroying his property. He was somewhat mollified when told that his goods had been rescued and were in storage in the fort.[14]

Still not persuaded that there was any serious danger of an Indian attack on his shallop, Tilly sailed three miles upriver, then anchored and went ashore to do some hunting with a companion. As soon as he fired his musket, Tilly and his shipmate were seized by Indians. His compatriot was killed on the spot, but Tilly was taken downriver to a spot in sight of the fort at Saybrook where, as John Underhill recounted, the Pequots "tied him to a stake, flayed his skin off, put hot embers between his flesh and the skin, cut off his fingers and toes, [to] make hatbands of them." In his journal, Winthrop recorded that Tilly "lived three days after his hands were cut off" and that he won the respect of his captors "because he cried not in his torture." Gardener, less impressed, named the place where Tilly was taken captive "Tilly's Folly." [15]

One of the visitors at Saybrook in the fall of 1636 was Edward Gibbon, an Old Planter and business associate of the Winthrops. Gibbon had been a member of the first party dispatched to the mouth of the Connecticut the previous year. After inspecting the fort, Gibbon reported to the younger Winthrop that Gardener did appear to be a conscientious and capable commander. He had placed the fort in a high state of military preparedness. The construction of the Saybrook complex was not, however, very far along, and the few buildings erected the previous year already looked quite dilapidated "for want of finishing." Gibbon saw little prospect of profit in the Saybrook venture. The shabby fort was surrounded by "insolent Indians" and had not received much support from its English sponsors. He declared that he had no desire to take up residence there and advised John Winthrop, Jr., not to do so. Gardener's fears of abandonment were well founded. [16]

Intimidated by the cannons mounted in the walls of the fort, the Pequots and western Niantics did not attempt a direct attack on Gardener's position. The early winter months thus passed quietly at Saybrook. On February 22, 1637, Gardener took a party of ten men, accompanied by three dogs, to a field on a narrow neck of land jutting into the river about a half-mile upstream from the palisade. He hoped to retrieve some twenty logs cut the summer before and float them downriver to the fort. He ordered his men to "burn the weeds, leaves, and reeds . . . every man carrying a length of match with brimstone matches with him to kindle the fire." As Gardener described the incident that followed, "when we came to the small of the neck, the weeds burning, I having before this set two sentinels on the small of the neck, I called to the men that were burning the reeds to come away, but they would not until they had burned up the rest of their matches." While Gardener argued with the men, four Pequots suddenly sprang out of the burning reeds. He tried to muster his company, "but Thomas Hurlbut cried out to me that some of the men did not follow me, for Thomas Rumble and Arthur Branch, threw down their two guns and ran away." A volley of arrows wounded two of the men standing in the burning reeds as the Indians tried to cut off the English party. Gardener ordered his men into a half-moon formation and slowly retreated back to the fort. "Thomas Hurlbut," he recorded, "was shot almost through the thigh, John Spencer in the back, into his kidneys, myself into the thigh, two more were shot dead." The Indians continued to attack throughout the retreat, "we defending ourselves with our naked swords, or else they had taken us all alive." He noted with some pride that the "two sore wounded men, by our slow retreat, got home with their guns" but added with disgust that "two sound men ran away and left their guns behind them." [17]

Once within the palisade, Gardener confronted Rumble and Branch, "the cowards that left us," telling them to draw lots to determine which of them should be hanged. Their actions were indefensible, he declared, for the Articles of War had been posted in the great hall of the fort, and they therefore were fully aware of the penalty for desertion during battle. But several "gentlemen" then at Saybrook, among them the Reverend Francis Higginson and the trader Matthew Mitchell, urged Gardener to grant a pardon. He agreed, reluctantly, recognizing that under the circumstances Saybrook needed every able-bodied man, even the cowardly. Of the wounded, Hurlbut and Gardener both recovered quickly. Hurlbut later claimed that in a subsequent engagement he had the pleasure of beheading the Indian who shot him through the thigh in the ambush near Saybrook. The other wounded man, shot through the kidneys, soon died. A member of Gardener's party who was captured by the Pequots perished under torture, his hands and nose severed from his body. [18]

Gardener's bitterness at the loss of his men and his anger at Boston for placing their lives in jeopardy were reflected in his account of the aftermath of ambush. "Within a few days after," he wrote, "when I had cured myself of my wound, I went out with eight men to get some fowl for our relief, and found the guns that were thrown away, and the body of one man shot through, the arrow going in the right side, the head sticking fast, half through a rib on the left side, which I took out and cleansed it, and presumed to send it to the Bay, because they had said that the arrows of the Indians were of no force." "The man's rib," Gardener declared, could serve as a "token" to Boston of the real nature of the war with the Pequots. [19]

Soon after the battle in the burning weeds, the Indian trader Thomas Stanton sailed downriver bound for Boston but was becalmed at Saybrook. Attracted by his ship, a large party of Pequots surrounded the fort, digging in within "musket shot" of the gate "behind a little rising hill and two great trees." Gardener ordered the carpenter to load the fort's two small cannons with musket balls and aim them at the Indians' position. "I told him," Gardener related, "that he must look towards me, and when he saw me wave my hat above my head, he should give fire to both guns." The Pequots, however, did not attack. Instead, "there came three Indians, creeping out and calling to us to speak with them." Grateful that Stanton, a trader fluent in the Algonquian dialects of the region, was present to assist him, Gardener grabbed his sword and a pistol and, with his interpreter at his side, "went ten or twelve poles without the fort to parlay with them." Before leaving the palisade, he ordered six men to precede him and stand guard outside the wall, so he would not be cut off outside. His suspicion of Pequot intentions was verified, as the guards "found a great number of Indians creeping behind the fort, or betwixt us and home." Seeing the armed Englishmen, the Pequots withdrew.[20]

Gardener instructed Stanton not to give the Indians any direct answers, as he was not authorized to grant concessions or terms without the consent of the authorities at Boston. The Pequots asked Gardener and Stanton to come closer, "but," Gardener recalled, "I would not let Thomas go any further than the great stump of a tree, and I stood by him." The Pequots first "asked who we were, and he answered, Thomas and Lieutenant. But they said he lied, for I was shot with many arrows, and so I was, but my buff coat preserved me, only one hurt me. But when I spake to them, they knew my voice, for one of them had dwelt three months with us, but ran away when the the Bay-men first came." The Pequots then asked if the English were at war with the western Niantics across the river, declaring that the western Niantics wanted English friendship and trade. Suspecting a trap, Gardener replied through Stanton that "we knew not the Indians one from another and therefore would trade with none." Then the Pequots asked, "Have you fought enough?" Gardener's reply to that peace feeler was evasive. "We said we knew not yet." The next Pequot inquiry reflected a telling uncertainty about the nature of their new enemy. "Then they asked if we did use to kill women and children? We said they should see thereafter. So they were silent for a small space, and then they said, We are Pequits, and have killed Englishmen, and can kill them as mosquitoes, and we will go to Conectecott, and kill men, women, and children, and we will take away the horses, cows, and hogs."[21]

At that point, young Stanton became agitated and demanded that Gardener "shoot that rogue." He had, Stanton cried, killed Englishmen, for he and his fellows were wearing clothes they had stripped from the corpses of their victims. Gardener calmed Stanton, telling him that they could not kill Indians during a parley but would take their revenge at an appropriate time. He told Stanton to challenge the Pequots to a battle on the grounds near Saybrook. Stanton, on Gardener's prompting, warned the Pequots that English women and livestock would be of no use to them, "for English women are lazy, and can't do their work; horses and cows will spoil your cornfields, and the hogs the clam banks, and so undo them." He added that if they took Fort Saybrook they would find a supply of hatchets, hoes, and trading cloth belonging to the English trader William Pynchon. On hearing that speech, the parleyers, Gardener recalled, ran back to the main body of the Pequots "mad as dogs. . . . I waved my hat above my head, and the two great guns went off so that there was a great hubbub amongst us." The Pequots disappeared.[22]

Two days after Gardener's acrimonious conference with the Pequots, Saybrook received reinforcements. The Connecticut towns upriver sent Captain John Mason, Robert Seeley, and five other armed men to the fort. Winthrop and his associates, informed by Gardener that without help Saybrook would fall into the hands of the enemy, dispatched "twenty armed soldiers" under the command of Captain John Underhill, a veteran of Endecott's raid. The captain, shocked at the weakness of the garrison, later wrote that "it was a special providence of God that they were not all slain." Morale was low. The Pequots, Underhill related, "put on the English clothes [they had taken from the men they killed] and came to the fort jeering of them, and calling, come and fetch your Englishmen's clothes again, come out and fight, if you dare, you dare not fight; you are all one like women. We have one amongst us that if he could kill but one of you more, he would be equal with God, and as the Englishmen's God is, so would he be. This blasphemous speech troubled the hearts of the soldiers, but they knew not how to remedy it, in respect to their weakness."[23]

Gardener, meanwhile, fretted over Connecticut's refusal to accept his guidance. He had earlier sent via a Dutch trader letters to the English settlements on the Connecticut River warning of an imminent Pequot attack and giving instructions on defensive measures. He received in reply "a scoff, [rather] than any thanks, for my care and pains."[24]

Gardener's fears for the safety of the Connecticut towns were well founded. In late April the Dutch trader came back down the river bearing news that Pequots had attacked Wethersfield and "killed fourteen English." In his narrative account of the Pequot War, Captain John Mason declared that the hundred warriors who took part in the raid had acted in league with "the Indians of that place." Sequin, the sachem of the Wangunk band, had sold land to the Wethersfield settlers, who promised that the sachem and his people, previously tributary to the Pequots, would be allowed to continue to live in the area under English protection. In early 1637, acting on that promise, Sequin tried to settle on a small patch of land near the English village. The settlers drove him away. He then turned to the Pequots for aid, inviting them to attack Wethersfield with Wangunk assistance. After the war, the Bay Colony magistrates, consulted by Connecticut concerning the question of punishing Sequin, advised that the Wangunk sachem had been unfairly treated and thus "by the law of nations" had waged a "just war" to remedy the violation of the "covenant" he had with the English. On that advice, Connecticut held Sequin blameless and "made a new agreement with the Indians of the river."[25]

The first report of the attack on Wethersfield, which had occurred on April 23, exaggerated the casualties. John Haynes later wrote to the senior John Winthrop that the Pequots "had killed six men, being then at their work [in the fields], and twenty cows and a mare, and had killed three women, and carried away two maids." Subsequent reports provided a more detailed account. On the morning of the attack, a horseman riding near Wethersfield came upon a number of warriors creeping toward the village. He galloped into the settlement crying that the Pequots were about to attack. Several of the women asked how the Pequots could possibly be so far north, but as they debated the matter the Indians suddenly entered the village. The women ran for cover, but three were captured. One, who resisted, was killed on the spot. Two others, both young girls, were carried off. Passing through the village, the warriors then surprised a work party in the nearby field, where they killed two more women and six men and slaughtered the cattle.[26]

A report that the Pequots, after leaving Wethersfield, had attacked Pynchon's settlement at Springfield upriver and massacred all its inhabitants turned out to be false. The Pequots next appeared at Saybrook. Underhill related that they brought "with them two maid captives, having put poles in their canoes, as we put masts on our boats, and upon them hung our English men's and women's shirts and smocks, instead of sails." As the Pequots approached the fort, "we gave fire with a piece of ordnance, and shot among their canoes. And though they were a mile from us, yet the bullet grazed not above twenty yards over the canoe, where the poor maids were." The shot missed, Underhill declared, because of "a special providence of God." Had the girls been killed by friendly fire, the Puritans "would have been deprived of the sweet observance of God's providence in their deliverance." [27]

Encouraged by their easy victory at Wethersfield, the Pequots taunted the English garrison at Saybrook. Edward Johnson recounted that they shouted that Englishmen were all squaws and their God no more than an insect. Johnson, who saw the war as a holy struggle between the people of God and the hosts of Satan, concluded that the Pequots' profane utterances, by revealing "their horrible pride . . . fitted themselves for destruction. The English having this report were now full assured that the Lord would deliver them into his hands to execute his righteous judgment upon these blasphemous murtherers, and therefore raised fresh soldiers for the war." [28]

In response to the attack at Wethersfield, the Connecticut General Court, comprising two magistrates and three commissioners from each of the three river towns, on May 16, 1637, declared an "offensive war" against the Pequot Indians. Although the three towns together contained no more than 250 inhabitants, the court ordered the conscription of an army of ninety men, with forty-two to come from Hartford, thirty from Windsor, and eighteen from Wethersfield. Hartford was to provide armor for fourteen men, and Windsor for six. Hartford was also directed to provide the army with eighty-four bushels of corn, three firkins of suet, two firkins of butter, four bushels of oatmeal, two bushels of pease, two bushels of salt, and 500 fish. Wethersfield was asked to furnish thirty-six bushels of corn and a single bushel of Indian beans. Windsor's task was to send fifty bushels of corn, fifty pieces of pork, thirty pounds of rice, and four cheeses. The war declaration specified that good beer should be provided to the officers and "sick men." Two gallons of sack were also to be sent with the army as well as "stronge water." [29]

Each soldier was to provide himself with a pound of gunpowder, four pounds of shot, twenty bullets, and a musket for the trip downriver. A barrel of powder per man would be issued once the company reached Saybrook. The war declaration requisitioned William Pynchon's trading shallop to transport the troops. Command of the Connecticut forces was entrusted to Captain John Mason, a tall, portly, vigorous soldier, thirty-seven years of age. Mason was a veteran of the continental wars, having served during the previous decade with the English expeditionary army in the Netherlands. Before migrating to Connecticut from the Bay Colony, Mason had represented Dorchester in the General Court for two years and had assisted in the planning of fortifications at Boston, Charlestown, and Castle Island. Second in command was Lieutenant Robert Seeley.[30] Assembling at Hartford for the journey downriver, Mason's troops attended church. The minister exhorted them "to execute those whom God, the righteous judge of all the world, hath condemned for blaspheming his sacred majesty, and murthering his servants . . . execute vengeance upon the heathen . . . binde their Kings in chaines, and Nobles in fetters of Iron . . . make their multitudes fall under your warlike weapons . . . your feet shall be set on their proud necks." [31]

The Massachusetts Bay Colony also made preparations to wage war against the Pequots. The General Court on April 18, 1637, had authorized a levy of 160 men, passing an emergency tax measure to raise 160 pounds to defray some of the anticipated costs. But the court directed the magistrates to enlist the help of the Plymouth Colony in bearing the burden of hostilities.[32] Plymouth's leaders, still offended by Boston's unilateral and irresponsible provocation of the Pequots, did not take kindly to the suggestion that they should now help underwrite the cost of the war. On May 12 Edward Winslow called at Boston. He stated, on behalf of Plymouth's governing council, that while they wished them well in their quarrel with the Pequots, there were four compelling reasons why Plymouth should not be expected to make any contribution to the war effort. The first was the Bay Colony's earlier refusal to aid Plymouth in its struggle with the French in Maine. The second was the Bay Colony's intrusion into Plymouth's trade there; the third, its interference with

Plymouth's rights in Connecticut; the fourth, Plymouth's poverty and
the Bay Colony's affluence. Moreover, since the Boston magistrates had
not bothered to consult with Plymouth prior to provoking the war, they
should not presume to ask them for help in extricating themselves from
the mess Endecott had made. Winslow added, however, that no final
decision would be made on Boston's request until the meeting of their
General Court three weeks later. In the meantime, they would be most
interested in their friends' response to their complaints about the Bay
Colony's past conduct.[33]

Governor Vane and his associates at once protested that Massachusetts
was not asking for aid for its own sake but wanted help in fighting "the
common enemy." They warned Plymouth that if the Pequots were not
quickly and decisively defeated the appearance of weakness "would cause
all the Indians in the country to join to root out all the English." They
explained that they regretted that they had not been of more assistance
to Plymouth in its efforts to maintain its position in Maine but at the
time thought it impolitic to antagonize "the king of France." As to
interference with Plymouth's trading activities in Maine and in the Connecticut River valley, those had been "private quarrels," not official Bay
Colony actions. Boston could hardly be expected to control traders on
the frontier. Finally, the Bay Colony raid that triggered the present war
had really been aimed only at the punishment of the Block Islanders, a
limited engagement for which, as Winthrop explained, "we thought it
not needful to trouble" Plymouth. Endecott's visit to the Pequots was not
intended to provoke hostilities; he had hoped "to draw them to parlay,
and so to some quiet end." That statement was very different in tone
from Winthrop's earlier boast that Endecott had avenged Englishmen
killed by the Pequots and had terrorized them into submission. It comes
close to an admission that Endecott's mission had in fact miscarried.[34]

Shortly after Winthrop's election as governor on May 17, he wrote to
his friend William Bradford to underscore his colleagues' explanations.
In the margin of Winthrop's letter, beside his denial of Bay Colony
misconduct in Maine, Bradford wrote an annotation to the effect that
Winthrop was lying. Boston was still involved in a clandestine trade
there. He added no comments to Winthrop's explanation of the Endecott
raid, but it is reasonable to surmise that he found it less than persuasive,
given Winthrop's earlier bellicose declarations on the subject.[35]

In response to Boston's repeated warning that the "Pequots and all other Indians" must be regarded as a common enemy, the Plymouth General Court finally agreed to contribute fifty foot soldiers and the crew of a bark to the war effort. They saw no action, as by the time they were mobilized the Pequots had been defeated at Fort Mystic, and Boston sent word that there was no longer any need of help from Plymouth.[36]

Plymouth's recalcitrance was not the only obstacle the magistrates encountered as they labored to implement the council's plan for mobilization. Dissension within the church hampered efforts to recruit troops in Boston and contributed to a nine-month delay in resuming the offensive against the Pequots. Anne Hutchinson and her followers, often called "antinomians" because of their attitude toward ecclesiastical authority, held that God's grace is made manifest in individual spiritual experience and that grace freed the faithful from the law. They had challenged the authority of some of the clergy, questioning whether certain of the Bay Colony's more learned and eminent divines were truly in a state of grace, given the legalism that characterized their preaching. They took exception to the appointment of the Reverend John Wilson as army chaplain, declaring that Wilson was under "a covenant of works" and therefore unfit to minister to the Lord's soldiers. Winthrop, replacing the pro-antinomian Henry Vane as governor in May, complained that as a result of that controversy Boston failed to send its best men to war but supplied instead only "the most refuse sort." Their "carelesse manner," Winthrop declared, "gave great disappointment to the service." Winthrop's complaint reflected his distaste for the unorthodox views of some of the men who did join in the war effort against the Pequots. A number of them were sympathetic to the schismatics.[37]

The dissension surrounding Pequot War recruitment in Boston may also have reflected a controversy concerning the organization of military forces in the Bay Colony. Prior to 1634, military preparations were in the hands of hired professional soldiers who drilled trainbands organized in each village. But fear of an invasion from England prompted by *quo warranto* proceedings against the colony's charter, brought by Sir Ferdinando Gorges and other enemies of the Puritan venture, impelled the magistrates to take direct charge of the military. The General Court accordingly established a war council composed of the governor, deputy governor, and nine deputies. The war council had sweeping powers to "dispose of all military matters whatsoever" and in time of emergency could "putt such person to death" as "they shall judge to be enemyes of the commonwealth." In response to the Pequot crisis, the magistrates reorganized the trainbands into three regiments, representing Suffolk, Middlesex, and Essex counties. The leaders of those regiments received the rank of colonel, but in making those appointments the war council by-passed the professional soldiers who had led the trainbands. The new commanding officers were magistrates, men of weight and orthodoxy who could be trusted to uphold the Puritan order. For Suffolk County, John Winthrop was appointed colonel; Thomas Dudley was designated lieutenant colonel. Middlesex's military forces were entrusted to Colonel John Haynes and Lieutenant Colonel Roger Harlakenden. John Endecott commanded the Essex County force, assisted by John Winthrop, Jr. With the exception of Endecott and Dudley, none of those new officers had any prior military experience whatsoever. With the exception of Ende-cott, none led Massachusetts Bay volunteers against the Pequots. But they retained their commands, for political reasons, while those who did the actual fighting had to settle for lesser rank. Several of the professional soldiers who might reasonably have expected their own commands—John Underhill, William Trask, and Daniel Patrick, for example—received the rank of "muster-master" and were placed under the close supervision of the magistrate commanders.[38]

Needless to say, the command situation produced tensions and resentments. John Underhill complained bitterly that, if professional officers were "of no better esteem" than "constables," he would "rather lay downe my commande." Underhill, of course, rendered the Bay Colony notable service throughout the Pequot War. However, his open sympathy for Anne Hutchinson, exiled in 1637, resulted in the termination of his career in Massachusetts. When Underhill returned to Boston at the war's end, he was disarmed and disenfranchised. A land grant promised in compensation for his military service was withheld, and Underhill was subsequently exiled. In justification of that action, Winthrop noted that Underhill had claimed to have received direct inspiration from God while "taking the moderate use of the creature called tobacco." He had also allegedly committed "incontinency with a neighbor's wife," a woman "young, and beautiful, and withal of a jovial spirit and behavior." Underhill claimed that he was simply offering the woman spiritual comfort "and that when the door was found locked upon them, they were in private prayer together." He subsequently served the Dutch in New

Netherland as an Indian fighter, employing the tactics he learned at Fort Mystic to terrorize the natives of western Long Island.[39]

The leader of the Mohegans was eager to contribute to the war against the Pequots. Shortly after Jonathan Brewster took charge of the Plymouth trading post on the Connecticut River, Uncas sought to ingratiate himself with Brewster and his associates. We remarked earlier on Uncas's rumor mongering and his use of his English contacts to inflame the colonists against the Pequots. Now, as Connecticut mobilized following the Pequot assault on Wethersfield, Uncas offered the services of some sixty warriors recruited primarily from the River Indian bands that had clashed with the Pequots some years earlier. Uncas's efforts to build an anti-Pequot coalition were not entirely successful. A number of Uncas's kinsmen were offended by his pandering to the English and sought to reattach themselves to the Pequots. But Sassacus was now so wary of Uncas's Mohegans that he refused to accept their professions of loyalty. He drove some of them away. Others remained in the Pequot villages.[40]

Despite his relationship with the Plymouth traders, the English military commanders did not trust Uncas and at first were inclined to keep him at arm's length. Captain John Mason wrote that "we were somewhat doubtful of his Fidelity." John Underhill recorded that during their trip down the Connecticut River the Connecticut militiamen were troubled by the thought that Uncas's men "in time of greatest need might revolt, and turn their backs against those they professed to be their friends, and join with the Pequeats." Underhill recalled that when he rowed upriver from Saybrook to meet Mason and his company, he found their chaplain leading them in prayer. "O Lord God," intoned the Reverend Mr. Stone, "if it be thy blessed will, vouchsafe so much favor to thy poor distressed servants, as to manifest one pledge of thy love that may confirm us of the fidelity of these Indians toward us, that now pretend friendship and service to us, that our hearts may be encouraged the more in this work of thine." Underhill informed the chaplain and the company that Uncas's forces had already reached Saybrook and that "those Indians had brought in five Pequeats' heads, one prisoner, and wounded one mortally." That news "did much encourage the hearts of all, and replenished them exceedingly, and gave them all occasion to rejoice and be thankful to God."[41]

The Mohegans had been goaded into attacking Pequots by the ever-skeptical Lieutenant Gardener. In conversations with Captain John Mason, Gardener had questioned not only the Connecticut militia's ability to mount a war against Indians but also their wisdom in trusting Uncas's Mohegans, "who had but that year come from the Pequits." Mason replied that he had no choice, as he needed Indian guides familiar with the Pequot country. Maybe so, Gardener replied, "but I will try them before a man of ours shall go with you or them." He then summoned Uncas "and said unto him: You say you will help Maj. Mason, but I will first see it; therefore send you twenty men to the Bass river, for there went yesternight six Indians in a canoe thither; fetch them now dead or alive, and then you shall go with Maj. Mason, else not." Uncas accepted the challenge. In addition to four Pequot heads, Uncas's men brought back to Fort Saybrook one live "traitor . . . whose name was Kiswas." Only one of the Indians Gardener asked Uncas to apprehend escaped. Delighted by that show of loyalty, Gardener presented Uncas with "fifteen yards of trading cloth on my own charge, to give unto his men according to their desert." [42]

The captive Kiswas had once lived among the English at Saybrook. Taunting his former friends, he shouted that they "durst not kill a Pequot." Enraged, Gardener turned him over to the Mohegans, who "tied one of his legs to a post, and twenty men, with a rope tied to the other, pulled him in pieces." Kiswas was finally dispatched with a pistol shot administered by Captain Underhill. [43]

Shortly thereafter, a Dutch trading ship anchored at Fort Saybrook. Invited ashore by the English, the captain and a trader in his company informed their hosts "that they were bound to the Pequeat [Thames] river to trade." Alarmed, Gardener and his colleagues exclaimed that they could not permit the Dutch to visit the Pequots, as they were about to march against them and did not want their men killed by Pequot arrowheads made from Dutch kettles. Although the Dutch were initially angered by this interference with their Indian trade, they soon reached an accommodation with the English. The Dutch captain promised that, in exchange for permission to call on the Pequots, they would endeavor to secure the release of the two English girls taken captive in the raid on Wethersfield. Gardener promised to pay the Dutch captain for his efforts. (He later complained that he received neither thanks nor recompense for the ten pounds he laid out to secure the girls' freedom.) In the meantime, the director general of New Netherland learned of the plight of the "captive maids" and dispatched a pinnace to overtake the trading vessel with orders that the girls be rescued, peaceably if possible, by force if necessary. He added that they were to be brought immediately to the Dutch colony, so that he might have "the first sight of them after their deliverance."[44]

Landing at Pequot harbor in the Thames River, the Dutch captain called on Sassacus and offered trade goods for the girls' freedom. Sassacus refused to release them. The Dutch then invited the Pequots to board their bark to trade. Seven Indians, including several lesser sachems, accepted that invitation. Once the Pequots were on board, the Dutch seized them and sent word to Sassacus that if the English captives were not delivered to him, at once, they would set sail and drown their Pequot prisoners in the ocean on the way home. The Pequots laughed at that suggestion, thinking the Dutch were joking. But as the bark drew anchor and headed for the mouth of the river, they ran after it, crying that they would give up the girls after all. The ship turned back, anchored again, took the "captive maids" on board, and released the Pequots. Stopping briefly at Saybrook, the captain explained to the English commander there that the director general at New Amsterdam had asked to be the first to interview the girls. Gardener agreed to that arrangement.[45]

After visiting with Director General Van Twiller, the "redeemed captives" were delivered to Saybrook, where they were questioned closely about their experiences among the Pequots. Captain Mason recorded that they had learned that the Pequots were armed with "sixteen guns with powder and shot." The Pequots had asked their prisoners to make more gunpowder for their arsenal and were disappointed to learn that they did not know how to do so. Captain John Underhill was more interested in the moral and religious aspects of their captivity. He recorded in his narrative of the Pequot War that the "captive maids" were asked if they had been raped or seduced. "The eldest of them," Underhill wrote, "was about sixteen years of age. Demanding of her how they had used her, she told us that they did solicit her to uncleaness, but her heart being much broken, and afflicted under the bondage she was cast in, had brought to her consideration these thoughts—How shall I commit this great evil and sin against my God? Their hearts were much taken up with the consideration of God's just displeasure to them." Underhill noted approvingly that the girls regarded their captivity as a sign of God's displeasure, realizing that God's "hand was justly upon them for their remissness in all their ways." Their release, they believed, was a sure sign of God's grace. The girls testified that the Pequots did not actually abuse them in any way, apart from tempting them sexually, but "carried them from place to place, and showed them their forts and curious wigwams and houses, and encouraged them to be merry." But they could not feel "any delight or mirth under so strange a king." Underhill assured his readers that "behind the rocks, and under the trees, the eldest spent her breath in supplication to her God." His account of the interview with the "captive maids" contains themes that later in the century would become standard motifs in narratives of Indian captivity.[46]

After the arrival at Saybrook in early May of the Connecticut forces commanded by John Mason, planning for an "offensive war" against the Pequots began in earnest. Mason's instructions from the Connecticut court directed him to proceed to Pequot harbor. But as his vessels "lay Windbound" at Saybrook from Wednesday until Friday, Mason discussed with Underhill and Gardener the risks of a direct attack on Sassacus's village. As Mason recalled their misgivings, the English troops were "altogether ignorant of the Country" and were therefore very uncertain "in what manner we should proceed in our Enterprize." One possibility was to by-pass Pequot harbor, sail to the Narragansett country, recruit a party of Narragansett warriors, and then attack the Pequots from the east. Several considerations persuaded the commanders of the wisdom of that plan. Mason pointed out that since the Pequots "kept a continual Guard upon the River Night and Day" there was virtually no chance that they could mount a surprise attack at the harbor. But without the element of surprise there was little hope of a victory, since "their Numbers far exceeded ours." A landing at Pequot harbor would expose men disembarking in unfamiliar territory to an immediate counterattack by a foe "swift on Foot" that would "impede" the operation "and possibly dishearten our Men." But, Mason continued, if the army sailed to Narragansett Bay and then marched overland from the east, "we should come upon their Backs, and possibly might surprize them unawares, at worst we should be on firm Land as well as they."

There was one difficulty with that plan. Mason had been ordered by the Connecticut General Court to "land our Men in Pequot River." Underhill and Gardener were both reluctant to sanction a violation of that order. Mason therefore asked the chaplain to "commend our Condition to the Lord, that Night, to direct how and in what manner we should demean ourselves." The Reverend Mr. Stone accordingly spent the evening aboard ship with the troops. The next morning he went ashore, made his way to Mason's room in the great hall in the fort, and informed him that after seeking the guidance of the Almighty he was persuaded that the attack should be mounted from Narragansett Bay. Underhill and Gardener then gave their consent to Mason's plan. Mason added to his report of their deliberations an editorial comment. Though he certainly did not wish "to encourage any Soldiers to act beyond their Commission, or contrary to it," battlefield commanders must have some discretion, as it is not possible for the civil authorities "to forsee all Accidents and Occurents that fall out in the Management and Pursuit of a War."[47]

The commanders then decided upon the deployment of their forces. Underhill committed nineteen of his men to the expedition against the Pequots, whereupon Mason sent twenty of the Connecticut troops home to help protect their villages from Indian attack. The English force now consisted of ninety soldiers accompanied by seventy Mohegans. Arriving at Narragansett Bay near Port Judith by sea on a moonlit Saturday evening (May 20, 1637), the invaders did not disembark but rather observed the sabbath aboard ship. On Monday, a gale-force wind rose from the southwest and kept them from landing. The wind blew until Tuesday night. Shortly after sunset, Captain Mason was finally able to make his way ashore "and Marched up to the Place of the Chief Sachem's Residence." He asked Miantonomi for free passage through the Narragansett country, as his troops were under orders to punish the Pequots for the "intolerable Wrongs and Injuries" they "had lately done unto the English." Miantonomi replied that he shared their ill feelings toward the Pequots but, as Mason recalled, "thought our Numbers were too weak to deal with the Enemy, who were (as he said) very great Captains and Men skilfull in War. . . . He spake somewhat slightingly of us."[48]

The Narragansetts may well have been irritated by the rejection of an offer they had sent to Boston through Roger Williams several weeks earlier. Miantonomi had proposed that the attack on the Pequots be entrusted to Narragansett warriors, with the English military role limited to providing sea transport for the striking force. The Pequots, he argued, were short of supplies and therefore vulnerable. Fearing an attack, they had planted new cornfields on Block Island and eastern Long Island and had gone to the coast "to take sturgeon and other fish." In payment for bringing the Pequots to their knees, Miantonomi had asked only that he be given some trading cloth and that the renegade Pequot Wequash, who would serve as guide, be presented with "a large coate." Williams urged the magistrates to accept Miantonomi's offer, but Boston was unwilling to entrust so vital a mission to Indians.[49]

On May 24, the day following his conference with the Narragansetts, Mason marched his troops to an eastern Niantic village near the "Frontier to the Pequots . . . eighteen or twenty miles" west of Miantonomi's residence. The eastern Niantics gave them a very cool reception. "They carryed very proudly toward us," Mason wrote, "not permitting any of us to come into their Fort." Alarmed by their demeanor, the English commanders posted "a strong Guard . . . about their Fort, giving Charge that no Indian should be suffered to pass in or out. We also informed the Indians, that none of them should stir out of the Fort upon peril of their Lives." Mason was aware that a number of eastern Niantics, once Pequot tributaries, had married Pequots and feared they would alert their in-laws to the impending English attack. If the Pequots were aroused, his expedition had little hope of success.[50]

The following morning, a band of Narragansett warriors arrived at the village and urged its inhabitants to join with them in helping the English defeat the Pequots. "Suddenly gathering into a Ring," Mason recalled, the Narragansetts one by one "made solemn Protestation how gallantly they would demean themselves, and how many Men they would Kill." The march began around eight in the morning. About 500 Indians initially accompanied the English expedition. The heat was oppressive, and the English were short of rations. Several soldiers passed out from heat prostration or hunger. Twelve miles down the trail, they came to the Pawcatuck River. The army stopped "at a Ford where our Indians told us the Pequots did usually fish." At that spot, Mason claimed, the Narragansetts "manifesting great Fear" began to desert in droves. He noted sarcastically that those same Indians had expressed contempt for the English troops, "saying, that we durst not look upon a Pequot" while boasting that they "themselves would perform great Things." Perplexed, Mason turned to the Mohegan sachem Uncas, whose seventy warriors had remained with the English, and asked "what he thought the Indians would do." Uncas replied that his people would remain true to their pledge and march with him against Sassacus, but "the Narragansetts would all leave us." With some exaggeration Mason added, "and so it proved."[51]

After a sparse meal, the march resumed. Three miles west of the Pawcatuck River, the army, now in Pequot country, "came to a Field which had lately been planted with Indian Corn." After pausing to confer with their Indian guides, Mason and Underhill determined "that the Enemy had two Forts almost impregnable; but we were not at all Discouraged but rather Animated, in so much as we were resolved to Assault both their Forts at once." On closer inquiry, however, they determined that Weinshauks "was so remote that we could not come up with it before Midnight, though we Marched hard." Since Sassacus was presumably at Weinshauks, some thought was given to by-passing Mystic, the closer fortified village, and striking Weinshauks first. But, as Mason related, "we were then constrained, being exceedingly spent in our March with extream Heat and want of Necessaries," to attack Fort Mystic instead.[52]

The army resumed its march "in a silent Manner." No admirer of Indian character, Mason claimed that those who had not already deserted "fell all into the Rear . . . being possessed with great Fear." He recalled that an hour after nightfall they came to "a little Swamp between two Hills; there we pitched our little Camp, much wearied with hard Travel, keeping great Silence, supposing we were very near the Fort: as our Indians informed us: which proved otherwise: the Rocks were our Pillows, yet rest was pleasant: the Night proved comfortable, being clear and Moon Light." The guards posted outside the camp heard singing from the Pequot fort. Mason's Indian informants claimed that the enemy was celebrating, "with great Insulting and Rejoycing," English cowardice. They had spotted "our Pinnaces sail by them some Days before" and "concluded that we were afraid of them and durst not come near them."[53]

In his account of the campaign against the Pequots, the Reverend Philip Vincent described the design of Fort Mystic, constructed, as he declared, through the tutelage of "natural reason and experience . . . without mathematical skill, or use of iron tools." He explained that in building a "military fortress" the Indians always "choose a piece of ground, dry and of best advantage, forty or fifty feet square." Fort Mystic was larger than usual, covering "at least two acres of ground." To protect the enclosure,

> they pitch, close together as they can, young trees and half trees, as thick as a man's thigh or the calf of his leg. Ten or twelve foot high they are above the ground, and within rammed three feet deep with undermining, the earth being cast up for their better shelter against the enemy's dischargements. Betwixt these palisadoes are divers loopholes, through which they let fly their winged messengers. The door for the most part is entered sideways, which they stop with boughs or birches, as need requireth. The space therein is full of wigwams, wherein the wives and children live with them. These huts or little houses are framed like our garden arbors, something more round, very strong and handsome, covered with close-wrought mats, made by their women, of flags [iris leaves], rushes, and hempen threads, so defensive that neither rain, though never so bad and long, nor yet the wind, though never so strong, can enter. The top through a square hold giveth passage to the smoke, which in rainy weather is covered.

Fort Mystic, Vincent reported, was "so crowded with numerous dwellings, that the English wanted foot room to grapple with their adversaries." [54]

The attack on the Pequot fort was mounted shortly after daybreak on Friday, May 26. Mason related that the English, wearied from the previous day's march, overslept and did not awaken until first light. He had planned to strike in the dark. Fearing loss of the advantage of surprise, he "rowsed the Men with all expedition" and, after a short prayer, hastened toward his objective, "the Indians shewing us a Path" which they claimed "led directly to the Fort." After marching two miles, the Indian village was not in sight, and Mason began to suspect that his Indian guides had deliberately misled him. But then they came to a cornfield at "the foot of a Great Hill." [55]

Uncas and Wequash, the renegade Pequot, were summoned. "We demanded of them, Where was the Fort? They answered, On Top of that Hill: Then we demanded, Where were the Rest of the Indians? They answered, Behind, exceedingly afraid." Mason gave word that the Indians need not run away. They should instead "stand at what distance they pleased, and see whether English men would now Fight or not." Captain

Underhill, commanding the Massachusetts troops, had been marching in the rear. He now joined Mason at the head of the line. After a prayer, Mason and Underhill divided their forces into two companies. The Pequot fort had two entrances. They decided "to enter both at once."[56]

Mason related that, as he led the attack through the northeast gate, he "heard a Dog bark, and an Indian crying Owanux! Owanux! which is Englishmen! Englishmen! We called up our Forces with all expedition, gave fire upon them through the Pallizado: the Indians being in a dead indeed their last sleep: then we wheeling fell upon the main Entrance, which was blocked up with Bushes about Breast high, Over which the Captain passed, intending to make good the Entrance, encouraging the rest to follow. Lieutenant Seeley endeavored to enter, but being somewhat cumbered, stepped back and pulled out the bushes and so entered." Their original intention, Mason claimed, was not to burn the village but "to destroy by the Sword and save the Plunder." Since the troops relied on the spoils of war for much of their compensation, his claim is believable.[57]

At the other gate, Captain Underhill and his men also found their passage blocked with piles of tree branches. Underhill recounted that he tried to break through but "found the work too heavy for me." He fell back and ordered his men to "pull out those breaks." (After the war, Underhill's enemies accused him of cowardice for hesitating at the gate.) Once the entrance was cleared, Underhill, as he recalled, led his men into the village, "our swords in our right hand, our carbines and muskets in our left hand."[58]

The Pequots put up a fierce resistance. Several of Underhill's men were struck by arrows as soon as they broke through the barrier blocking the gate. Some were pierced "through the shoulder, some in the face, some in the legs." Underhill himself "received a shot in the left hip" but was protected by his thick buff coat. At the other gate, Mason's life was saved by his helmet, which deflected a barrage of arrows. Two of the English invaders were killed; twenty others were wounded in their effort to take Fort Mystic by storm. Underhill praised the Pequots for their courage, declaring, "mercy did they deserve for their valor, could we have had the opportunity to have bestowed it."[59]

Captain John Mason disagreed. Far from commending the Pequots' gallantry, he claimed that they would not come out and fight in the open. Blaming the victims for presumably inciting a massacre, Mason charged that the behavior of the Pequot warriors gave the English no choice but to put the village to the torch. Rather than facing English steel, some of the Pequots fled through the crowded alleyways within the palisade. "Others crept under their beds." Entering a wigwam, Mason "was beset by many Indians." Beating them off and stumbling back into the crowded alleyway, Mason encountered a large band of warriors, who turned and ran from him. At the "end of the lane," with Mason in pursuit, the Pequots encountered "Edward Patterson, Thomas Barber, with some others." Patterson and his compatriots killed seven of the Indians; the rest escaped.[60]

Out of breath, frustrated by the course of the battle, Mason "marched at a slow Pace" back up the lane. Near the gate, he "saw two Soldiers standing close to the Pallizado with their Swords pointed to the Ground." As Mason related, "I told them We should never kill them after that manner. . . . We must burn them." Mason ducked into a nearby wigwam and "brought out a Firebrand." Thrusting the smoldering stick "into the Matts with which they were covered," he set the wigwams lining the narrow alley ablaze. Two of his soldiers, Lieutenant Thomas Bull and Nicholas Olmstead, quickly followed Mason's lead. Soon flames were coursing through the village.

Captain Underhill then "set fire on the south end with a train of powder. The fires of both meeting in the center of the fort, blazed most terribly, and burnt all in the space of half an hour." Of the trapped Pequots, Underhill wrote, "Many courageous fellows were unwilling to come out, and fought most desperately through the palisadoes so as they were scorched and burnt with the very flame, and were deprived of their arms . . . the fire burnt their very bowstrings." The Pequots at Fort Mystic, Underhill declared, "perished valiantly." But Mason offered a different account of their behavior. The Pequots, he wrote, were "most dreadfully amazed . . . indeed, such a dreadful Terror did the Almighty let fall upon their Spirits, that they would fly from us and run into the very Flames, where many of them perished."[61]

After the fires were set, Mason and Underhill ordered their men to "fall off and surround the Fort." One man, Arthur Smith, was so badly wounded in the earlier skirmishing that "he could not move out of the Place," so he was carried from the burning village by Lieutenant Bull. A number of the Pequots, overcoming their momentary panic, ran through an alley lined with flaming wigwams and regrouped "windward" of the conflagration. Temporarily out of harm's way, they began "pelting at us with their Arrows, and we repaid them with our small shot." Another group of forty Pequots suddenly ran out of the fort and "perished by the Sword." Others who attempted to escape the flames were shot down.[62]

Most of the residents of Fort Mystic were burned alive. Mason estimated that "six or seven Hundred" Pequots were killed that morning. Among the dead were 150 warriors from Weinshauks whom Sassacus had dispatched to intercept the English troops. Mason attributed their decision to stop overnight at the doomed village to the intervention of the Almighty. Underhill claimed the Pequots themselves reported losing around 400, but Mason's estimate is probably more accurate. Except for seven who were taken prisoner and seven who escaped, those who broke through the flames were systematically killed by the troops surrounding the village. That deliberate, cold-blooded slaughter of women and children as well as warriors suggests that the burning of Fort Mystic cannot be dismissed or excused, as some have claimed, as a military necessity. No military necessity requires that noncombatants fleeing a burning village be shot or impaled. The massacre at Fort Mystic was an act of terrorism intended to break Pequot morale. So intense was the musket fire outside the fort that a number of Narragansetts in the outer perimeter were killed or wounded. Roger Williams later deplored the fact that only a few of the army's Indian allies had been issued yellow identification bands.[63]

In their accounts of the destruction of Fort Mystic, the English commanders paused to provide their readers with an ideological justification for their massacre of its inhabitants. Captain Mason declared the incineration of the Pequots was an act mandated by God to punish "savages" guilty of arrogance and of treachery against God's Chosen. The Pequots, he wrote, "not many Hours before [had] exalted themselves in their great Pride, threatening and resolving the utter Ruin and Destruction of all the English, Exulting and Rejoycing with Songs and Dances. But God was above them, who laughed his Enemies and the Enemies of his People to scorn making them as a fiery Oven. . . . Thus did the Lord judge among the Heathen, filling the Place with dead Bodies."[64]

Captain Underhill remarked that "young soldiers that had never been in war" were distressed by the cold-blooded slaughter of Indians fleeing the burning village. He granted that "great and doleful was the bloody sight . . . to see so many souls lie gasping on the ground, so thick in some places, that you could hardly pass along." After musing for a moment on the possible immorality of their butchering women and children, Underhill found reassurance in Scripture. "It may be demanded," he wrote, "Why should you be so furious (as some have said). Should not Christians have more mercy and compassion? But I would refer you to David's war. When a people is grown to such a height of blood, and sin against God and man, and all confederates in the action, there he hath no respect to persons, but harrows them, and saws them, and puts them to the sword, and the most terriblest death that may be. Sometimes the Scripture declareth women and children must perish with their parents. Sometimes the case alters, but we will not dispute it now. We had sufficient light from the word of God for our proceedings." [65]

Puritan spokesmen echoed Underhill's judgment. Governor William Bradford of Plymouth drew inspiration from Leviticus. "It was a fearful sight," he wrote, "to see them thus frying in the fire and the streams of blood quenching the same, and horrible was the stink and scent thereof; but the victory seemed a sweet sacrifice, and they gave praise to God, who had wrought so wonderfully for them, as to enclose their enemy in their hands and give them so speedy a victory over so proud and insulting an enemy." Edward Johnson also declared the immolation of the Pequots at Fort Mystic God's will. "The Lord," he wrote, "would look out of the cloudy pillar upon them." Johnson claimed that some of the English soldiers had difficulty piercing Pequot bodies with their swords and therefore sensed "the devil was in them" as they "could work strange things with the help of Satan." [66]

Bradford claimed that the Narragansetts who accompanied the Puritan army taunted the dying Pequots. But Underhill placed the attitude of the Narragansett and Mohegan auxiliaries in a different light when he recorded that they were horrified by the massacre at Fort Mystic and complained to the commanders about "the manner of the Englishmen's fight . . . because it is too furious, and slays too many men." [67]

English casualties at Mystic were higher than is sometimes realized, belying both Mason's claim that the warriors defending the village were cowardly and Jennings's assertion three centuries later that the village contained only women, children, and elderly men. Although only two Englishmen were killed in the fighting inside the palisade, twenty out of seventy-seven were wounded, some severely. The Bay Colony chronicler Edward Johnson declared that, "assuredly, had the Indians knowne how much weakned our Souldiers were at present," they might well have mounted an immediate counterattack and wiped them out. He credited "the Lord" with withholding that deadly knowledge from them. As Captain Underhill recalled conditions that morning, "we were forced to cast our eyes upon our poor maimed soldiers, many of them lying upon the ground, wanting food and such nourishable things as might refresh them in this faint state. But we were not supplied with any such things whereby we might relieve them, but only were constrained to look up to God, and to entreat him for mercy toward them. Most were thirsty, but could find no water. The provision we had for food was very little." Some of the wounded, Mason recalled, "fainted by reason of the sharpness of the weather, it being a cool morning." The ill-prepared army lacked medical support, for the surgeon engaged to accompany the troops, a man named Pell from Saybrook, "not accustomed to war," had remained with the ships at Narragansett Bay. Though in "great misery and pain," the wounded pulled through despite (or, given the state of seventeenth-century surgical practice, perhaps because of) his absence.[68]

The English entrusted a skirmish with a handful of Pequots on an open field near the smoldering fort to their Indian allies. The commanders, Underhill related, wanted to "see the nature of the Indian war." If the Narragansetts and Mohegans were horrified by English warfare, the Puritans were contemptuous of its Indian counterpart. "I dare boldly affirm," Underhill wrote, "they might fight seven years and not kill seven men. They came not near one another, but shot remote, and not point blank, as we often do with our bullets, but at rovers, and then they gaze up in the sky to see where the arrow falls, and not until it is fallen do they shoot again. This fight is more for pastime, than to conquer and subdue enemies." Captain Mason scoffed at the Indians' "feeble Manner," declaring that it "did hardly deserve the Name of Fighting."[69]

Soon after that desultory engagement, the Narragansetts who had remained with the Puritan army decided that it was time to return home. But as they made their way down the trail to the east, they were attacked by Pequots. Underhill related: "Then came the Narragansetts to Captain Mason and myself, crying, Oh help us now, or our men will all be slain. We answered, How dare you crave aid of us, when you are leaving of us in this distressed condition, not knowing which way to march out of the

country?" Underhill then lectured his Indian allies on the contrast between English virtue and savage vice: "But yet you shall see it is not the
nature of Englishmen to deal like heathens, to requite evil for evil, but we
will succor you." Underhill then led thirty of the English troops down
the trail and rescued the beleaguered Narragansetts. He claimed that the
English "in a space of an hour . . . slew and wounded above a hundred
Pequeats, all fighting men, that charged us both in rear and flanks" as the
English retreated with the Narragansetts in tow. Underhill's account of
Pequot ferocity in this action contrasts vividly with his description of
the lackadaisical Pequot-Narragansett confrontation in the field by Fort
Mystic quoted earlier. Underhill simply did not comprehend the real
nature of Indian warfare, which valued individual initiative and cunning
and sought to achieve advantage through stealth and ambush. In common with many later English observers, he judged the Indian warrior by
European standards.[70]

Despite the victory at Mystic, the success of the mission was now in
doubt. Many of the Narragansetts, Underhill's exhortations notwithstanding, had returned home. Low on food and munitions, accompanied
only by Uncas, his small band of Mohegans, and a handful of Narragansetts, the Puritan army no longer had the means to mount an attack
on Sassacus at Weinshauks. The main Pequot stronghold remained intact. As they were pondering their course of action, outnumbered in "the
enemies Country," they looked to sea and, as Mason recalled, saw "to our
Great Rejoycing . . . our Vessels [coming] to us before a fair Gale of
Wind, sailing into Pequot Harbour." But as the English started toward
the Thames River to the west and relief, they encountered some 300
Pequot warriors from Weinshauks. Mason led a detachment of his more
able-bodied men to confront the enemy, "chiefly to try what temper they
were of." Wary of the better-armed English, the Pequots backed off.[71]

The evacuation proved difficult. Several of the soldiers were so badly
wounded they could not walk but had to be carried by their hungry and
fatigued comrades. "We also being faint, were constrained to put four to
one Man." As others had to carry the arms and supplies of the wounded,
"we had not above forty Men free." Several Mohegans were then persuaded to carry the nonambulatory. The Pequots who followed nearby
sent a party a quarter of a mile up the hill and saw the smoking ruins of
Fort Mystic. They "stamped and tore the Hair from their Heads" in rage
and grief and then charged down the hill toward the retreating English.

The men in the rear of the column wheeled and fired. Several Pequots were hit, and the others held back for a moment, then scattered and shot their arrows "at Random." At the foot of the hill, the English found "a small Brook, where we rested and refreshed ourselves."[72]

Resuming their march, they came upon several isolated wigwams, which were put to the torch. The Pequots followed close behind and from time to time sent scouts in advance of the Puritan column to wait "in Ambush behind Rocks and Trees." To clear the line of march, the troops fired into the underbrush. Several Pequots were struck by that blind fire and, Mason added, "probably more might, but for want of Munition." The Mohegans, with "a great Shout," beheaded the Pequots as soon as they fell. Underhill recalled that "one Sargeant Davis, a pretty courageous soldier, spying something black upon the top of a rock, stepped forth from the body with a carbine of three feet long, and, at a venture, gave fire, supposing it to be an Indian's head, turning him over with his heels upward. The Pequeats were much daunted at the shot, and forebear approaching so near upon us."[73]

About two miles east of Pequot harbor on the Thames River, the Pequots who had been dogging the retreat "gathered together and left us." To make an appropriate impression on the relief party at the river, Mason and his men marched to the top of a hill near the harbor and unfurled their banners. (The captain regretted that their drum had been left behind.) They found at anchor the shallop they had left in Narragansett Bay, now commanded by Captain Daniel Patrick of the Massachusetts Bay Colony and carrying forty newly recruited troops. Patrick's forces had just raided Block Island, which the Pequots had occupied and planted with corn the previous spring.[74]

Immediately after their arrival at Pequot harbor, Mason and Underhill clashed with the commander of the Bay Colony expedition. Patrick announced that he had come to rescue the hapless Connecticut troops, "supposing," Mason observed acerbically, "we were pursued, though there did not appear any the Least sign of such a Thing." But when Mason asked him to disembark his men to make room aboard the bark for the wounded, Patrick at first refused, finally giving in when Mason and Underhill angrily reminded him that "it was our own Boat in which he was." After the casualties were finally taken on board, Underhill and Patrick became embroiled in a shouting match over who was in command of the ship and how it should now be used. With some difficulty, they reached a compromise agreement. Patrick would stay with the vessel in question at Pequot harbor in order to protect the few Narragansetts remaining with the English from Pequot reprisals. Underhill would transport the wounded to Saybrook in a small pinnace, then return, pick up the Narragansetts, and take them home.[75]

But as soon as Underhill was underway, Patrick changed his mind, declaring that he needed to go to Saybrook immediately to rendezvous with a Bay Colony fleet now on its way to the Connecticut River. He told Mason that he should look after his Indians, and his own men, as best he could. In his memoir of the war, Mason complained bitterly that Patrick had refused to provide adequate transport for his troops and his Indian allies. "To march by Land was very Dangerous; it being near Twenty Miles in the Enemies Country, our Numbers being much weakened, we were then about twenty Men, the rest we had sent home for fear of the Pequots Invasion." But they had no choice. So Mason set out, accompanied by Uncas, his Mohegans, and the remaining Narragansetts. The volatile Captain Patrick, perhaps fearing that he would be blamed if Mason and his men were killed by the Pequots, now insisted on marching his own men to Saybrook by land. "In truth," Mason wrote, "we did not desire or delight in his Company, and so we plainly told him: However he would and did March along with us."[76]

Their route took them through the homeland of the western Niantics who, on the approach of the English troops, "fled to a Swamp for Refuge." Hoping to punish them for their adherence to the Pequots, Mason gave pursuit, but his wearied troops could not catch up with the fleeing Niantics. They "burned and spoiled the country," then on the eve of the sabbath encamped on the east bank of the Connecticut River. Across the water, Gardener and his seventy-seven-man garrison fired their cannons to celebrate the victory at Mystic and the safe arrival of the Puritan warriors. "On the morrow," Mason recorded, "we were all fetched over to Saybrook, receiving many courtesies from Lieut. Gardener."[77]

The mood at Weinshauks was hardly festive. Even though the Pequots still possessed a fairly formidable striking force, and in fact greatly outnumbered the English troops then in Connecticut, the disaster at Mystic broke their will to resist. They did not understand their adversary or sense his weakness but rather saw only the power and the ruthlessness that had turned Fort Mystic into a flaming funeral pyre. Their anxious questions as to whether the English would kill women and children had now been answered. Moreover, gunfire from the retreating English army had also taken its toll. Indian informants later told the English that about 100 of the 300 Pequots who stalked Mason's forces had been killed or wounded. The claim seems exaggerated, but it does convey some sense of the panic and despair that gripped the Pequot villages in the wake of the burning of Mystic. English power seemed invincible.

In their confusion and rage, the Pequots turned on those Mohegan kinsmen of Uncas who were still living among them. Most were killed. Seven escaped and made their way to Saybrook. A party of 100 Pequot warriors was dispatched eastward to punish the Narragansetts for their collusion with the enemy. But it encountered "a great mist," lost its way (or its nerve), and returned to Weinshauks empty-handed. Sassacus called for renewed hostilities against the English, but his hold over his people was slipping. Held responsible for the catastrophe at Mystic, Sassacus was now a target of popular wrath. Only "the Intreaty of their Counsellors . . . spared his Life." But despite their protection of Sassacus, the Pequot sachems were now persuaded that they could not survive a continued war with the English, and they determined to save their people by abandoning their villages and seeking refuge with other Indians. About a hundred made their way to the Montauks on Long Island. Seventy surrendered to the Narragansetts. Williams learned from Asso-temuit, Miantonomi's messenger, that Sassacus and some of his support-ers were "wroth" with those who intended to "beg" the Narragansetts for their lives. "A skirmish past betweene them when some were wounded, but away they got and each Company packt up and departed their intended journeyes." The largest party, numbering several hundred men, women, and children led by Sassacus, Mononotto, and most of the other sachems, moved westward, hoping to join the Mohawks in New York. Crossing the Connecticut River, they killed the three-man crew of a small shallop bound downriver for Saybrook. But one group of about forty Pequots after striking out toward the Connecticut River panicked, turned around, returned to Pequot country, and sought safety in a swamp north of Weinshauks known as *ohomowauke*, meaning "the Owl's Nest."[78]

Three days after the burning of Fort Mystic, Wyandanch, "next brother to the old Sachem of Long Island," called at Saybrook to ask, as

Gardener related, "if we were angry with all Indians." Gardener assured them that they were at war with only those that "had killed Englishmen." But when Wyandanch asked if they might "come to trade with us," Gardener declared that as long as they sheltered Pequots on Long Island they could not do business at Saybrook. If the Long Islanders really wanted friendship with the English, Gardener suggested, they should first kill all the Pequot refugees in their midst and "send me their heads." Wyandanch promised to convey that suggestion to his brother. Soon thereafter, a messenger from Long Island brought five Pequot heads to Saybrook.[79]

As Sassacus moved westward, rumors that he had used his very substantial cache of wampum to buy the support of the Mohawks spread through the Narragansett country. Williams reported that he had received "tidings" that Mohawks and Pequots "have slaine many both English and Native" in Connecticut. (These reports were false.) The Mohawks, he warned, "are most savage, their weapons more dangerous, and their crueltie dreadfull, roasting alive, etc." They were reputed to be "man eaters." "I sadly feare," he wrote, "if the lord please to let loose these Mad dogs, their practice will render the Pequts Caniballs too." Williams thought the rumor of Pequot-Mohawk cohesion was probably false but suggested that it would be prudent to send envoys to the Mohawks to secure their adherence to the English.[80]

Determined to eradicate the presumed Pequot menace once and for all, the Massachusetts Bay Colony and Connecticut raised a fresh body of troops. In June the Bay Colony dispatched 120 men under the command of Israel Stoughton and William Trask. The Mohegans turned over to Stoughton a number of Pequot stragglers left behind when Sassacus and his party crossed the Connecticut River. Aided by Indian guides, Stoughton rooted out the small band that had taken refuge in the Owl's Nest. The Narragansetts, required by an earlier agreement with the English to turn over Pequot prisoners to Stoughton, appealed to the Puritan authorities through Roger Williams to treat those captives "kindly." Those who had surrendered without a fight, they advised, should have their lands and possessions restored. That advice was ignored. Most of the adult male prisoners in Stoughton's hands, about thirty in all, were put to death. Two sachems were spared, on condition that they assist in locating the remaining Pequots. The Pequot women and children were enslaved. The more fortunate were given to other Indian tribes. The Narragansetts received thirty, the Massachusetts, three. The remainder were sent to Boston. A number tried to escape but were captured by Indians friendly to the English and "branded on the shoulder." The Puritans sold some of their Pequot prisoners to Caribbean slave traders.[81]

Roger Williams expressed misgivings over the Bay Colony's treatment of the Pequot captives, warning that the Old Testament precedents concerning the Lord's command to destroy Amalekites then being invoked to justify their execution or enslavement were not really applicable. The magistrates, he declared, should heed instead the message in 2 Kings 2:6, which forbids the punishment of the innocent for the sins of their fathers or children. Many of the Pequot captives, Williams argued, were blameless. Puritan severity toward Indians has embarrassed even some of their apologists. A nineteenth-century historian not noted for his sympathy for the Pequots was moved to exclaim of the treatment of Pequot prisoners: "All this is truly horrible; and, if a historian were not, like a witness on oath, under strict obligation to tell the whole truth as well as nothing but the truth, I should be tempted to pass the transaction over in charitable silence."[82]

After rounding up all of the Pequots who had remained near their villages, Stoughton then marched to Saybrook where he was joined by Captain Mason and forty soldiers from Connecticut. Uncas and his Mohegans, accompanied by the captive Pequot sachems and a few English, set out by land to intercept Sassacus and the main body of Pequots. The refugees had made slow progress in their march westward, being burdened by "their Children and want of Provision." Hungry and tired, they hugged the coastline, subsisting by digging clams and foraging in the woods. They were closely pursued by Uncas, who picked off stragglers. The Pequot sachems spared by Stoughton earlier were not particularly helpful, so they were executed at a place later named "Sachem's Head."[83]

The main body of the English force went by sea, landing at New Haven Harbor, then called Quinnipiac. Six Pequots were captured near the landing spot. Two were executed, two spared, one of whom promised to lead the English forces to Sassacus. "He went, and found him not far off," Winthrop related, "but Sassacus, suspecting him, intended to kill him, which the fellow perceiving, escaped in the night, and came to the English." Sassacus, accompanied by Mononotto and other close followers, hastily abandoned his encampment. The English forces marched westward from Quinnipiac and on July 14 discovered a large body of Pequots near "a most hideous swamp, so thick with bushes and so quagmiry, as men could hardly crowd into it." As the English approached, they spotted several Pequots standing on a hill just beyond a cornfield. The Pequots fled, and the English rushed up the hill. Looking down in the direction of the fleeing Indians, they saw the swamp, later named the Sadque, separated into two parts of unequal size and, just beyond the thickets, a small settlement of about twenty wigwams. The wigwams were deserted, for the Pequots, along with some local Indians who had given them haven, had taken refuge within the swamp. A small party led by Lieutenant Davenport tried to force their way in but were repulsed by volleys of arrows and then by charging Pequots. Slashing at the Indians with their swords, Davenport and his detachment beat a hasty retreat.[84]

Surrounding the swamp, the English fired into the thicket. Hoping to take captives and therefore seeking a means to reduce noncombatant casualties, the commanders determined to offer the Pequots an opportunity to surrender. Thomas Stanton, who had served as Gardener's interpreter at Saybrook, called the Indians in the swamp to a parley and assured them that those who were not guilty of killing Englishmen would be spared. During a two-hour lull in the fighting that followed that offer, about 200 Indians left the swamp and threw themselves on the mercy of the English troops. But most, perhaps all, of the Pequot warriors refused to surrender. The battle resumed and raged through the night. The English entered the thicket and systematically shot down the Pequots, some of whom drowned in the muck. Winthrop recorded that the Pequots "coming up behind the bushes very near our men . . . shot many arrows into their hats, sleeves and stocks, yet (which was a very miracle) not one of ours was wounded." Toward morning, in a heavy fog, a number of the surviving Pequots rushed the English position commanded by Captain Daniel Patrick. Many were cut down by musket fire. Others, wounded in the attempt, were found dead on the trail the following day. Some made good their escape.

The soldiers seized Pequot wampum, and some kettles and trays, as booty. The local Indians, some twenty in number who with their sachem had joined the Pequots in the swamp, were freed, but the 180 Pequots who surrendered were treated as spoils of war and divided among the

Connecticut and Massachusetts Bay troops. Fifteen Pequot boys and two women were sold to a slave trader bound for Bermuda. Blown off course, he delivered his captives to Providence Isle, a Puritan colony off the coast of Nicaragua. Sassacus was not among the prisoners or the dead at the swamp fight. Along with his close associate Mononotto and forty or so warriors, the Pequot grand sachem reached the Hudson River valley but found no refuge there. John Winthrop noted in his journal that several traders from Connecticut in early August brought to Boston "part of the skin and lock of hair of Sassacus and his brother and five other Pequot sachems, who, being fled to the Mohawk for shelter, with their women, were by them surprised and slain, with twenty of their best men. Mononotto was also taken, but escaped wounded." As the Narragansett sachem Miantonomi had predicted in a conversation with Roger Williams some weeks earlier, the Mohawks respected English power, perceived Sassacus's weakness, and understood that their own self-interest required that they also kill Pequots.[85]

The victorious Puritans moved quickly to establish English hegemony. Soon after the death of Sassacus, several of the surviving Pequot sachems sought to negotiate a peace, offering, as Mason recalled, "that If they might but enjoy their Lives, they would become the English Vassals, to dispose of them as they pleased." The Puritan response to that plea was far from generous. As an object lesson to other Indian groups that might contemplate opposing the Puritan colonies, the victors moved to obliterate the Pequots as a political and social entity. The surviving Pequots were forbidden to return to their villages or use the tribal name. No mercy was shown to Pequots who had actively waged war on the English. In treaty negotiations between the English and their Indian allies at Hartford, Connecticut, in September 1638, the Mohegan and Narragansett sachems agreed to offer no sanctuary to Indian enemies of the English and promised to apprehend and execute any surviving Pequot warriors guilty of killing Englishmen and deliver their heads or hands to the Puritan authorities. Those Pequot noncombatants not yet disposed of were awarded as prizes of war to Uncas of the Mohegans and Miantonomi of the Narragansetts, each of whom received eighty. Ninigret, leader of the eastern Niantics, received a provisional award of twenty Pequots, conditional on his paying for "a Mare of Edward Pomroye's killed by his men." The most important provision of the agreement, however, obligated Uncas and Miantonomi to submit all intertribal conflicts to the English and abide by their decisions. The Puritans thus made clear their intention to control Indian affairs in southern New England.[86]

The Hartford agreement exiled the Pequots from "their Native country." Nonetheless, late in 1638, a band of Pequots reestablished a village at Pawcatuck near the Rhode Island boundary. Captain John Mason and forty Connecticut soldiers, aided by Uncas and a hundred Mohegans, sailed to Pawcatuck Bay to destroy the settlement and return the Pequots to their new masters. The Pequots had placed themselves under the protection of the eastern Niantics, who objected to their dispossession, offering to fight Uncas and the Mohegans but not the English, whom they believed to be "Spirits" possessed of supernatural power. Mason and his men proceeded to loot and burn the Pequot village, to the beat of a drum. "As we marched," Mason recalled, "there were two Indians standing upon a Hill jeering and reviling . . . us." Mason's hotheaded interpreter, Thomas Stanton, demanded permission to shoot them. Mason agreed, saying "let fly," but thinking they were out of range. But Stanton "shot one of them through both his Thighs; which was to our Wonderment, it being at such a distance." As serious opposition to the mission never materialized, Mason and Uncas loaded the Connecticut army's bark and the Mohegans' canoes with their loot: "Corn . . . Kettles, Trays, Mats." The Pequots were turned over to the Mohegans. The Narragansetts, enraged by Mohegan incursions into their sphere of influence, claimed that the Pawcatuck Pequots belonged to them. Uncas then "challenged the Naragansett Sachem out to a single conflict, but he would not fight without all his men." With difficulty, Gardener noted, the English "mediated between them and pacified them," but the "grudge remained still."[87]

The surrender terms generally offered Pequots in the latter stages of the war promised clemency to those who had not killed Englishmen. But we must bear in mind that in judging Pequot captives the Puritans recognized no distinction between acts committed in peacetime, such as the murder of Stone and his crew, and acts of war. As we have seen, adult Pequot males were executed by Stoughton's troops, and tribes desiring friendly relations with the English were placed under an obligation to deliver to the Puritan authorities the heads or hands of any Pequot warriors who sought refuge in their midst. A notorious court case in 1639 gave further expression to the principle of Indian culpability for acts of violence committed in time of war. On October 26 in the newly established English settlement at Quinnipiac (later named New Haven), an Indian named Nepaupuck was arrested and charged with murder. Nepaupuck, it was alleged, had participated in the Pequot raid on Wethersfield and in an assault on an English shallop during Sassacus's flight across the Connecticut River. After a trial, which the nineteenth-century Connecticut historian John W. De Forest rightly described as "a mere farce," Nepaupuck was convicted of having killed Englishmen. On October 30, a day after Nepaupuck's trial, his head was cut off and stuck on a pole in the town square. The judicial murder of Nepaupuck was the logical outgrowth of Puritan fear of Indian treachery and of their determination to achieve peace by dealing severely with those Indians whom they perceived as threats to their security.[88]

The English profited greatly from the Pequot War. Soon after the Hartford agreement, Uncas, eager to curry favor and win support in his own struggle for hegemony among the Indian sachems of the region, ceded most of eastern Connecticut to the English, reserving for himself only the villages and fields on the Thames River occupied by the Mohegans and their newly acquired Pequot subjects. The River Indian sachems soon followed suit, ceding vast tracts of land in exchange for token remuneration. The war also filled the coffers of the Massachusetts Bay Colony with Indian wampum. Not only did the Bay Colony forces seize a fair amount of Pequot wampum as booty, but tribes once tributary to the Pequots, and some who were not, now bought peace and protection from the Puritans and paid their annual wampum tribute to Boston. The Massachusetts Bay Colony effectively blocked Narragansett and Mohegan efforts to claim that tribute. In addition, the Hartford agreement of 1638 stipulated that the Mohegans, Narragansetts, and eastern Niantics make annual wampum payments to the English for each of the Pequots they received. Moreover, after the war Indians were required to pay fines in wampum for various offenses. Although the records are too fragmentary to permit an accurate analysis of the economic impact of this new income, Lynn Ceci is undoubtedly correct in observing that one outcome of the Pequot War "was, in effect, the partial underwriting of New England colonization costs by the conquered natives."[89]

The defeat of the Pequots did not bring to Puritan New England any real sense of security. One is struck, in reading New England correspondence, diaries, journals, chronicles, and legal records from the four decades between the defeat of the Pequots and the outbreak of King Philip's War, by the persistent fear of Indian conspiracy. Though sometimes characterized as a period of "social harmony" between Puritan and Indian, those years were marked not only by a relative absence of interracial violence but, paradoxically, by a profound lack of trust. Puritan New England's Indian policy throughout the seventeenth century was governed by the assumption that a satanically inspired Indian war of extermination against the Saints was a very real possibility and could be averted only by constant intimidation of potential adversaries.[90]

In the years immediately following the Pequot War, the leaders of the Puritan colonies were troubled by the suspicion that erstwhile Indian allies might be treacherous and, given the opportunity, might yet make common cause with surviving Pequots. Puritans interpreted the occasional reluctance of some sachems to kill surrendering Pequots or turn them over to the English as evidence not of compassion but of malign intent toward the English. In the summer of 1639, Connecticut officials were so angered by reports that the Wangunks had given refuge to Pequot warriors that they considered sending a military expedition against them. The leaders of both Connecticut and the Massachusetts Bay Colony were particularly distrustful of the Narragansetts. They suspected that Miantonomi had incorporated Pequot warriors into his fighting force, intending to use them in a future war against the Puritan colonies. Roger Williams's persistent efforts to assure Boston that the Narragansett sachem had not broken his promise not to shelter Pequot belligerents were only partially successful. Suspicion of Narragansett intentions persisted. Captain Daniel Patrick had told Williams in 1637 that his men had "a great Itch" to attack Narragansetts. Patrick himself later concluded that the Narragansetts aspired to "be the onelye Lords of the Indians" and thus were a natural threat to Puritan security. A rumor that the Narragansetts were trying to bribe the Mohawks to join them in a war of extermination against the English exacerbated the Puritan leaders' anxieties.[91]

Uncas, leader of the Mohegans, and the Montauk sachem Wyandanch both shrewdly exploited English distrust of the Narragansetts to enhance their own power. Rumors of an impending Narragansett uprising were rampant. The two sachems did all that they could to keep those rumors alive. Their influence with the Puritan leaders in Connecticut prompted that colony in 1642 to call for a preventive war against the Narragansetts. The Massachusetts Bay Colony, however, counseled caution, finding the evidence of a Narragansett conspiracy too flimsy to warrant such extreme action. The Massachusetts leaders observed that, as Uncas and Miantonomi "continually sought to discredit each other with the English," their allegations should not be taken at face value. Miantonomi was summoned to Boston in September and interrogated but claimed he was "Innocent of any ill intentions."[92]

Winthrop and his colleagues accepted the Narragansett sachem's explanation, but Lion Gardener at Saybrook was skeptical. He related that Wyandanch had reported that Miantonomi had recently asked for 250 Long Island warriors to join in a campaign to eject the English. Calling for pan-Indian unity, Miantonomi had presumably declared that all Indians must be united, "as the English are. . . . otherwise we shall be all gone shortly, for you know our fathers had plenty of deer and skins, our plains were full of deer, as also our woods, and of turkies, and our coves full of fish and foul. But these English having gotten our land, they with scythes cut down the grass, and with axes fell the trees; their cows and horses eat the grass and their hogs spoil our clam banks, and we shall all be starved." The solution, Miantonomi allegedly declared, was for all of the Indians to "fall on" the English "and kill men, women and children." Cattle, however, were to be spared, "for they will serve to eat till our deer be increased again." That speech, a rough precursor to the grandiloquent translations of the exhortations of Indian resistance leaders commonplace in later historical literature, may be the product of anti-Narragansett rumor mongering. Though there are many indications that Miantonomi resented English slights and insults, there is no conclusive evidence to indicate that he was actually plotting an attack on the Puritan colonies. Roger Williams continued to plead his cause with Winthrop and other magistrates.[93]

Miantonomi was, however, clearly implicated in several plots to kill his rival, Uncas. To cover his tracks, he beheaded a Pequot conspirator whom he had promised to send to the Puritans for interrogation. The Pequot had earlier, on Miantonomi's instigation, stabbed Uncas. The rivalry of Miantonomi and Uncas was essentially a power struggle for influence over the Indians of the Connecticut River valley. It represented a continuation of the Pequot-Narragansett rivalry, with Uncas now playing the role of the Pequot grand sachem. When the Mohegans killed several members of a River Indian band that had accepted Narragansett protection, Miantonomi and a force of a thousand warriors invaded Uncas's territory. Though they outnumbered their adversaries, the Narragansetts were defeated. Miantonomi, encumbered by heavy English armor given him by his friend Samuel Gorton, was taken prisoner. Receiving an appeal from Gorton to spare his life, Uncas, realizing that his own power depended on English goodwill, delivered the Narragansett sachem to the Connecticut authorities at Hartford.[94]

Miantonomi's fate was decided by the commissioners of the newly formed United Colonies, a military alliance of Puritan colonies in southern New England. (Rhode Island, the "place of the otherwise-minded," was excluded.) The commissioners were bothered by the lack of clear evidence proving Uncas's allegations that the Narragansett sachem had plotted against the English. They suspected, however, that he was guilty. Moreover, the commissioners believed that "Uncas cannot be safe while Myantonomo lives." Equally important was the fact that Miantonomi had broken that provision of the Treaty of Hartford which required that intertribal conflicts be settled by the English. The commissioners suspected that Miantonomi intended "to make himself universall sagamore or Governor of all these parts." Hence, though he might not be planning the extermination of the English as his enemies charged, Miantonomi nonetheless threatened English hegemony. Uncas, by contrast, owed his position to English patronage and could be relied upon, the commissioners believed, to uphold that hegemony. Although the Narragansetts had aroused English suspicions of Uncas in 1638 by spreading rumors that he was sheltering Pequot prisoners, the Mohegan sachem had very shrewdly humbled himself to Boston. As John Winthrop related, Uncas protested that "this heart (laying his hand upon his breast) is not mine but yours, I have no men; they are all yours; command me in any difficult thing; I will do it, I will not believe any Indian's words against the English; if any man shall kill an Englishman, I will put him to death, were he never so dear to me." Miantonomi, by contrast, had pursued a more independent policy, urging the Algonquian communities on Long Island not to pay tribute to the English. There was another consideration that may have swayed the commissioners. Miantonomi had recently undercut the authority of the Massachusetts Bay Colony by granting land to Samuel Gorton and other arch-heretics who dissented from the New England way. Uncas, by contrast, had been of great assistance in the establishment of orthodox Puritan communities in Connecticut.[95]

The first official act of the commissioners of the United Colonies in September 1643 was to declare that the Narragansett sachem should die. In their resolution, the commissioners gave credence to rumors that he had engaged in "mischievous plots to root out the body of the English nation." Miantonomi was turned over to Uncas for execution. The Mohegans were told that he was to be killed humanely, not tortured. On the road between Hartford and Windsor, Uncas killed Miantonomi with a sharp blow to the head.[96] Although the documents do not record his last words, we may well assume that Miantonomi now felt, if he did not express, more than a little regret for his decision, seven years earlier, to ally himself with the English and the Mohegans in their war against the Pequots.

5

The Pequot War and
the Mythology of the Frontier

Although the Pequot War was a small-scale conflict of short duration, it cast a long shadow. The images of brutal and untrustworthy savages plotting the extermination of those who would do the work of God in the wilderness, developed to explain and justify the killing of Pequots, became a vital part of the mythology of the American frontier. Celebration of victory over Indians as the triumph of light over darkness, civilization over savagery, for many generations our central historical myth, finds its earliest full expression in the contemporary chronicles and histories of this little war. The myth from its inception was grounded in a distorted conception of Indian character and behavior. The Pequot War was not waged in response to tangible acts of aggression. It cannot be understood as a rational response to a real threat to English security. It was, however, the expression of an assumption central to Puritan Indian policy. Puritan magistrates were persuaded that from time to time violent reprisals against recalcitrant savages would be necessary to make the frontier safe for the people of God. The campaign against the Pequots was driven by the same assumption that had impelled Plymouth to massacre Indians suspected of plotting against them at Wessagusett in 1623. The incineration of Pequots at Fort Mystic served the same symbolic purpose as the impalement of Wituwamet's head on Plymouth's blockhouse. Both were intended to intimidate potential enemies and to remind the Saints that they lived in daily peril of massacre at the hands of Satan's minions.

Two letters written by clergymen to civil authorities in 1637 tell us much about the Puritan mind-set. Both warn of the dangers of hesitation or leniency in dealing with the Pequots. The Reverend Thomas Hooker, responding to the attack on Wethersfield, predicted that any delay in undertaking a punitive war against them would lead other Indians to conclude that Englishmen were cowards. If that happened, Hooker predicted, all of the tribes would "turne enemyse against us."[1] In a similar vein, the Reverend John Higginson, writing from Fort Saybrook, declared that "the eyes of all the Indians of the country are upon the English. If some serious and very speedie course not be taken to tame the pride and take down the insolency of these now insulting Pequots . . . we are like to have all the Indians in the country about our ears."[2] The assumption, voiced here by Hooker and Higginson, that all Indians are natural enemies of Christians and that the English frontier in Connecticut can therefore be made secure only through the employment of extreme measures against the Pequots, was obviously shared by the English commanders whose cruelty to noncombatants and prisoners of war shocked their Indian allies.

In their reflections on the Pequot War, Puritan apologists argued that English troops were instruments of divine judgment. Early Puritan historians portrayed the war as a key episode in the unfolding of God's plan for New England. Captain John Mason, who believed that the English had been saved from a general Indian uprising only by divine intervention, ended his "Brief History of the Pequot War" with praise of the Almighty: "Let the whole Earth be filled with his Glory! Thus the lord was pleased to smite our Enemies in the hinder Parts, and give us their land for an Inheritance." Mason's colleague, Captain John Underhill, concurred. Through God's providence, "a few feeble instruments, soldiers not accustomed to war," defeated a "barbarous and insolent nation," putting to the sword "fifteen hundred souls." Underhill rejoiced that through God's will "their country is fully subdued and fallen into the hands of the English," and he called on his readers to "magnify his honor for his great goodness." A dissenting note was struck by Lieutenant Lion Gardener who, in a work written in 1660, wondered why the Bay Colony leaders made war against the Pequots to avenge the worthless old reprobate Stone, while the Narragansetts, whom he presumed guilty of the murder of the worthy Captain Oldham, went scot-free. But Gardener, no less a Puritan than his colleagues, warned against trusting Indians and complained about lax military preparedness. After describing Indian tortures, he predicted that hundreds of Englishmen would die in agony and dishonor, "if God should deliver us into their hands, as justly he may for our sins."[3]

No other Puritan writer expressed any misgivings about whether the English had attacked the right adversary in 1637. The Massachusetts Bay Colony historian Edward Johnson, writing of the English massacre of Pequots at Fort Mystic, declared that "by this means the Lord strook a trembling terror into all the Indians round about, even to this very day." Through righteous violence, Johnson believed, God had pacified the forces of Satan in the wilderness.[4] That theme dominated Puritan thinking about Indian wars. The commissioners of the United Colonies of New England in 1646 called for the writing of histories that would record how God "hath cast the dread of his people (weak in themselves) upon the Indians."[5] Increase Mather, in his *Brief History of the War with the Indians in New England* (1676), wrote that the defeat of the Pequots in 1637 "must be ascribed to the wonderful Providence of God, who did (as with Jacob of old, and after that with the children of Israel) lay the fear of the English and the dread of them upon all the Indians. The terror of god was upon them round about."[6] Incorporating that notion into his grand history of New England, Cotton Mather later declared that, through God's providence, the Puritans were enabled to achieve not only "the utter subduing" of the Pequots but "the affrighting of all the other Natives" as well, and thereby secured several decades of peace.[7]

As the evidence reviewed in this study demonstrates, Puritan preoccupation with the idea that Indians were part of a satanic conspiracy against God's true church in the wilderness led them to interpret Pequot recalcitrance as evidence of malevolent intent. But it does not follow that we can therefore explain the Pequot War solely and simply as the result of an unfortunate misunderstanding about certain specific occurrences, for the conflict was more fundamentally the outgrowth of a profound incompatibility of cultures.[8] Puritan ideology precluded long-term coexistence with a "savage" people unwilling to acknowledge Christian hegemony. Clarification of Pequot intentions in the short run would not necessarily have changed the long-term outcome. A reading of their commentaries on Indian affairs suggests that our assumptions about the desirability of peaceful coexistence were not necessarily shared by the founders of Puritan New England or by their immediate successors. Although they feared Indian war and prayed that they be spared its horrors, they also suspected that it was both necessary and inevitable. Apologists for the Fort Mystic massacre did not invent the image of the Indian as a savage killer to excuse the Pequot War, nor did Pequot actions inspire a new view of Indian character. There is ample evidence, as we noted in the first chapter of this study, that from the founding of the first English settlements in North America onward, Englishmen in general and Puritans in particular saw in Native American culture only the "degeneracy" of those who follow the Devil rather than God; they accordingly were predisposed to regard Indians as untrustworthy and treacherous and were thus prone to overreact to rumors of impending Indian attacks.

Their acceptance of customary English anti-Indian prejudice in itself does not fully explain Puritan behavior. We must also examine Puritan ideas about the role of Indians in God's providential plan for New England. Here we encounter concepts quite alien to modern sensibilities, embedded in explanations so far removed from our sense of historical processes that it is tempting to dismiss them as irrelevant. But let us look more closely, for we must try to understand the seventeenth century on its own terms. Fundamental to the Puritan understanding of the dynamics of New England history was the assumption that only through God's special protection of his people could Christians survive in a wilderness realm dominated by Satan and inhabited by satanic savages. God intervened early to soften the hearts of the godless heathens who lurked in New England's forests and wastelands. Ultimately, he controlled their behavior. It therefore followed that troubled Indian relations might well be a frightening sign that God's protection had been, or was about to be, withheld for some reason. Throughout the seventeenth century, rumors of impending Indian attack occasioned deep soul-searching and calls for reformation in Puritan New England.

The Pequot War inspired the earliest expressions of the idea that Indian wars were providentially ordained events intended to test and chastise God's people. John Higginson suggested that the Lord had set "the Indians upon his servants, to make them cleave more closely together, to prevent contentions of brethern."[9] Edward Johnson hinted that God had unleashed the Pequots in order to punish the Puritans for their lack of proper severity in dealing with Anne Hutchinson and the antinomians.[10] Those suggestions foreshadowed the portrayals of the role of divine providence in Indian warfare that would dominate the literature inspired by King Philip's War half a century later. Historians of that conflict spoke of God's need to test his Saints in the fire of battle, punish his people for straying from the true way, and give them also opportunity to serve as the vehicles of God's wrath in exterminating heathen who refused to embrace the Gospel.[11] Those themes were exploited most thoroughly by Puritan divines who, in later years, warned of the fearful consequences of declension. Thus, Increase Mather in a sermon preached in 1676 declared King Philip's War God's "heavy judgment," a punishment of the "sin of man's unfaithfulness. . . . Alas that New England should be brought so low in so short a time (for she is come down wonderfully) and that by such vile enemies by the Heathen, yea by the worst of the Heathen."[12] Cotton Mather, in his 1689 election sermon, declared that the "molestations" the English in New England had suffered at the hands of the Indians had come about because God was angry that his people had "indianized"; in other words, they had allowed themselves to succumb to what Mather regarded as Indian vices: idleness, self-indulgence, and dishonesty.[13] The belief that God used Indians as a rod with which to discipline his people became an enduring and vital aspect of the Puritan sense of the past. In his election sermon of 1730, the Reverend Thomas Prince, reviewing more than a century of New England history, exclaimed, "how often has he made the eastern Indians the rod of his anger and the staff of indignation with us! He has sent them against us and given them the charge to take the spoil and tread us down as the mire of the street. They came with open mouth upon us; they thrust thro' everyone they found abroad; they ensnared and slew our mighty men who went forth for our defense; they spoil'd our fields and pastures; they burnt up our houses; they destroy'd our towns and garrisons; they murdered our wives; they carried our young men and virgins into captivity; they had no pity on the fruit of the womb; their eyes spared not our children, they dashed them in pieces." Prince reminded the citizenry that they had survived only because the Lord, although rightly provoked, finally took pity on his own true people and turned against the savages. "He rebuk'd them and set them one against another . . . as wax melteth before the fire, so they perished at the presence of God." But his favor and protection were not to be taken for granted.[14]

God's wrath, in Puritan formulations of the providential view of New England's history, was not reserved for errant Saints. Historians of King

Philip's War assured their readers that, although the war was in part intended to punish the English in New England for straying from the true way, the Lord's anger against the Indians was far greater. For our purposes, perhaps the most revealing statement in the later Indian war literature was a declaration from the Bay Colony's superintendent of Indian affairs that God had ordained the war against King Philip in order to punish the Indians who had refused to embrace Puritan Christianity.[15] This was not an entirely new theme. Although lack of receptivity to the Christian Gospel was not stated explicitly as a reason for killing Pequots by any of the chroniclers of that early war, the preacher's charge to the Connecticut militia to "execute vengeance against the heathen" rested upon the assumption that the English were indeed called upon by the Almighty to visit his wrath upon a very sinful people. Puritan literary celebrations of the Fort Mystic massacre, which strike us as rather grotesque, are grounded in the belief that the burning of Pequots was a righteous act of divine retribution.

Assessments of the causes and consequences of the Pequot War must take into account Puritan ideas about God's attitude toward the unregenerate. The Pequots were not the last indigenous group in New England to suffer what the Puritans believed to be divinely mandated punishment. The Narragansetts and the Wampanoags, friends of the English in 1636–37, both discovered, before the seventeenth century ended, that the Puritan conception of God's providential plan for New England ultimately left no room for vigorous assertions of Native American autonomy, for such assertions offended the Puritan sense of mission. Puritan toleration of Indian independence was never anything more than an expedient; as the population ratio between Englishmen and Native Americans in New England shifted in favor of the English, the Puritan authorities grew increasingly overbearing in their dealings with their Indian counterparts. Puritan Indian policy from its inception was driven by the conviction that, if the Puritans remained faithful to their covenant with the Almighty, they were destined to replace the Indians as lords of New England. Puritan ideology required that Indian control of land and resources be terminated, on the grounds that "savages" did not exploit natural bounty in the manner that God intended. The pressures created by the burgeoning of the English population in the latter half of the seventeenth century reinforced that ideological imperative. Economic changes, such as the declining importance of the fur trade and the expansion of English agriculture and industry, which reduced the need for Indian commerce, further jeopardized the status of Native American communities in a New England dominated by Euro-Americans. The Indian uprising led by Metacom (King Philip) in 1675 represented a desperate, belated, and ultimately futile effort to protect the last remnants of Indian sovereignty in southern New England.

Although Puritan apologists for the war against the Pequots provided one of the earliest English statements of the belief in Indian war as a divinely sanctioned means of extending the light of civilization and true religion into the wilderness, their version of the frontier drama contained some elements that later generations would find strange and uncongenial. Over the years, the myth of heroic struggle against savagery underwent some important changes in emphasis as secular doctrines of scientific progress and historical evolution, along with a new sense of "manifest destiny," largely but not entirely replaced Puritan notions of divine providence. The idea that Indians might be used by the Almighty to punish the sins of Christians fell from favor. Puritan misgivings about the wilderness as a place of spiritual peril gave way to a more optimistic and uncritical celebration of the frontier as the birthplace of uniquely American virtues. Indian rejection of progress replaced their disinterest in the Gospel or their presumed alliance with Satan as the reason most often advanced to explain their imminent extinction. But in one important particular, the central theme remained the same. On a succession of frontiers, as Winthrop Jordan reminds us, "conquering the Indian symbolized and personified the conquest of American difficulties, the surmounting of the wilderness. To push back the Indian was to prove the worth of one's own mission, to make straight in the desert a highway for civilization." [16]

Once the eastern Indians were no longer a threat, some nineteenth-century writers transformed the Native American into a victim rather than a villain. In their pages, the American "savage" emerged as an innocent and hapless primitive doomed by the imperatives of historical progress, an object of pity for whom the sentimental might shed a tear. Historians, novelists, and dramatists now sometimes castigated Puritans and other pioneers for their mistreatment of such a simple and defenseless people. It goes without saying that such sympathy for the Indian as a "much injured race" is not to be found in seventeenth-century Puritan commentaries on Indian wars. But we must not assume that its appearance in later historical writing necessarily meant abandonment of the idea that the conquest and dispossession of Indians were historical imperatives. Until quite recently, the attitude of paternalistic benevolence cultivated by architects of Indian policy as well as by their critics was generally qualified by a condition: The Indian must now cease to be an Indian, must embrace the values, culture, and religion of his dispossessors, if he is to be deemed worthy of survival. Here we are once again face to face with the premise that drove Puritan Indian policy: denial of the validity and viability of Native American life. Whether the Indian was to be displaced by the workings of divine providence or by the inexorable march of progress, the outcome was much the same. Moreover, it did not matter whether Indians were portrayed as noble or degraded; white Americans over the years generally thought of them as a backward people without history and without a future.

While the frontier struggle for control of land continued, misgivings about mistreatment of Native Americans had only a very limited impact upon events. As Michael Paul Rogin notes, "not the Indians alive . . . but their destruction, symbolized the American experience." Violence against Indians cannot be explained fully as the outgrowth of the white man's acquisitive instincts. There were other motives at work. Rogin argues that Native American societies in their communal aspects "posed a severe threat," as they inspired "forbidden nostalgia for the nurturing, blissful and primitively violent connection to nature that white Americans had to leave behind." Hence, "the only safe Indians were dead, sanitized, or completely dependent upon white benevolence." Indians were "at once symbols of a lost childhood bliss, and, as bad children repositories of murderous negative projections." [17] Those Indians who physically survived plague, war, and dispossession were therefore not only relegated to reservations, where they lived in abject poverty, but subjected to an onslaught on their cultural integrity through measures such as the so-called Religious Crimes Acts, which outlawed the sun dance and other expressions of Native American spirituality.

Intolerance of Indian cultures reflected the persistence of essential elements of the Puritan vision of the struggle between heathen savagery and Christian civilization. Puritan ideology as it pertained to encounters with Indians contained three premises which later provided vital elements in the mythology of the American frontier. One was the image, not original with the Puritans but embellished by them, of the Indian as the Other, primitive, dark, and sinister. Another was the portrayal, first developed in the Pequot War narratives, of the Indian fighter as the agent of God and of progress, redeeming the land through righteous violence. And finally, it is to the apologists for the Pequot War that we owe the justification of the expropriation of Indian resources and the extinction of Indian sovereignty as security measures necessitated by their presumed savagery.

Few historians today confuse these elements of our founding myth with historical fact. The "triumphalist" tone that once characterized the narration of Euro-American victories over presumably savage foes is now muted, or silenced, as scholars struggle to come to terms with the ambiguities as well as the cruelties and injustice now perceived in the encounters of indigenous peoples and European invaders. What place should the Pequots occupy in the new history of intercultural conflict? Despite the ample evidence of arrogance, ignorance, and brutality in the English treatment of Sassacus and his people, it will not do to cast them in the role of passive victims. They were not guilty of the enormities, real or anticipated, with which they are charged in the traditional, pro-Puritan literature. They were not a threat to the survival of the Puritan colonies. But in their efforts to establish and maintain a far-flung tributary network and to control European trade, the Pequots provoked powerful Indian opposition. Their murder of Indian rivals en route to trade at the House of Good Hope in 1632, the exile of the Mohegan sachems shortly thereafter and the occupation of their hunting preserves, along with the subsequent treatment of Mohegans living in Pequot villages after the final defection of Uncas, all give evidence of a ruthless determination to maintain power that suggests that Sassacus would be seriously miscast were we now to describe him simply as an inoffensive noble savage wronged by the white man. He was inept; he lost, but he was hardly a hapless innocent. Neither were the Mohegan, River Indian, and Narragansett sachems who engineered his downfall.

In seeking to use the English as pawns in their power struggles, the sachems made a serious miscalculation. The consequences of alliance with the Puritan colonies were not immediately apparent. The sachems no doubt believed that they could maintain control. The English, as we have seen, were susceptible to manipulation by those who knew how to play on their expectations and anxieties. It was a game that Uncas easily mastered, that Sassacus never learned how to play, and that Miantonomi ultimately lost. But the final outcome was loss of Algonquian autonomy. A revisionist history of the Pequot War written from the Native American point of view—and this present study does not pretend to accomplish that—might well deemphasize decisions made at Boston, Plymouth, Saybrook, and Hartford and focus instead on the miscalculations and blunders in Pequot, Mohegan, and Narragansett councils that paved the way for the early establishment of English hegemony in southern New England. Unfortunately, given the limitations in the source materials, such a reconstruction would be highly conjectural. But we do know enough about Native American politics in southern New England in the early seventeenth century to realize that viewing the conflict from an Algonquian perspective would immediately expose the absurdity of the English belief that they were engaged in some sort of holy war against murderous heathens determined to exterminate Christians. Although the Puritans believed that their actions were driven by their own security needs, and by divine providence, the conflicts that culminated in the Pequot War originally were the outgrowth of the ambitions of rival sachems, not of an anti-English conspiracy. Believing themselves endangered, the Puritan colonies, to the later sorrow of many of their Indian allies, transformed the quarrel with the Pequots into a successful campaign to establish English dominance.

In their justification of the war against the Pequots, Puritan mythmakers invoked old images of treacherous savages and told tales of diabolical plots. It is now clear that their portrayals of the Pequots bear little resemblance to reality. The Puritans transformed their adversary into a symbol of savagery. Rumors of Pequot conspiracy, although flimsy in substance and of dubious origin, reinforced expectations about savage behavior and justified preemptive slaughter and dispossession. Not only did the Pequot War engender its own myths in reinforcement and embellishment of Puritan ideology; it was the fulfillment of a prewar mythology that foretold conflicts in the wilderness between the people of God and the hosts of Satan. The fact that the triumph of Christians in such conflicts would open the way to English control of land and trade, and to the receipt of tribute, provided powerful material incentives to maintain intact ideas about savagery that justified the domination of indigenous peoples. Puritan apologists for their assault on the Pequots made a significant contribution to the development of an ideological rationale for Christian imperialism. The images they framed of their adversary have been remarkably persistent but now should be recognized as the products of wartime propaganda.

The Pequot War in reality was the messy outgrowth of petty squabbles over trade, tribute, and land among Pequots, Mohegans, River Indians, Niantics, Narragansetts, Dutch traders, and English Puritans. The Puritan imagination endowed this little war with a metahistorical significance it hardly deserved. But the inner logic of Puritan belief required creation of a mythical conflict, a cosmic struggle of good and evil in the wilderness, and out of that need the Pequot War epic was born.

Notes

Introduction

1. Laurence M. Hauptman, "The Pequot War and Its Legacies," in *The Pequots in Southern New England: The Fall and Rise of an Indian Nation,* ed. Laurence M. Hauptman and James D. Wherry (Norman, Okla., 1990), p. 69.

2. The most recent detailed narrative of the war is to be found in Herbert M. Sylvester, *Indian Wars of New England,* 3 vols. (Cleveland, 1910), 1:183–339. Sylvester's work is of limited use, out of date, and seriously flawed by its anti-Indian bias and lack of understanding of Native American culture. The native of New England, as Sylvester described him, was "in all his tendencies animalistic; his natural desire was solely the satisfying of his stomach and the sustaining of his energies by the slothfulness of sleep. On the opposite, his acquired tastes were but a few steps from actual debauchery" (1:36). Sylvester's overall assessment of Indian life reflected the same degree of prejudice and misunderstanding. The most extensive modern accounts of the Pequot War are Alden T. Vaughan, *New England Frontier: Puritans and Indians, 1620–1675* (Boston, 1965), pp. 93–154, and Francis P. Jennings, *The Invasion of America: Indians, Colonialism, and the Cant of Conquest* (New York, 1976), pp. 177–227. Although differing radically in their assessments of the causes of this conflict, neither provides a full-scale history of the war. Vaughan and Jennings both focus primarily on Puritan policy and behavior; neither offers a thorough analysis of the Pequot response. Neal Salisbury, *Manitou and Providence: Indians, Europeans, and the Making of New England, 1500–1643* (New York, 1982), pp. 203–24, provides some exceedingly valuable ethnohistorical insights into the background of this conflict. Salisbury's careful analysis of the relationship of the Pequot sachem Sassacus to his rivals and of the Pequots to other Indian bands in the region has deflated customary claims regarding Pequot dominance and provides the basis for a reinterpretation of the origins of the Pequot War. The following also offer

some provocative suggestions regarding the nature of the Pequot War: Peter N. Carroll, *Puritanism and the Wilderness* (New York, 1969), pp. 148–50; William Cronon, *Changes in the Land: Indians, Colonists, and the Ecology of New England* (New York, 1983), pp. 96–97; Karen Ordahl Kupperman, *Settling with the Indians: The Meeting of English and Indian Cultures in America, 1580–1640* (London, 1980), p. 175; Richard Drinnon, *Facing West: The Metaphysics of Indian-Hating and Empire Building* (Minneapolis, 1980), pp. 35–61; Richard Slotkin, *Regeneration through Violence: The Mythology of the American Frontier, 1600–1860* (Middletown, Conn., 1973), pp. 76–78; Gary B. Nash, *Red, White, and Black: The Peoples of Early America*, 2nd ed. (Englewood Cliffs, N.J., 1982), pp. 85–86; Charles M. Segal and David C. Stineback, eds., *Puritans, Indians, and Manifest Destiny* (New York, 1977), pp. 105–12; Anne Kibbey, *The Interpretation of Material Shapes in Puritanism: A Study of Rhetoric, Prejudice, and Violence* (Cambridge, Mass., 1986), pp. 92–120; Lynn Ceci, "The Effect of European Contact and Trade on the Settlement Patterns of the Indians in Coastal New York, 1524–1665: The Archaeological and Documentary Evidence" (Ph.D. diss., City University of New York, 1977), pp. 208–18; Richard John Burton, "Hellish Fiends and Brutish Men: Amerindian-European Interaction in Southern New England, an Interdisciplinary Analysis" (Ph.D. diss., Kent State University, 1976), pp. 106–46; P. Richard Metcalf, "Who Should Rule at Home? Native American Politics and Indian-White Relations," *Journal of American History* 61 (December 1974): 651–65; Adam Hirsch, "The Collision of Military Cultures in Seventeenth Century New England," *Journal of American History* 74 (March 1988): 1187–1212.

3. Charles Orr, ed., *History of the Pequot War: The Contemporary Accounts of Mason, Underhill, Vincent, and Gardiner* (Cleveland, 1897); the quotation is from Underhill's account, p. 81.

4. Ibid., pp. 23, 81, 119, 147; the quotation is from Underhill, p. 81. See also Edward Johnson, *Wonder-Working Providence of Sion's Saviour in New England* (1654), ed. J. Franklin Jameson (New York, 1910), p. 148.

5. William J. McTaggart and William K. Bottorff, eds., *The Major Poems of Timothy Dwight* (Gainesville, Fla., 1969), pp. 454–56.

6. Francis Parkman, *France and England in North America*, ed. David Levin (New York, 1983), 1:1084.

7. John Gorham Palfrey, *History of New England during the Stuart Dynasty*, 3 vols. (Boston, 1865), 1:456–67.

8. John Fiske, *The Beginnings of New England* (Boston, 1899), pp. 128–34. Other examples of nineteenth-century portrayals of Pequot savagery include Benjamin Trumbull, *A Complete History of Connecticut, Civil and Ecclesiastical*, 2 vols. (New Haven, 1818), 1:69–93; Abiel Holmes, *Annals of America*, 2 vols. (Cambridge, Mass., 1829), 1:235–41; George Bancroft, *History of the United States of America*, 10 vols. (1834; New York, 1912), 1:402–4; John A. Goodwin, *The Puritan Republic* (1888; New York, 1970), pp. 132, 174. A somewhat more ambivalent defense of the Puritan attack on the Pequots is to be found in John W.

De Forest, *History of the Indians of Connecticut from the Earliest Known Period to 1650* (1852; St. Clair Shores, Mich., 1970), pp. 138–40.

9. Thomas Hutchinson, *The History of the Colony and Province of Massachusetts Bay* (1783), 3 vols., ed. Lawrence Shaw Mayo (Cambridge, Mass., 1936), 1:52–59.

10. Richard Hildreth, *The History of the United States of America*, 6 vols. (New York, 1856), 1:237–42.

11. William Apess, *A Son of the Forest* (1831), reprinted in Barry O'Connell, ed., *On Our Own Ground: The Complete Writings of William Apess. A Pequot* (Amherst, Mass., 1992), pp. 55–56. Unfortunately, Apess did not provide any details to support his suggestion that the Puritans, not the Pequots, were responsible for the war but relied on quotations from William Robertson, an eighteenth-century Scottish historian critical of the colonists' mistreatment of Indians.

12. Quotation from Evarts P. Greene, *The Foundations of American Nationality* (New York, 1922), pp. 123–24. Greene, like most writers in the early twentieth century, believed that the Pequots were the aggressors. For another view, see James Truslow Adams, *The Founding of New England* (1921; New York, 1965), pp. 199–205. Adams describes the Bay Colony's response to Oldham's murder as "a course of blundering stupidity and criminal folly" (p. 200). An equally severe assessment of Puritan conduct is found in William Christie Macleod, *The American Indian Frontier* (New York, 1928), pp. 209–19.

13. Vaughan, *New England Frontier*, pp. 123–54. See also Vaughan's article, "Pequots and Puritans: The Causes of the War of 1637," *William and Mary Quarterly*, 3rd ser. 21 (1964): 256–69. For other twentieth-century examples of the persistence of the demonic image of the Pequots, see Woodrow Wilson, *A History of the American People*, 5 vols. (New York, 1902), 1:153–55; Edward Channing, *A History of the United States*, 6 vols. (New York, 1912), 1:402; Howard Bradstreet, *The History of the War with the Pequots Retold* (New Haven, 1933); George F. Willison, *Saints and Strangers* (New York, 1945), pp. 394–405.

14. Jennings, *Invasion of America*, pp. 177–227. Jennings's early work has often been faulted for his lack of attention to the Native American side of the story. His account of the Pequot War is essentially an exposé of the Puritans. For a very perceptive analysis of Jennings's strengths and weaknesses, see James P. Ronda, "Beyond Thanksgiving: Francis Jennings' *The Invasion of America,*" *Journal of Ethnic Studies* 7 (1978): 88–94. Jennings has recently published a large-scale ethnohistorical survey of the conflict of Native American and European cultures, *The Founders of America* (New York, 1993), which nicely complements his *Invasion of America*. It does not, however, contain any new information on the Pequot War. For an ethnohistory of the Puritan-Pequot conflict, one must look elsewhere. Of particular value are the articles in Bruce Trigger, ed., *The Handbook of North American Indians: Northeast* (Washington, D.C., 1978), and in Hauptman and Wherry, *Pequots in Southern New England.* As

noted earlier, the analysis of the Pequot War in Salisbury's *Manitou and Providence* draws very skillfully on ethnohistorical data to demonstrate that the Pequots were far weaker and much less aggressive than generally recognized. The findings of this present study provide additional evidence to support Salisbury's conclusion.

15. Drinnon, *Facing West*, p. 46.

16. Alvin M. Josephy, *Now that the Buffalo's Gone* (New York, 1982), pp. 53, 57–58. Josephy draws upon Ceci's Ph.D. dissertation, "Effect of European Contact." Also of value on this issue is Ceci, "Native Wampum as a Peripheral Resource in the Seventeenth Century World System," in Hauptman and Wherry, *Pequots in Southern New England*, pp. 48–64.

17. Cronon, *Changes in the Land*, p. 97.

18. Salisbury, *Manitou and Providence*, pp. 203–35; quotation on p. 225.

19. Nash, *Red, White, and Black*, pp. 85–86.

20. Larzer Ziff, *Puritanism in America: New Culture in the New World* (New York, 1973), pp. 90–91.

21. Kibbey, *Interpretation of Material Shapes*, pp. 92–120.

22. Kupperman, *Settling with the Indians*, p. 175.

23. Slotkin, *Regeneration through Violence*, pp. 69–78; quotation on p. 77. Slotkin offers a very provocative, psychohistorical reading of the Pequot War chronicles.

24. See, for example, Anna P. Monguia, "The Pequot War Reexamined," *American Indian Culture and Research Journal* 1 (1975): 13–21; Paul Marasnio, "Puritan and Pequot," *Indian Historian* 3 (1970): 9–13; Francis E. Ackerman, "A Conflict over Land," *American Indian Journal* 7 (March 1981): 8–18. College-level textbooks published since 1945 have also frequently portrayed the Pequots as defenders of their homeland against Puritan aggression. For examples, see Oliver P. Chitwood and Frank L. Owsley, *A Short History of the American People* (New York, 1945), pp. 61–62; Richard N. Current and Frank Freidel, *American History: A Survey* (New York, 1961), p. 59; Peter N. Carroll and David W. Noble, *The Free and the Unfree: A New History of the United States* (New York, 1988), pp. 45–47; George B. Tindall and David E. Shi, *America: A Narrative History* (New York, 1992), p. 153; Richard Middleton, *Colonial America: A History, 1607–1760* (Cambridge, Mass., 1992), pp. 62–63. While placing the onus of aggression on the Puritans, those texts have also sometimes accepted traditional stereotypes of Pequot behavior that, as we shall see in this study, are remnants of Puritan propaganda not supported by the evidence.

25. Alden T. Vaughan, *New England Frontier: Puritans and Indians, 1620–1675,* 2nd ed. (New York, 1979), p. xxix; Vaughan, "Pequots and Puritans: The Causes of the War of 1637," in *Roots of American Racism: Essays on the Colonial Experience* (New York, 1995), p. 194.

26. Arrell Morgan Gibson, *The American Indian: Prehistory to Present* (Lexington, Mass., 1980), pp. 187–89. Other writers on American Indian history

have generally emphasized Pequot resistance to English expansionism. See, for example, William T. Hagan, *American Indians* (Chicago, 1961), p. 13; Angie Debo, *A History of the Indians of the United States* (Norman, Okla., 1970), pp. 46–47; Wilcomb E. Washburn, *The Indian in America* (New York, 1975), pp. 129–31; William Brandon, *The Last Americans* (New York, 1974), pp. 202–5.

27. Andrew Delbanco, *The Puritan Ordeal* (Cambridge, Mass., 1989), p. 106. Delbanco and numerous others who have repeated the story that Pequot means "destroyers of men" have generally not noted that they are dealing with a theory, not a proven fact. Frank Speck, the leading authority on the Pequot-Mohegan language, acknowledged that an earlier student of Algonquian linguistics had argued that the name Pequot is derived from "Paquatauoq" and thus means "destroyers." Speck, however, declined to confirm that conjecture; see his "Native Tribes and Dialects of Connecticut: A Mohegan-Pequot Diary," *Annual Reports of the U.S. Bureau of American Ethnology* 43 (1928): 218. Subsequent studies have not resolved the question, and the exact derivation and meaning of the word remain obscure.

28. Steven T. Katz, "The Pequot War Reconsidered," *New England Quarterly* 64 (1991): 211.

29. Roy Harvey Pearce, *Savagism and Civilization: A Study of the Indian and the American Mind* (1953; Berkeley, 1988), pp. x, 24, 20 (first published as *The Savages of America: A Study of the Indian and the Idea of civilization*). See also Pearce, " 'The Ruines of Mankind': The Indian and the Puritan Mind," *Journal of the History of Ideas* 13 (1952): 200–217, and "The Metaphysics of Indian Hating," *Ethnohistory* 4 (1957): 27–40.

30. Pearce, *Savagism and Civilization*, pp. 254–55. In addition to Pearce, I have found the following works particularly valuable in their explanation of Puritan concepts of savagery: Carroll, *Puritanism and the Wilderness*; Slotkin, *Regeneration through Violence*; the foreword by Sacvan Bercovitch and the introduction to Segal and Stineback, *Puritans, Indians, and Manifest Destiny*; the introduction to Richard Slotkin and James K. Folsom, eds., *So Dreadful a Judgment: Puritan Responses to King Philip's War, 1676–1677* (Middletown, Conn., 1978); and Mitchell Robert Breitwieser, *American Puritanism and the Defense of Mourning: Religion, Grief, and Ethnology in Mary White Rowlandson's Captivity Narrative* (Madison, Wisc., 1990). For a broader perspective on the development and evolution of Anglo-American concepts of savagery, see Bernard Sheehan, *Savagism and Civility: Indians and Englishmen in Colonial Virginia* (New York, 1980); Kupperman, *Settling with the Indians*; and Robert F. Berkhofer, Jr., *The White Man's Indian: Images of the American Indian from Columbus to the Present* (New York, 1978). The literature on Puritan thought is enormous. The classic work of Perry Miller and his followers and others generally ignored Puritan responses to the Indian. Recent writers have been more perceptive. To risk naming a single writer, I have found Sacvan Bercovitch, *The American Jeremiad* (Madison, Wisc., 1978), and *The Puritan Origins of the American Self* (New

Haven, 1979), of particular value. Although neither work deals at length with Indian policy, together they provide vital insights into the overall Puritan world view, insights essential for placing Puritan responses to Native Americans in their proper context. Equally important, for the insight it provides into the language of possession, is Stephen Greenblatt's *Marvelous Possessions: The Wonders of the New World* (Chicago, 1991), a remarkably incisive analysis of sixteenth-century accounts relating to early European encounters with the people of the Americas.

31. Quotation from Michael Shanks and Christopher Tilley, "Ideology, Symbolic Power, and Ritual Communication: A Reinterpretation of Neolithic Mortuary Practices," in Ian Hunter, ed., *Symbolic and Structural Archaeology* (Cambridge, 1982), p. 30. For a very useful collection of essays on the role of ideology in social conflict, see David Apter, ed., *Ideology and Discontent* (New York, 1964). In using the term "ideology," I am mindful of the distinction often made between ideology, which is "rhetorical and philosophical in form," and mythology, which is grounded in "the logic of narrative" and seeks to transform "contingent" events "into the absolute and eternally recurring" (Slotkin and Folsom, *So Dreadful a Judgment*, p. 7). But I do not find it at all useful to stress that distinction in explaining the Puritans' response to Indian wars. In their explanation of the unfolding of divine providence in time, philosophical assumptions and religious beliefs (ideology) were embedded within their historical narratives (mythology). The myths that arose out of their efforts to explain the Pequot War and later Indian-white conflicts were driven by ideology.

32. Bercovitch, foreword to Segal and Stineback, *Puritans, Indians, and Manifest Destiny*, p.17.

33. Breitwieser, *American Puritanism and the Defense of Mourning*, p. 94.

1. Preconceptions and Misperceptions

1. Edward A. Arber, ed., *The First Three English Books on America* (Birmingham, 1885), p. 70; H. C. Porter, *The Inconstant Savage: England and the North American Indian, 1500–1660* (London, 1979), pp. 133–34. The secondary literature on this topic is extensive. See, for example, Margaret T. Hodgen, *Early Anthropology in the Sixteenth and Seventeenth Centuries* (Philadelphia, 1964); Lee Eldridge Huddleston, *Origins of the American Indians: European Concepts, 1492–1729* (Austin, 1967); Lewis Hanke, *Aristotle and the American Indians: A Study of Race Prejudice in the Modern World* (Bloomington, Ind., 1959); Anthony Pagden, *The Fall of Natural Man: The American Indian and the Origins of Comparative Ethnology* (London, 1982); Sheehan, *Savagism and Civility*; Fredi Chiappelli et al., eds., *First Images of America: The Impact of the Old World on the New,* 2 vols. (Berkeley, 1976); Benjamin Keen, *The Aztec Image in Western Thought* (New Brunswick, N.J., 1971); Tzvetan Todorov, *The Conquest of America: The Question of the Other* (New York, 1984); Greenblatt, *Marvelous Possessions*.

2. Kupperman, *Settling with the Indians,* argues that Englishmen who visited the New World abandoned many of the misconceptions of armchair travelers but notes that belief that Native American religion was diabolical in nature persisted.

3. Richard Hakluyt, *The Principal Navigations, Voyages, Traffiques, and Discoveries of the English Nation,* 8 vols. (Glasgow, 1904), 6:302, 7:373–74, 397, 8:100–120, 301–82. For a summary of the portrayals of the American Indian in Hakluyt's compendium, see Alfred A. Cave, "Richard Hakluyt's Savages: The Influence of 16th Century Travel Narratives on English Indian Policy in North America," *International Social Science Review* 60 (Winter 1985): 3–24.

4. John Smith, *A Map of Virginia* (1612), in Philip Barbour, ed., *The Jamestown Voyages under the First Charter, 1606–1609* (London, 1969), 2:354, 364, 367, 372; John Smith, *A Description of New England* (1616), in Peter Force, ed., *Tracts and Other Papers Relating Principally to the Origin, Settlement, and Progress of the Colonies in North America from the Discovery of the Country to the Year 1776* (Gloucester, Mass., 1963), 2:1, 15, 17, 18, 33, 34; Alexander Whitaker, *Good Newes from Virginia* (London, 1613), p. 40. On Smith's attitudes toward Indians, see Sheehan, *Savagism and Civility,* pp. 43–46, 51–69, 144–45, 163–68; Kupperman, *Settling with the Indians,* pp. 17–19, 23–24, 30–31, 36–40, 43–45, 50–61, 66–78, 80–95, 111–25, 171–81; Keith Glenn, "Captain John Smith and the Indians," *Virginia Magazine of History and Biography* 52 (1944): 228–48; William Randel, "Captain John Smith's Attitudes toward the Indians," *Virginia Magazine of History and Biography* 47 (1939): 218–29.

5. George Abbot, *A Briefe Description of the Whole World* (London, 1605); *Works of Sir Walter Raleigh* (Oxford, 1829), 4:693–94; Mede quoted in John Canup, *Out of the Wilderness: The Emergence of an American Identity in Colonial New England* (Middletown, Conn., 1990), p. 74.

6. Johnson, *Wonder-Working Providence,* p. 48.

7. William Bradford, *Of Plymouth Plantation, 1620–1647,* ed. Samuel Eliot Morison (New York, 1976), pp. 61–62; Johnson, *Wonder-Working Providence,* pp. 52, 115.

8. Bradford, *Of Plymouth Plantation,* pp. 25–26.

9. Ibid., p. 84. Salisbury comments that Bradford's "description betrays his fear of witchcraft as it was understood by Europeans rather than a comprehension of Indian beliefs and customs. More likely the Pokanoket were ritually purging themselves of their hostilities toward the English as a prelude to their diplomatic reversal." They had decided that "the time was ripe to befriend the settlers instead of maintaining a hostile distance" (*Manitou and Providence,* p. 114).

10. Edward Winslow, "Good Newes from New England" (1624), reprinted in Edward Arber, ed., *The Story of the Pilgrim Fathers* (New York, 1969), pp. 513–14.

11. On the Native American as the "Other," three works previously cited are of particular value: Todorow, *Conquest of America;* Greenblatt, *Marvelous Possessions;* Slotkin, *Regeneration through Violence.*

12. Sheehan, *Savagism and Civility,* p. 48; John Brinsley, *A Consolation for our Grammar Schools* (London, 1622), seg. A3; Richard Eburne, *A Plain Pathway to Plantations* (1629), ed. Louis B. Wright (Ithaca, N.Y., 1962), p. 137.

13. This idea received its fullest exploration in the writings of Robert Johnson and William Strachey. See Alfred A. Cave, "Canaanites in a Promised Land: The American Indian and the Providential Theory of Empire," *American Indian Quarterly* 12 (Fall 1988): 284–87.

14. John White, *The Planter's Plea* (New York, 1968), pp. 54–55; Canup, *Out of the Wilderness,* pp. 69–73.

15. Delbanco, *Puritan Ordeal,* p. 14.

16. Thomas Prince, "The People of New England Put in Mind of the Righteous Acts of the Lord to them and Their Fathers, and Reasoned with Concerning Them," in A. W. Plumstead, ed., *The Wall and the Garden: Selected Massachusetts Election Sermons, 1670–1775* (Minneapolis, 1968), p. 202.

17. David D. Smits, " 'We Are Not to Grow Wild': Seventeenth Century New England's Repudiation of Anglo-Indian Intermarriage," *American Indian Culture and Research Journal* 11 (1987): 1–32.

18. Cotton Mather, *Good Fetch'd out of Evil* (Boston, 1706). On sexual themes in the captivity narratives, see Alden T. Vaughan and Edward W. Clark, *Puritans among the Indians: Accounts of Captivity and Redemption, 1676–1724* (Cambridge, Mass., 1981), pp. 14–15, 19, 70, 121, 242.

19. On Gray and his contemporaries, see Cave, "Canaanites in a Promised Land," pp. 285–92.

20. Winslow, "Good Newes," pp. 581–92. On Winslow and other early-contact-period observers of Native American spirituality, see Frank Shuffelton, "Indian Devils and Pilgrim Fathers: Squanto, Hobomok, and the English Conception of Indian Religion," *New England Quarterly* 49 (1976): 108–16. For an excellent analysis of the influence of Calvinist concepts of history on Puritan expectations of Indian behavior, see William S. Simmons, "Cultural Bias in the New England Puritans' Perceptions of the Indians," *William and Mary Quarterly,* 3rd ser. 38 (1981): 56–72.

21. William Wood, *New England's Prospect (1634),* ed. Alden T. Vaughan (Amherst, Mass., 1977), pp. 100–102.

22. John Eliot and Thomas Mayhew, "Tears of Repentence; or, A Further Narrative of the Progress of the Gospel amongst the Indians in New England ...," *Massachusetts Historical Society Collections,* 3rd ser. 4 (1834): 201–2. William Hubbard, *A General History of New England from the Discovery to MDCLXXX* (Cambridge, Mass., 1815), pp. 34–35; Paul J. Lindholt, ed., *John Josselyn, Colonial Traveller: A Critical Edition of Two Voyages to New England* (Hanover, N.H., 1988), p. 95; Cotton Mather, *Magnalia Christi Americana; or, The Ecclesiastical History of New England,* 2 vols. (1702; New York, 1967), 1: 256.

23. In addition to the standard biographies of Williams, see Kathleen David-

son March, "Uncommon Civility: The Narragansett Indians and Roger Williams" (Ph.D. diss., University of Iowa, 1985).

24. Roger Williams, *The Complete Writings of Roger Williams* (New York, 1963), 1:152–53.

25. John A. Grim, *The Shaman* (Norman, Okla., 1983), pp. 3–33. The literature on shamanism is vast. The most valuable general study remains Mircea Eliade, *Shamanism: Archaic Techniques of Ecstasy* (Princeton, N.J., 1964). The basic assumptions and principles underlying shamanic practices throughout the world are essentially identical, but there are great variations in local practices. For a review of the evidence relating to New England, see William S. Simmons, "Southern New England Shamanism: An Ethnographic Reconstruction," in William Cowan, ed., *Papers of the Seventh Algonquian Conference* (Ottawa, 1976), pp. 217–56. Also of value is Frank G. Speck, "Penobscot Shamanism," *Memoirs of American Anthropological Association* 6 (1919): 237–88.

26. On witchcraft in Puritan New England, the following secondary accounts are particularly valuable: Marion Starkey, *The Devil in Massachusetts: A Modern Inquiry into the Salem Witch Trials* (Garden City, N.Y., 1961); Paul Boyer and Stephen Nissenbaum, *Salem Possessed: The Social Origins of Witchcraft* (Cambridge, Mass., 1974); Chadwick Hansen, *Witchcraft at Salem* (New York, 1969); John Putnam Demos, *Entertaining Satan: Witchcraft and the Culture of New England* (New York, 1982); Carol F. Karlsen, *The Devil in the Shape of a Woman: Witchcraft in Colonial New England* (New York, 1987). Some recent studies have explored the relationship of attitudes toward witchcraft and folk magic in both England and New England in the early seventeenth century. See Keith Thomas, *Religion and the Decline of Magic* (New York, 1971); Richard Weisman, *Witchcraft, Magic, and Religion in 17th Century Massachusetts* (Amherst, Mass., 1984); David Hall, *Worlds of Wonder, Days of Judgment: Popular Religious Belief in Early New England* (New York, 1989); Richard Godbeer, *The Devil's Dominion: Magic and Religion in Early New England* (New York, 1991). Those studies emphasize Puritan association of both malevolent witchcraft and the magical healing practices of the English "cunning folk" with the devil. Although Indians were subject to English laws against witchcraft, which prescribed the death penalty, there is no record that any Puritan magistrate, missionary, or Indian commissioner ever brought any legal charge of malevolent sorcery against any shaman. See Demos, *Entertaining Satan*, p. 71; Yasuhide Kawashima, *Puritan Justice and the Indian* (Middletown, Conn., 1986); Lyle Koehler, "Red-White Power Relations and Justice in the Courts of Seventeenth-Century New England," *American Indian Culture and Research Journal* 3 (1979): 1–31; James P. Ronda, "Red and White at the Bench: Indians and the Law in the Plymouth Colony, 1620–1691," *Essex Institute Historical Collections* 110 (1974): 200–215; Alfred A. Cave, "Indian Shamans and English Witches in Seventeenth Century New England," *Essex Institute Historical Collections* 128 (Fall 1992): 239–54.

27. Harold W. Van Lonkhuyzen, "A Reappraisal of the Praying Indians: Acculturation, Conversion, and Identity at Natick, Massachusetts, 1646–1730," *New England Quarterly* 63 (September 1990): 400.

28. Increase Mather, "Angelgraphia," quoted in Hansen, *Witchcraft at Salem,* p. 198; Cotton Mather, *Decennium Luctuosum* (1699), in Wilcomb E. Washburne, ed., *The Garland Library of Narratives of North American Indian Captivities,* 111 vols. (New York, 1978), 3:103.

29. Williams, *Complete Writings,* 1:148–50.

30. Hall, *Worlds of Wonder, Days of Judgment,* p. 238.

31. Henry Warren Bowden, *American Indians and Christian Missions: Studies in Cultural Conflict* (Chicago, 1981), p. 119.

32. Ake Hultkrantz, *The Religions of the American Indians* (Berkeley, 1980), p. 41; Gregory Evans Dowd, *A Spirited Resistance: The North American Indian Struggle for Unity, 1745–1815* (Baltimore, 1992), p. 9.

33. Bowden, *American Indians and Christian Missions,* p. 105.

34. Williams, *Complete Writings,* 1:36, 50, 58, 81.

35. Ibid., pp. 152–54.

36. Ibid., pp. 150–52.

37. Quoted in Elizabeth Tooker, ed., *Native North American Spirituality of the Eastern Woodlands* (New York, 1979), p. 17.

38. Christopher L. Miller and George R. Hamill, "A New Perspective on Indian-White Contact: Cultural Symbols and Colonial Trade," *Journal of American History* 73 (1986): 311–28.

39. Some authorities, such as Paul Radin, have argued that Native Americans possessed no concept of the supernatural. That view is extreme, as manifestations of manitou were clearly differentiated from the ordinary and the mundane. On this point, see Hultkrantz, *Religions of the American Indians,* pp. 9–14.

40. On the contrast between Puritan piety and Algonquian spirituality, Bowden, *American Indians and Christian Missions,* pp. 111–33, is particularly useful. The literature on the Puritan conversion experience is extensive, but two older works remain useful: Edmund Morgan, *Visible Saints: History of a Puritan Idea* (New York, 1963); and Norman Pettit, *The Heart Prepared: Grace and Conversion in Puritan Spiritual Life* (New York, 1968). See also Charles L. Cohen, *God's Caress: The Psychology of Puritan Religious Experience* (New York, 1986).

41. Bowden, *American Indians and Christian Missions,* p. 121.

42. Eliot and Mayhew, "Tears of Repentence," pp. 229–60. On the notion that "the exemplary conduct of settlers rather than preaching" would be the means that would bring Indians to civility and Christianity, see Salisbury, *Manitou and Providence,* p. 178.

43. The most comprehensive and useful studies of Puritan missionary activities are James Axtell, *The Invasion Within: The Contest of Cultures in Colonial North America* (New York, 1985); Neal Salisbury, "Conquest of the 'Savage':

Puritans, Puritan Missionaries, and Indians" (Ph.D. diss., UCLA, 1976); Elise Melanie Brenner, "Strategies for Autonomy: An Analysis of Ethnic Mobilization in Seventeenth Century Southern New England" (Ph.D. diss., University of Massachusetts, 1984). The Puritans made little effort to convert the Indians during the first two decades of colonization. Jennings, *Invasion of America,* pp. 228–53, charges that the later efforts of John Eliot and his associates were insincere, prompted by a desire to enjoy the income provided to missionaries by English benefactors and by the need to counter English criticism of Puritan neglect of Indian well-being. For another view, see Richard W. Cogley, "John Eliot in Recent Scholarship," *American Indian Culture and Research Journal* 14 (1990): 77–92. The following articles are of value in assessing Puritan missionary efforts: Neal E. Salisbury, "Red Puritans: The Praying Indians of Massachusetts Bay and John Eliot," *William and Mary Quarterly,* 3rd ser. 31 (1974): 27–54; Gary B. Nash, "Notes on the History of Seventeenth Century Missionization in Colonial America," *American Indian Culture and Research Journal* 2 (1978): 3–8; James B. Ronda, " 'We Are Well as We Are': An Indian Critique of Seventeenth Century Christian Missions," *William and Mary Quarterly,* 3rd ser. 34 (1977): 66–82; Kenneth B. Morrison, " 'That Art of Coyning Christians': John Eliot and the Praying Indians of Massachusetts," *Ethnohistory* 21 (1974): 77–92; William S. Simmons, "Conversion from Indian to Puritan," *New England Quarterly* 52 (1979): 197–218; Robert James Naeher, "Dialogue in the Wilderness: John Eliot and the Indian Exploration of Puritanism as a Source of Meaning, Comfort, and Ethnic Survival," *New England Quarterly* 62 (1989): 346–68; Van Lonkhuyzen, "A Reappraisal of the Praying Indians," pp. 396–428.

44. Thomas Morton, *The New English Canaan* (1634), in Force, *Tracts,* 2, no. 5:38–39; Wood, *New England's Prospect,* p. 96. The following provide useful summaries of current information about the material culture of the Indians of southern New England: Howard S. Russell, *Indian New England before the Mayflower* (Hanover, N.H., 1980); Dean R. Snow, *The Archaeology of New England* (New York, 1980); Cronon, *Changes in the Land*; Charles C. Willoughby, *Antiquities of the New England Indians* (Cambridge, Mass., 1935); Regina Flannery, *An Analysis of Coastal Algonquian Culture* (Washington, D.C., 1939); Salisbury, *Manitou and Providence,* pp. 13–84; Froelich G. Rainey, "A Compilation of Historical Data Relating to the Ethnography of Connecticut and Southern New England Indians," *Bulletin of the Archaeological Society of Connecticut,* rpt. 3 (1956): 3–49.

45. Williams, *Complete Writings,* 1:66; Christopher Levitt, "Voyage into New England" (1628), in *Massachusetts Historical Society Collections,* 3rd ser. 3 (1833): 178; Francis Higginson, *New England's Plantation* (1630), in *Massachusetts Historical Society Proceedings* 62 (1929): 316; Wood, *New England's Prospect,* p. 113.

46. Daniel Gookin, "Historical Collections of the Indians in New England," in *Massachusetts Historical Society Collections,* 1st ser. 1 (1792): 149.

47. Russell, *Indian New England before the Mayflower,* pp. 72–184; Snow, *Archaeology of New England,* pp. 25–100; Cronon, *Changes in the Land,* pp. 34–53.

48. Gookin, "Historical Collections," pp. 152–53; Williams, *Complete Writings,* 1:59–76, 188–93; Wood, *New England's Prospect,* pp. 108–9. French observers shared English misperceptions of Native American gender roles. The Jesuit Joseph Jouvency declared of the Indian women of Canada: "their duties and position are those of slaves, laborers, and beasts of burden." He believed that "the women, although naturally prolific, cannot on account of their occupation in their labors, either bring forth fully developed offspring, or properly nourish them after they have been brought forth; therefore they either suffer abortion, or forsake their new-born children, while engaged in carrying water, securing wood and other tasks, so that scarcely one infant in thirty survives until youth." Fr. Pierre Biard, to cite another example, reported of the natives of Canada: "Their wives are regarded and treated as slaves"; see Reuben Gold Thwaites, ed., *The Jesuit Relations and Allied Documents,* 73 vols. (Cleveland, 1896–1901), 1:257–59, 2:79. The Jesuits' celebrated capacity to comprehend and appreciate Native American culture sometimes failed them.

49. Cronon, *Changes in the Land,* p. 46.

50. Williams, *Complete Writings,* 1:141.

51. Salisbury, *Manitou and Providence,* p. 44; Williams, *Complete Writings,* 1:151, 153, 197; Salisbury, *Manitou and Providence,* p. 44; Wood, *New England's Prospect,* pp. 103–4.

52. Nicholaes van Wassenaer, "Historisch Verhael" (1624), in J. Franklin Jameson, ed., *Narratives of New Netherland, 1609–1664* (New York, 1911), p. 87; Johann De Laet, "The New World" (1625), in Jameson, ed., *Narratives of New Netherland,* p. 44. Champlain's comment is quoted in Salisbury, *Manitou and Providence,* p. 66.

53. Joseph G. Cogswell, ed., "The Voyage of John de Verrazano along the coast of North America from Carolina to Newfoundland, A.D. 1624," *New York Historical Society Collections,* 2nd ser. 1 (1841): 45–49.

54. "A Relation, or Journal, of the Beginning and Proceedings of the English Plantation Settled at Plymouth in New England" (1622), in Arber, *Story of the Pilgrim Fathers* (New York, 1969), pp. 414, 419.

55. There has been some controversy of late as to whether the technique of planting corn with fish as fertilizer, taught by Squanto (whose full name was Tisquantum), was in fact an Indian practice. There are no other reports of the use of fish fertilizer in contemporary European descriptions of the horticultural methods of the indigenous inhabitants of southern New England. Lynn Ceci argues that Squanto learned to use fish fertilizer during an earlier sojourn among Europeans. But Neal Salisbury suggests that the method might well have been "a strictly local adaptation by which the Patuxet and, perhaps, a few other coastal groups with high, concentrated populations, small amounts of farmland, and an

abundance of fish, had increased their agricultural yields before the depopulation of the late 1610's." See Lynn Ceci, "Fish Fertilizer: A Native North American Practice?" *Science* 188 (April 1975): 26–30; Salisbury, *Manitou and Providence,* p. 252. Recent research challenges Ceci's thesis and supports Salisbury's suggestion. Nanepashemet, "It Smells Fishy to Me: An argument supporting the use of Fish Fertilizer by the Native People of New England," in *Algonkians of New England: Past and Present, Annual Proceedings of the Dublin Seminar for New England Folklore* 16 (1993): 42–50.

56. Cronon, *Changes in the Land,* pp. 51–52.

57. Allyn B. Forbes, ed., *Winthrop Papers, 1623–1630* (Boston, 1931), 2:91, 140–41.

58. "New Englands Plantation," in Force, *Tracts,* 1, no. 12: 12. Most scholars now maintain that, the Puritans' reputation for rapacity notwithstanding, they did recognize a legal obligation to respect the Indians' right to their *cultivated* lands. See Charles E. Eisinger, "The Puritan Justification for Taking the Land," *Essex Institute Historical Collections* 84 (1948): 131–43; Ruth Barnes Moynihan, "The Patent and the Indian: The Problem of Jurisdiction in Seventeenth Century New England," *American Indian Culture and Research Journal* 2 (1977): 8–18; James Warren Springer, "American Indians and the Law of Real Property in Colonial New England," *American Journal of Legal History* 30 (1986): 25–58; Kawashima, *Puritan Justice and the Indian,* pp. 42–71. But Jennings, *Invasion of America,* p. 135, argues that while "morally and pragmatically Winthrop's Puritans were obligated to leave individual Indians in possession of tract actually under tillage . . . legally they recognized as real property only those lands whose claimants could show deeds from grants made by the Massachusetts Bay Company." Kawashima, however, has demonstrated that Jennings confused the legal issues of jurisdiction and ownership, noting that, "in unoccupied and vacant regions, the Crown's charter established both jurisdiction and land ownership at once, but in the areas occupied and controlled by Indian tribes, the charter simply established the claim to superiority, or the right to control the Indians, a right that could only be established against other European or neighboring English colonies" (*Puritan Justice and the Indian,* pp. 46–47). On the evolution of English theories concerning Indian land rights, see Fred M. Kimmey, "Christianity and Indian Lands," *Ethnohistory* 7 (1960): 44–60; and Cave, "Canaanites in a Promised Land," pp. 277–97.

59. Robert Cushman, "Reasons and Considerations Touching the Lawfulness of Removing out of England into the Parts of America" (1621), in Young, *Chronicles of the Pilgrim Fathers, of the Colony of New Plymouth from 1602 to 1625* (Boston, 1841), p. 243; John Cotton, "God's Promise to His Plantations" (1630), in *Old South Leaflets* (Boston, n.d.) 3, no. 53:6.

60. "Master John Cotton's answer to Master Roger Williams," in Williams, *Complete Writings,* 2:46–48. Williams's argument is known only in Cotton's summary, as he destroyed his tract on Indian land rights.

61. William Pynchon to Thomas Dudley, June 5, 1648, in Henry Morris, *Early History of Springfield, 1636–1675* (Springfield, Mass., 1876), pp. 68–71; Vaughan, *New England Frontier,* p. xviii.

62. Thomas Lechford, "Plain Dealing: or, Newes from New England," *Massachusetts Historical Society Collections,* 3rd ser. 3 (1833): 103; Williams, *Complete Works,* 1:164; Gookin, "Historical Collections," 1:154.

63. Salisbury, *Manitou and Providence,* pp. 41–49; Anthony F. C. Wallace, "Political Organization and Land Tenure among the Northeastern Indians, 1600–1830," *Southwestern Journal of Anthropology* 13 (1957): 301–21; Raymond D. Fogelson, "The Context of American Indian Political History: An Overview and a Critique," in *The Struggle for Political Autonomy: Papers and Comments from the Second Newberry Library Conference on Themes in American Indian History,* ed. Frederick E. Hoxie (Chicago, 1989), pp. 14–18; Morton H. Fried, "The Myth of the Tribe," *Natural History* 84 (1974): 12–20. Salisbury finds that the degree of political consolidation in New England was limited; "the 'chiefdom' and 'tribe' of political anthropology were not to be found in southern New England; the only permanent, supra-familial organization was the band" (*Manitou and Providence,* p. 48). Others suggest that Marshall Sahlin's term "segmentary tribe" for a confederation less stable than the unified tribe best describes the Narragansetts and the Pequots; see Marshall Sahlins, *Tribesmen* (Englewood Cliffs, N.J., 1968), p. 20; Peter Allen Thomas, "In the Maelstrom of Change: The Indian Trade and Cultural Process in the Middle Connecticut River Valley, 1635–1665" (Ph.D. diss., University of Massachusetts, 1979), pp. 33–34; Paul Alden Robinson, "The Struggle Within: The Indian Debate in Seventeenth-Century Narragansett Country" (Ph.D. diss., State University of New York at Binghamton, 1990).

64. Brenner, in "Strategies for Autonomy," p. 41, remarks that "southern New England communities appear to have recognized distinctions of hereditary right (ascribed status) as well as of individual accomplishment (achieved status). In coastal areas the system of political succession through inheritance was, perhaps, more rigidly maintained than in non-coastal areas. It was the rare sachem, however, who was able to command allegiance and the resulting tribute all of the time. Therefore, political applications were fluid, resulting in dynamic political events." See also William Burton and Richard Lowenthal, "The First of the Mohegans," *American Ethnologist* 1 (1974): 588–99.

65. Gordon Day, "English-Indian Contacts in New England," *Ethnohistory* 9 (1962): 68.

66. Trumbull, *Complete History of Connecticut,* 1:40.

67. Mary Guilette Soulsbey, "Connecticut Indian Ethnohistory: A Look at Five Tribes" (M.A. thesis, University of Connecticut, 1981), pp. 4–9. Mathias Spiess, "The Indians of Connecticut," *Tercentenary Commission of the State of Connecticut, Committee on Historical Publications, No. 19* (New Haven, 1935), listed among the "River Tribes" the Tunxis, the Podunks, the Wangunks, the

Hammonassets, the Poquonocks, the Saukiogs, and the Massacoes. The claim that these "tribes" were closely related to the so-called Wappinger Confederacy is now discredited. See Ives Goddard, "The Ethno-historical Implications of Early Delaware Linquistic Materials," *Man in the Northeast* 1 (1971): 14–26, and "Eastern Algonquian Languages," in Trigger, *Handbook*, 15: 70–78. As to a more recent practice of referring to the River Indians as the "Mattabesec" tribe or confederacy, see John R. Swanton, *The Indian Tribes of North America* (Washington, D.C., 1952), p. 33. Bert Salwen, however, rightly comments: "this usage does not seem to fit the 17th century situation"; see his "Indians of Southern New England and Long Island, Early Period," in Trigger, *Handbook*, 15:173.

68. Salwen, "Indians of Southern New England," in Trigger, *Handbook*, 15:175.

69. Spiess, "Indians of Connecticut," p. 8.

70. Williams, *Complete Writings*, 1:204; R. Brian Ferguson, "Tribal Warfare," *Scientific American*, January 1992, p. 108. See also Wendell S. Haddock, "War among Northeastern Woodland Indians," *American Anthropologist* 49 (1947): 204–21; R. Brian Ferguson and Neil L. Whitehead, *War in the Tribal Zone: Expanding States and Indigenous Warfare* (Sante Fe, N.M., 1992); Eric R. Wolf, *Europe and the People without History* (Berkeley, 1982), pp. 127–262. One recent writer suggests that the pandemics following early contacts with Europeans may have lowered the level of violence among New England's indigenous inhabitants by reducing "the pressure for land in the region" and impressing "on the survivors the folly of unnecessary bloodshed"; see Hirsch, "Collision of Military Cultures," p. 1191, n. 11.

71. John Winthrop, *Winthrop's Journal, History of New England, 1630–1639*, ed. James K. Hosmer, 2 vols. (New York, 1908), 1: 61; Bradford, *Of Plymouth Plantation*, pp. 257–58.

72. Wood, *New England's Prospect*, p. 80.

73. Orr, *History of the Pequot War*, pp. 23, 99, 119, 147, 166 (the quotation from Vincent is on p. 99); Johnson, *Wonder-Working Providence*, p. 147; William Hubbard, *The History of the Indian Wars in New England*, ed. Samuel G. Drake (Roxbury, Mass., 1845), 2:6–7.

74. See, for example, Vaughan, *New England Frontier*, p. 123.

75. Speck, "Native Tribes and Dialects," pp. 216–18; "Notes on the Mohegan and Niantic Indian," *Anthropological Papers, American Museum of Natural History* 3 (1909): 183–210; interview with Gladys Tantequideon, May 15, 1987.

76. Speck, "Native Tribes and Dialects," pp. 213–16, 222–23; Truman D. Michelson, "Notes on Algonquian Language," *International Journal of American Linguistics* 1 (1917): 56–57; Goddard, "Eastern Algonguian Languages," in Trigger, *Handbook*, 15:72–76. The overall evidence on the question of Pequot origins is reviewed and analyzed in Carroll Alton Means, "Mohegan-Pequot Relationships, as Indicated by the Events Leading to the Pequot Massacre of 1637 and Subsequent Claims in the Mohegan Land Controversy," *Archaeological Society of*

Connecticut Bulletin 21 (1947): 26–33; Bert W. Salwen, "A Tentative 'In Situ' Solution to the Mohegan-Pequot Problem," in *An Introduction to the Archaeology and History of the Connecticut Valley Indian,* ed. William R. Young (Springfield, Mass., 1969), pp. 81–89; Alfred A. Cave, "The Pequot Invasion of Southern New England: A Reassessment of the Evidence," *New England Quarterly* 62 (1989): 27–44.

77. Lucianne Lavin, "Pottery Classification and Cultural Models in Southern New England Prehistory," *North American Archaeologist* 7 (1986): 1–2.

78. Irving Rouse, "Ceramic Traditions and Sequences in Connecticut," *Archaeological Society of Connecticut Bulletin* 21 (1947): 25; Kevin McBride, "Prehistory of the Lower Connecticut Valley" (Ph.d. diss., University of Connecticut, 1984), pp. 126–28, 199–269.

79. Snow, *Archaeology of New England,* p. 85.

80. Means, "Mohegan-Pequot Relationships," pp. 26–33; Charles J. Hoadly, "Pedigree of Uncas," *New England Historical and Genealogical Register and Antiquarian Journal* 10 (1856): 227–28.

81. Snow, *Archaeology of New England,* pp. 39, 83–87; William A. Starna, "The Pequots in the Early Seventeenth Century," in Hauptman and Wherry, *Pequots in Southern New England,* pp. 33–47; Kevin McBride, "The Historical Archaeology of the Mashantucket Pequots, 1637–1900," ibid., pp. 96–116. Snow has determined that his earlier population estimate of 13,300 was in error; the 16,000 total is explained in Dean R. Snow and Kim M. Lamphear, "European Contact and Indian Depopulation in the Northeast: The Timing of the First Epidemics," *Ethnohistory* 35 (1988): 16–38. See also Sherburne F. Cook, "The Significance of Disease in the Extinction of the New England Indians," *Human Biology* 45 (1973): 485–508; Arthur E. Spiero and Bruce D. Spiess, "New England Pandemic of 1616–1622: Cause and Archaeological Implication," *Man in the Northeast* 35 (1987): 71–83. Henry Dobyns, *Their Number Became Thinned* (Knoxville, 1983), pp. 38, 318–19, cites Roger Williams's reports of Narragansett recollections of sixteenth-century earthquakes as proof of pandemics caused by occasional contact with European sailors or traders in the century prior to European contact. Dobyns believes that the Narragansetts generally associated earthquakes with epidemic disease. His claim has not won much acceptance. For discussion of this aspect, see Snow and Lamphear, "European Contact and Indian Depopulation; David Henige, "Primary Source by Primary Source? On the Role of Epidemics in New World Depopulation," *Ethnohistory* 33 (1986): 293–312; Henry Dobyns, "More Methodological Perspectives on Historical Demography," *Ethnohistory* 36 (1989): 284–99; Dean R. Snow and Kim M. Lamphear, "More Methodological Perspectives: A Rejoinder to Dobyns," ibid., pp. 299–307. For other useful studies of the problem of Indian depopulation, see Alfred W. Crosby, Jr., "Virgin Soil Epidemics as a Factor in Aboriginal Depopulation in America," *William and Mary Quarterly,* 3rd ser. 33 (1976): 289–99; and *The Columbian Exchange: Biologi-*

cal and Cultural Consequences of 1492 (Westport, Conn., 1972); Russell Thornton, *American Indian Holocaust and Survival: A Population History since 1492* (Norman, Okla., 1987); Ann F. Ramenofsky, *Vectors of Death: The Archaeology of European Contact* (Albuquerque, 1987). For a vivid eyewitness account of the aftermath of the epidemic of 1616–19, see Morton, *New English Canaan*, pp. 18–19: "The hand of God fell heavily upon them, with such a mortall stroke, that they died on heapes, as they lay in their houses, and the living; that were able to shift for themselves would runne away, and let them by, and let there carkases ly above the ground without buriall. For in a place where many inhabited, there hath been but one left a live, to tell what became of the rest, the livinge being (as it seems) not able to bury the dead, they were left for Crowes, Kites and vermin to pray upon. And the bones and skulls upon the severall places of their habitations, made such a spectacle after my coming into those partes, that as I travailed in that Forrest, near the Massachusetts, it seemed to mee a new found Golgotha."

82. McBride, "Historical Archaeology of the Mashantucket Pequots," pp. 99–104.

83. Starna, "Pequots in the Early Seventeenth Century," p. 43.

84. Wood, *New England's Prospect*, pp. 95–96.

85. Thomas Shepard, "The Clear Sun-Shine of the Gospel Breaking Forth upon the Indians in New England" (1648), reprinted in *Massachusetts Historical Society Collections*, 3rd ser. 4 (1834): 44.

86. Williams, *Complete Writings*, 1:185–86.

87. William S. Simmons, *Spirit of the New England Tribes: Indian History and Folklore, 1620–1684* (Hanover, N.H., 1986), p. 72.

88. Quoted in ibid.

89. Winslow, "Good Newes," p. 557.

90. Ibid., pp. 557–74; Salisbury, *Manitou and Providence*, pp. 125–33; Jennings, *Invasion of America*, pp. 186–87.

91. Morton, *New English Canaan*, p. 76; Bradford, *Of Plymouth Plantation*, pp. 204–6. Morton's side of the story is found in *New English Canaan*, pp. 89–125. For recent perspectives, see Karen Ordahl Kupperman, "Thomas Morton, Historian," *New England Quarterly* 50 (1977): 660–64; and Michael Zuckerman, "Pilgrims in the Wilderness: Community, Modernity, and the Maypole at Merry Mount," *New England Quarterly* 50 (1977): 255–77.

92. Quotation from Ronald Takaki, "The *Tempest* in the Wilderness: The Racialization of Savagery," *Journal of American History* 79 (December 1992): 909.

93. Everett Emerson, ed., *Letters from New England: The Massachusetts Bay Colony, 1629–1639* (Amherst, Mass., 1976), p. 64; Morton, *New English Canaan*, p. 71; John H. Humins, "Squanto and Massasoit: A Struggle for Power," *New England Quarterly* 60 (1987): 54–70; Salisbury, *Manitou and Providence*, pp. 166–202; Vaughan, *New England Frontier*, pp. 93–121.

2. Wampum, Pelts, and Power

1. Both Massasoit of the Pokanokets and Chickataubut of the Massachusetts used their connection with the English to block Narragansett expansion. See Morton, *New English Canaan*, pp. 32–33; Salisbury, *Manitou and Providence*, pp. 110–65; Eric Spencer Johnson, " 'Some by Flatteries and Others by Threatenings': Political Strategies among Native Americans of Seventeenth Century New England" (Ph.D. diss., University of Massachusetts, 1993), pp. 100–107.

2. On the incorporation of the peoples of North America into the European-dominated world trade network, see Immanuel Wallerstein, *Capitalist Agriculture and the Origin of the European World Economy, 16th Century*, vol. 1 of *The Modern World System* (New York, 1974); Wolf, *Europe and the People without History*; Denys Delâge, *Bitter Fruit: Amerindians and Europeans in Northeastern North America*, trans. Jane Brierley (Vancouver, 1993).

3. van Wassenaer, "Historisch Verhael," in Jameson, *Narratives of New Netherland*, p. 86; Salisbury, *Manitou and Providence*, pp. 148–50. Adriaen Block had explored the Connecticut River valley in 1614 and listed the Pequots among the Indian groups indigenous to the region. Block, according to the Dutch chronicler Johann De Laet, found the "Pequatoos" living on a small river, which the Dutch named "the river of Seccanamos after the name of the Sagmos or Sacmos [Sagamore]" ("New World," in Jameson, *Narratives of New Netherland*, pp. 42–43).

4. van Wassenaer, "Historisch Verhael," *Netherland*, pp. 86–87.

5. Winthrop, *Journal*, 1:131; Edmund B. O'Callaghan, *History of New Netherland*, 2 vols. (New York, 1845), 1:145–50.

6. O'Callaghan, *History of New Netherland*, 1:149–50.

7. Gookin, "Historical Collections," 1:147; Salisbury, *Manitou and Providence*, pp. 147–52.

8. Arnold J. F. van Laer, ed. and trans., *Documents Relating to New Netherland, 1624–1626, in the Henry E. Huntington Library* (San Marino, Calif., 1924), pp. 223–24. On the early history of the New Netherland colony, see Clef von Bachman, *Peltries or Plantations: The Economic Policies of the United West India Company in New Netherland, 1623–1639* (Baltimore, 1969); Simon Hart, *The Prehistory of the New Netherland Company: Amsterdam Notarial Records of the First Dutch Voyages to the Hudson* (Amsterdam, 1959); Oliver Rink, *Holland on the Hudson: An Economic and Social History of Dutch New York* (Ithaca, N.Y., 1986); Alan W. Trelease, *Indian Affairs in Colonial New York: The Seventeenth Century* (Ithaca, N.Y., 1960). The claim that the Dutch established an outpost on the Connecticut River prior to the founding of New Amsterdam is not supported in the contemporary source materials and is quite implausible.

9. Lynn Ceci, "The First Fiscal Crisis in New York," *Economic Development and Cultural Change* 28 (1980): 325–47; Francis Jennings, "Dutch and Swedish Indian Policies," in Wilcomb E. Washburn, ed., *Handbook of North American*

Indians: History of Indian-White Relations (Washington, D.C., 1988), 4:13–19; Isaack de Rasieres to Samuel Blommaert, 1628, in Jameson, *Narratives of New Netherland*, pp. 103–13; Bradford, *Of Plymouth Plantation*, pp. 203–4; Francis X. Maloney, *The Fur Trade of New England, 1620–1676* (Cambridge, Mass., 1931), pp. 26–27; Bernard Bailyn, *The New England Merchants in the Seventeenth Century* (New York, 1955), p. 13; William I. Roberts III, "The Fur Trade of New England in the Seventeenth Century" (Ph.D. diss., University of Pennsylvania, 1958), pp. 36, 64–65.

10. The literature on wampum and the wampum trade is extensive. For New England, the following are particularly useful: Salisbury, *Manitou and Providence*, pp. 147–65, 200–214; Frank Speck, "The Functions of Wampum among the Eastern Algonkian," *American Anthropological Association Memoirs* 6 (1919): 3–71; Ceci, "Effect of European Contact"; Ceci, "Native Wampum," in Hauptman and Wherry, *Pequots in Southern New England*, pp. 48–64; Mary W. Herman, "Wampum as Money in Northeastern North America," *Ethnohistory* 3 (1956): 21–33; George S. Snyderman, "Functions of Wampum," *American Philosophical Society Proceedings* 98 (1954): 469–94, and "The Function of Wampum in Iroquois Religion," ibid., 105 (1961): 571–608; T. S. Slotkin and Karl Schmitt, "Studies of Wampum," *American Anthropologist* 51 (1949): 223–36; Marshall Joseph Becker, "Wampum: The Development of an Early American Currency," *Bulletin of the Archaeological Society of New Jersey* 36 (1980): 1–11. Also still useful is William Weeden's classic *Indian Money as a Factor in New England Colonization* (Baltimore, 1884).

11. Speck, "Functions of Wampum," p. 6.

12. Williams, *Complete Writings* 1:176.

13. Slotkin and Schmitt, "Studies of Wampum," p. 225. As to the technical difficulties of their manufacture by a Stone Age people, Slotkin and Schmitt remind us that "other precontact artifacts exhibit more complex perforation problems than do shell beads. Stone pipes associated with the Hopewell horizons of the eastern United States possess borings of very narrow diameter and often of two to four inches in length. The tubular jasper beads of the Lauderdale focus present similar examples of difficult drilling."

14. Ralph Hamor, *A True Discourse on the Present State of Virginia* (1614; Albany, 1840), p. 41.

15. Rasieres, in Jameson, *Narratives of New Netherland*, p. 109.

16. Miller and Hamill, "A New Perspective," p. 318.

17. Salisbury, *Manitou and Providence*, pp. 147–65.

18. Speck, "Functions of Wampum," p. 56.

19. Salisbury, *Manitou and Providence*, p. 149; Rasieres, in Jameson, *Narratives of New Netherland*, pp. 103–6.

20. Bradford, *Of Plymouth Plantation*, pp. 139, 379–80. On the economic problems of the Plymouth Colony, see Ruth A. McIntyre, *Debts Hopeful and Desperate: Financing the Plymouth Colony* (Plymouth, Mass., 1963).

21. William Bradford, "Governor Bradford's Letter Book," *Massachusetts Historical Society Collections,* 1st ser. 3 (1849): 52–53; Forest Morgan, ed., *Connecticut as a Colony and as a State* (Hartford, 1904), 1:82.

22. Bradford, *Of Plymouth Plantation,* pp. 203–4; Van Laer, *Documents Relating to New Netherland,* pp. 223–24; Jameson, *Narratives of New Netherland,* pp. 100, 109–10; Rink, *Holland on the Hudson,* pp. 86–88. Rasieres married the niece of a director of the West India Company in 1633 and campaigned unsuccessfully to replace the ineffectual Wouter Van Twiller as director general of New Netherland. Rasieres subsequently traveled in Brazil, lived in Barbados, and served as governor of Tobago.

23. Ceci, "First Fiscal Crisis," pp. 829–47.

24. Jameson, *Narratives of New Netherland,* pp. 109–10; Bradford, *Of Plymouth Plantation,* pp. 203–5.

25. Jameson, *Narratives of New Netherland,* pp. 111–12.

26. Ibid., p. 112.

27. Bradford, *Of Plymouth Plantation,* pp. 203–4; Winthrop, *Journal,* 1:129, 131.

28. Bradford, *Of Plymouth Plantation,* pp. 203–4.

29. Winthrop, *Journal,* 1:131.

30. O'Callaghan, *History of New Netherland,* 1:149–50.

31. E. B. O'Callaghan and Berthold Fernow, eds., *Documents Relative to the Colonial History of the State of New York* (Albany, 1849), 1:287, 2:139–40.

32. Ibid.; De Forest, *History of the Indians of Connecticut,* p. 72.

33. David Pietersz De Vries, "Short Historical and Journal Notes," in Cornell Joray, ed., *Historical Chronicles of New Amsterdam, Colonial New York, and Early Long Island* (Port Washington, N.Y., 1968), pp. 86–88; Charles McKew Parr, *The Voyages of David De Vries* (New York, 1969), p. 174.

34. De Forest, *Indians of Connecticut,* p. 73, claims that the Pequot grand sachem murdered by the Dutch was Wopigwooit, but the Uncas genealogy cited earlier (Hoadly, "Pedigree of Uncas") indicates that Wopigwooit died some years earlier. De Forest believed that Tatobem and Wopigwooit were the same person. Historians have often repeated his error.

35. John Underhill, "Newes from America," in Orr, *History of the Pequot War,* pp. 56–57; O'Callaghan, *History of New Netherland,* 1:149–51.

36. Winthrop, *Journal,* 1:138–140; John Winthrop to John Winthrop, Jr., December 1634, in *Winthrop Papers, 1630-,* ed. Allyn B. Forbes (Boston, 1943), 3:177.

37. Underhill, "Newes from America," pp. 56–57.

38. Here I follow the reconstruction of events suggested in Cyclone Covey, *The Gentle Radical: Roger Williams* (New York, 1966), pp. 95–97.

39. For a general analysis of homicide and retribution in Native American cultures, see Harold E. Driver, *Indians of North America* (Chicago, 1969), pp. 309–29. On the nature of Algonquian warfare, see Haddock, "War among Northeastern Woodland Indians," pp. 204–21, and Hirsch, "Collision of Military

Cultures," pp. 1187–1212. Francis Jennings argues that Stone was not killed in retribution for Tatobem, as the killers were not Pequots. Basing his case on a line in John Mason's war chronicle, Jennings holds that the western Niantics were solely responsible; see *Invasion of America*, p. 194. But Puritan sources generally reported that the Pequots admitted responsibility, and as some of that testimony was recorded prior to the deterioration of Anglo-Pequot relations, I find it credible. The English in 1634 had no motive to fabricate a story implicating the Pequots. For a detailed analysis of the evidence on this point, see Alfred A. Cave, "Who Killed John Stone? A Note on the Origins of the Pequot War," *William and Mary Quarterly*, 3rd ser. 49 (July 1992): 509–21.

40. Bradford, *Of Plymouth Plantation*, p. 270; Winthrop, *Journal*, 1:118; John Mason, "Brief History of the Pequot War," in Orr, *History of the Pequot War*, p. 17.

41. Wilcomb E. Washburn, "Symbol, Utility, and Aesthetics in the Indian Fur Trade," *Minnesota History* 40 (Winter 1966): 198. See also Alfred G. Bailey, *The Conflict of European and Algonquian Cultures* (Toronto, 1937), p. 4; Ronnie G. McEwan and Jeffrey M. Mitchem, "Indian and European Acculturation in the Eastern United States as a Result of Trade," *North American Archaeologist* 5 (1984): 271–85. The nonutilitarian aspects of trade must not be overestimated. Bruce Trigger, "Early Native North American Responses to European Contact: Romantic versus Rationalistic Interpretation," *Journal of American History* 77 (1991): 1195–1215, argues that some writers, in stressing the persistence of traditionalism in Indian utilization of trade goods, have underestimated "the ability of native people to monitor new situations and to devise strategies that allowed them to respond in a rational fashion to the opportunities as well as the descriptive challenges of a European presence" (p. 1215). But in many accounts, Indian abandonment of traditional crafts and their presumed abject dependency on trade goods have been even more exaggerated.

42. John Smith, *A Map of Virginia, with a Description of the Country, the Commodities, People, Government, and Religion* (Oxford, 1612), p. 20.

43. Hakluyt, *Principal Navigations*, 8:299–308.

44. Frank G. Speck, *Naskapi: The Savage Hunters of the Labrador* (Norman, Okla., 1935), p. 36. For a comparable example among the Sioux, see William K. Powers, *Oglala Religion* (Lincoln, Nebr., 1977), p. 47.

45. Roberts, "Fur Trade of New England," p. 50.

46. Miller and Hamill, "A New Perspective," p. 325. Both French and English traders commented on the Indians' demand for red or blue items and on their refusal to accept lighter colors. See, for example, Marc Lescarbot, *The History of New France* (1609), trans. W. L. Frant, 3 vols. (Toronto, 1907–14), 2:323–24; "The Third Voyage of Master Henry Hudson Toward Nova Zambia," in Samuel Purchas, ed., *Hakluytus Posthumus; or, Purchas His Pilgrimes* (Glasgow, 1904), 13:347; Francis Kirby to John Winthrop, Jr., February 26, 1634, *Winthrop Papers*, 3:150–52. Miller and Hamill believe that European trade objects were desired

because of their resemblance to items of Native American manufacture that were believed to possess manitou, but Constance Crosby argues that all European material goods, and other artifacts of culture, were regarded as sources of power precisely because they were different. See Constance A. Crosby, "From Myth to History; or, Why King Philip's Ghost Walks Abroad," in Mark Leone and Parker Potter, eds., *The Recovery of Meaning in Historical Archaeology* (Washington, D.C., 1988), pp. 183–209.

47. Mason, "Brief History," p. 21.

48. Johnson, *Wonder-Working Providence,* pp. 40–41; Robinson, "The Struggle Within," p. 82.

49. Bradford, *Of Plymouth Plantation,* p. 87.

50. Robinson, "The Struggle Within," p. 77.

51. Winthrop, *Journal,* 1:65, Robinson, "The Struggle Within," pp. 77, 97.

52. Wood, *New England's Prospect,* pp. 80–81.

53. Burton and Lowenthal, "The First of the Mohegans," pp. 589–99.

54. William S. Simmons, "Narragansett," in Trigger, *Handbook,* pp. 190–97; Robinson, "The Struggle Within," pp. 84–85.

55. Winthrop, *Journal,* 1:76.

56. Bradford, *Of Plymouth Plantation,* pp. 257–58; Winthrop, *Journal,* 1:61; Salisbury, *Manitou and Providence,* p. 205.

57. Salisbury, *Manitou and Providence,* p. 210.

58. Glenn W. LaFantasie, ed., *The Correspondence of Roger Williams* (Hanover, N.H., 1988), 1:93–94; hereafter cited as Williams, *Correspondence.*

59. Laurie Weinstein-Farson, "Land, Politics, and Power: The Mohegan Indians in the Seventeenth and Eighteenth Centuries," *Man in the Northeast* 42 (1991): 9–16; Johnson, "Some by Flatteries," pp. 44–53.

60. Carroll Alton Means, "Mohegan-Pequot Relations," pp. 26–33.

61. The map is, however, inaccurate, and in places may have misread Block's notes. For that reason, some authorities decline to accept it as evidence of Mohegan autonomy. The name Mohegan meant "people of the river" and was used by other groups as well.

62. Burton, "Hellish Fiends and Brutish Men," p. 127.

63. Metcalf, "Who Should Rule at Home?" p. 657. For an excellent analysis of the evidence on Uncas's early career, see Johnson, "Some by Flatteries," pp. 53–60. See Hoadly, "Pedigree of Uncas," pp. 227–28, for his own claims about his lineage.

64. In Lorraine Williams's "Ft. Shantok and Ft. Carcharg: A Comparative Study of Seventeenth Century Culture Contact in the Long Island Sound Area" (Ph.D. diss., New York University, 1972), pp. 27–30, it is argued that the rejection of Uncas reflected a recent shift from a matrilineal to a patrilineal mode of succession and that Uncas and his followers fought to restore tradition. But the burden of evidence about the selection of sachems in southern New England

offers no support for the view that rigid rules of heredity succession were ever followed.

65. This account of Uncas's machinations is based upon Indian testimony in litigation in an English court many years later. See Means, "Mohegan-Pequot Relationships," pp. 26–29; J. Hammond Trumbull, and C. J. Hoadly, eds., *Public Records of the Colony of Connecticut* (New York, 1968), 3:479–80; Salisbury, *Manitou and Providence*, p. 206.

66. Means, "Mohegan-Pequot Relationships," p. 26.

3. Pequots and Puritans

1. Winthrop, *Journal*, 1:138–39.

2. Ibid., 1:140.

3. Ibid., 1:139–40; John Winthrop to John Winthrop, Jr., December 1634, *Winthrop Papers*, 3:177.

4. Winthrop, *Journal*, 1:40. Jennings interprets Winthrop's remarks about a defensive alliance somewhat differently, writing that, "emphatically, the Pequots had not permitted Massachusetts to assume a protectorate over them" (*Invasion of America*, p. 196). But in the context of 1634, the Pequots, being on the defensive and, as the record indicates, desirous of English diplomatic intervention to end their conflict with the Narragansetts, were far more likely to have requested an alliance than were the English, whose responses to Pequot overtures, as we shall see, were guarded.

5. Jennings, *Invasion of America*, pp. 191–96.

6. Winthrop, *Journal*, 1:138–39; John Winthrop to John Winthrop, Jr., December 1634, *Winthrop Papers*, 3:177; Bradford, *Of Plymouth Plantation*, p. 291.

7. Parr, *Voyages of David De Vries*, p. 241; Vaughan, *New England Frontier*, pp. 123–25; Jennings, *Invasion of America*, pp. 188–90; De Forest, *Indians of Connecticut*, p. 77.

8. Bradford, *Of Plymouth Plantation*, pp. 268–69.

9. Winthrop, *Journal*, 1:102; Bradford, *Of Plymouth Plantation*, p. 269.

10. Winthrop, *Journal*, 1:108.

11. "Captain Roger Clap's Memoirs," in Alexander Young, ed., *Chronicles of the First Planters of the Colony of Massachusetts Bay* (1845; Baltimore, 1979), p. 363; Winthrop, *Journal*, 1:118. Clap's account differed from Winthrop's, as Clap believed that Stone had successfully fled the colony prior to his trial but was captured "in a great cornfield; where we took him and carried him to Boston." His acquittal on the adultery charge, a capital offense, Clap attributed to the fact that there was only one witness, two being required.

12. Winthrop, *Journal*, 1:139; Bradford, *Of Plymouth Plantation*, p. 291. The Reverend John Eliot of Roxbury opposed the Pequot treaty, but his objections were based on the claim that treaties should not be negotiated without seeking

the approval of the people as a whole. See Winthrop, *Journal*, 1:142; Salisbury, *Manitou and Providence*, pp. 92–93.

13. John Ashley to John Winthrop, March 6, 1632/33, *Winthrop Papers*, 3:107; Winslow, "Good Newes," pp. 561–74; Jennings, *Invasion of America*, pp. 186–87; Willison, *Saints and Strangers*, pp. 214–30.

14. Segal and Stineback, *Puritans, Indians, and Manifest Destiny*, p. 36.

15. Bradford, *Of Plymouth Plantation*, p. 258.

16. Ibid., pp. 245–46; Winthrop, *Journal*, 1:82, 146; Bradford, *Of Plymouth Plantation*, pp. 241–55, 275; Winthrop, *Journal*, 1:177.

17. Bradford, *Of Plymouth Plantation*, pp. 276–77.

18. Ibid, pp. 277–79, 394–96. Plymouth never received support from Boston for its Maine ventures. In the spring of 1637, Edward Winslow informed Winthrop that he had learned, from Sir Ferdinando Gorges, that the French traders in Maine did not actually have a patent from the king of France but were rather "a base people" whom Paris would disclaim. Winslow pressed for joint action "to expell them." He never received an answer. See Edward Winslow to John Winthrop, 1637, *Winthrop Papers*, 2:391–93.

19. Bradford, *Of Plymouth Plantation*, p. 263; Winthrop, *Journal*, 1:129.

20. Bradford, *Of Plymouth Plantation*, pp. 262–68; Winthrop, *Journal*, 1:129.

21. Winthrop, *Journal*, 1:124, 128–29, 131, 137; *Winthrop Papers*, 3:167; Bradford, *Of Plymouth Plantation*, pp. 262–68.

22. Bradford, *Of Plymouth Plantation*, pp. 258–59.

23. Winthrop, *Journal*, 1:103.

24. Bradford, *Of Plymouth Plantation*, p. 258.

25. Winthrop, *Journal*, 1:109; Jennings, *Invasion of America*, pp. 188–89.

26. Winthrop, *Journal*, 1:109.

27. Bradford, *Of Plymouth Plantation*, pp. 148–57; Winthrop, *Journal*, 1:107–8.

28. Winthrop, *Journal*, 1:109–11; Morton, *New English Canaan*, p. 68.

29. Bradford, *Of Plymouth Plantation*, p. 259.

30. Ibid., pp. 258–60.

31. Ibid., pp. 258–59.

32. Ibid., pp. 259–60.

33. Ibid., pp. 260–61.

34. Ibid., p. 270.

35. Ibid., pp. 270–71; Winthrop, *Journal*, 1:118.

36. Jennings, *Invasion of America*, p. 189.

37. Winthrop, *Journal*, 1:124.

38. Ibid., 1:128; Bradford, *Of Plymouth Plantation*, pp. 280–81.

39. Bradford, *Of Plymouth Plantation*, p. 281; Charles McLean Andrews, *The Colonial Period of American History* (New York, 1936), 2:72.

40. Bradford, *Of Plymouth Plantation*, p. 282; Andrews, *Colonial Period*, 2:73; Henry R. Stiles, *The History and Genealogies of Ancient Windsor* (Hartford, 1891), p. 37.

41. Bradford, *Of Plymouth Plantation*, p. 290.

42. The text of the so-called Warwick patent may be found in Trumbull, *Complete History of Connecticut, Civil and Ecclesiastical* (New London, Conn., 1898), 2:423–24. On the question of the patent's authenticity, see Albert C. Bates, *The Charter of Connecticut: A Study* (Hartford, 1932), pp. 8–10; Robert C. Black III, *The Younger John Winthrop* (New York, 1966), pp. 85–87.

43. Bartholomew Greene to Richard Saltonstall, December 20, 1635, in *Massachusetts Historical Society Collections*, 5th ser. 1 (1897): 216–17; Winthrop, *Journal*, 1:157, 174–75; *Winthrop Papers*, 3:217–18; Bradford, *Of Plymouth Plantation*, p. 190.

44. Winthrop, *Journal*, 1:164; "Agreement of the Saybrook Company with John Winthrop, Jr.," *Winthrop Papers*, 3:198; Black, *Younger John Winthrop*, pp. 71–81.

45. Winthrop, *Journal*, 1:161, 165; Lion Gardener, "Relation of the Pequot War," in Orr, *History of the Pequot War*, p. 122.

46. Winthrop, *Journal*, 1:162; Andrews, *Colonial Period*, 2:77.

47. Covey, *Gentle Radical*, pp. 151–52. On the career of Henry Vane, see J. H. Adamson and H. F. Folland, *Henry Vane* (New York, 1973).

48. Winthrop, *Journal*, 1:165–66. On the founders of Saybrook, see Karen O. Kupperman, "Definitions of Liberty on the Eve of the Civil War: Lord Say and Sele, Lord Brook, and the American Puritan Colonies," *Historical Journal* 37 (1989): 17–34. Nineteenth-century writers changed the spelling of Gardener's name to "Gardiner," a practice followed by the editor of Winthrop's *Journal*. I use the original spelling.

49. Parr, *Voyages of David De Vries*, p. 169.

50. "Grievances of the Servants at Saybrook," *Winthrop Papers*, 3:281–82; Black, *Younger John Winthrop*, pp. 96–97, 137.

51. Richard Saltonstall to John Winthrop, Jr., February 27, 1635, *Winthrop Papers*, 2:229–30; Winthrop, *Journal*, 1:124.

52. Winthrop, *Journal*, 1:132–34.

53. Ibid.; Palfrey, *History of New England*, 1:449.

54. Nathaniel B. Shurtleff, ed.; *Records of the Governor and Company of the Massachusetts Bay in New England* (Boston, 1853), 1:146, 148, 160; Winthrop, *Journal*, 1:163, 165.

55. Shurtleff, *Records*, 1:170; Winthrop, *Journal*, 1:180–81. Jennings argues that the restriction of Connecticut military action to the waging of defensive war was intended to prevent an attack on the Pequots, which would have permitted the Connecticut towns to annex Pequot land by right of conquest, and that Mason's subsequent expedition against the Pequots was designed to outflank the Bay Colony's designs (*Invasion of America*, pp. 186–201). His argument is ingenious. Given the personal conflicts and trade rivalries among the English claimants to the Connecticut valley, it is somewhat plausible. But it must also be noted that it is not supported by much tangible evidence. In fact, the only real proof Jennings

offers is the fact that the Massachusetts Bay Colony, in delegating authority to the Connecticut towns, restricted its right to wage war to defensive actions. But Jennings has not demonstrated that the magistrates intended that provision as a safeguard against a Connecticut attack on the Pequots. We have no reason to believe that either the Bay Colony magistrates or the Connecticut settlers anticipated the Pequot War at the time the thorny question of legal jurisdiction was adjudicated with Saybrook. As to the subsequent action against the Pequots, none of the primary source materials—correspondence, journal entries, legislative actions—give any support at all to Jennings's argument that blocking Connecticut's expansion was the real reason for Endecott's raid on the Pequots or that Connecticut attacked the Pequots at Mystic in order to strike at Boston. Jennings asserts that Winthrop and others systematically destroyed incriminating evidence. That may be so. But we must ask why the Connecticut leaders, the presumed victims of the Bay Colony's machinations, left no record of their outrage at the presumed fabrication of an Indian war to block their expansion. Although the Connecticut authorities complained that Endecott's raid was clumsy and provocative, in neither private correspondence nor public statement do we find even a hint that they suspected the Massachusetts authorities of acting from the motives attributed to them by Jennings. Connecticut's involvement in the war is best explained as a response to the Pequot raid on Wethersfield, not, as Jennings suggests, as an attempt to counter a Bay Colony scheme to annex territory Connecticut also coveted. It is, of course, always difficult to prove a negative proposition. Thus we cannot prove categorically that Jennings is wrong. But, at best, the Scottish verdict "not proven" is in order here. Most authorities regard Jennings's claim on this matter as an interesting speculation, but at least one writer assumes that it is a proven fact that the Pequot War was the product of Massachusetts-Connecticut rivalries. See Neil Asher Silverman, "The Pequot Massacres," *Journal of Military History* 1 (Spring 1989): 73–81.

56. Shurtleff, *Records*, 1:170.

57. Andrews, *Colonial Period*, 2:77–78.

58. Jennings, *Invasion of America*, p. 198; John Winthrop to John Winthrop, Jr., June 10, 1636, *Winthrop Papers*, 3:268.

59. John Winthrop, Jr., to John Winthrop, May 16, 1636, *Winthrop Papers*, 3:260; George Fenwick to John Winthrop, Jr., May 21, 1636, ibid., pp. 260–62, 268; Gardener, "Relation," pp. 121–22.

60. Edward Winslow to John Winthrop, Jr., June 23, 1636, *Winthrop Papers*, 3:274; Black, *Younger John Winthrop*, p. 97; John Haynes to John Winthrop, Jr., June 1636, *Winthrop Papers*, 3:263–64; Israel Stoughton to John Winthrop, Jr., June 1636, ibid., pp. 264–65.

61. Bradford, *Of Plymouth Plantation*, p. 291; William Pynchon to John Winthrop, Jr., June 2, 1636, *Winthrop Papers*, 3:267. On Pynchon, see Thomas, "In the Maelstrom of Change."

62. Jonathan Brewster to John Winthrop, Jr., June 18, 1636, *Winthrop Papers,* 3:270–71, 271–72.

63. Ibid.; Sir Henry Vane to John Winthrop, Jr., "Commission and Instructions from the Colony of the Massachusetts Bay to John Winthrop, Jr., for Treating with the Pequots," July 1636, ibid., pp. 282–83, 284–85.

64. Gardener, "Relation," pp. 123–24, 124; *Winthrop Papers,* 3:513, 4:20–21.

65. Gardener, "Relation," p. 132; Jennings, *Invasion of America,* p. 206.

66. Gardener, "Relation," pp. 124–25.

67. Ibid., pp. 125–26.

68. Winthrop, *Journal* 1:183–84; Underhill, "Newes from America," p. 50; Winthrop, *Journal,* 1:184–85.

69. Winthrop, *Journal,* 1:184.

70. Ibid., 1:185. Vane's letter to Williams has not survived. We have only Winthrop's summary of its content.

71. Ibid. Again, we know of the correspondence only through Winthrop's *Journal.*

72. Gardener, "Relation," p. 139; Underhill, "Newes from America," p. 51; Winthrop, *Journal,* 1:184–85; Bradford, *Of Plymouth Plantation,* p. 294; Johnson, *Wonder-Working Providence,* pp. 162–63; Hubbard, *Indian Wars in New England,* 2:7, 11; Burton, "Hellish Fiends and Brutish Men," p. 130.

73. *Winthrop Papers,* 3:412.

74. Underhill, "Newes from America," p. 50; Williams, *Correspondence,* 1:72.

75. Philip Vincent, "A True Relation of the Late Battel Fought in New England, between the English and the Pequot Savages," in Orr, *History of the Pequot War,* pp. 109–10.

76. Winthrop, *Journal,* 1:186.

77. Winthrop, *Papers,* 3:25–26; Shurtleff, *Records,* 1:86; Johnson, *Wonder-Working Providence,* p. 255. The only modern study of Endecott is Lawrence S. Mayo, *John Endecott: A Biography* (Cambridge, Mass., 1936), which is rather dated.

78. Winthrop, *Journal,* 1:186; Underhill, "Newes from America," p. 51.

79. Winthrop, *Journal,* 1:187; Underhill, "Newes from America," p. 52–53.

80. Winthrop, *Journal,* 1:187–88.

81. Underhill, "Newes from America," p. 54.

82. Ibid., pp. 54, 55.

83. Ibid., p. 55; Winthrop, *Journal,* 1:188, 266; Shurtleff, *Records,* 1:181.

84. Gardener, "Relation," pp. 126–27.

85. Underhill, "Newes from America," p. 55.

86. Ibid., pp. 55–56.

87. Ibid., pp. 57–58.

88. Ibid.

89. Ibid., p. 59.

90. Ibid., pp. 59–60.
91. Ibid., p. 60.
92. Ibid.; Winthrop, *Journal,* 1:189–90.
93. Gardener, "Relation," p. 127.
94. Ibid.
95. Winthrop, *Journal,* 1:191–92: Gardener, "Relation," p. 127.
96. Winthrop, *Journal,* 1:194.
97. Ibid., 1:212.

4. The Pequots Humbled

1. Johnson, "Some by Flatteries," p. 120.
2. Roger Williams to Deputy Governor John Winthrop [c. August 1636], in Williams, *Correspondence,* 1:54–55.
3. Williams to Winthrop [October 24, 1636?], in Williams, *Correspondence,* 1:69; on the dating of the letter, see Glenn LaFantasie's editorial comment, pp. 60–65.
4. Winthrop, *Journal,* 1:190; Bradford, *Of Plymouth Plantation,* pp. 294–95; Mason, "Brief History," pp. 19, 24.
5. Salisbury, *Manitou and Providence,* pp. 212–13.
6. Williams to Major John Mason and Governor Thomas Prence, June 23, 1670, in Williams, *Correspondence,* 2:611–12.
7. Williams to Winthrop, May 1, 1637, in Williams, *Correspondence,* 1:72.
8. Ibid., 1:73; Salisbury, *Manitou and Providence,* pp. 214–15. Salisbury believes that Cutshamekin was "the most effective single agent in dissuading the Narragansetts from neutrality."
9. Johnson, *Wonder-Working Providence,* pp. 162–63.
10. Winthrop, *Journal,* 1:191–93.
11. Gardener, "Relation," pp. 128–29; Winthrop, *Journal,* 1:192.
12. Winthrop, *Journal,* 1:192; Gardener, "Relation," pp. 128–29, 134. Winthrop claims that the captive was "a godly young man called Butterfield (whereupon the meadow was named Butterfield Meadow)," but Gardener recalled that he was Mitchell's brother. Gardener's account and Winthrop's differ in other particulars. Winthrop claims that the hay-gathering episode occurred immediately after the return of the shallop from the Pequot (Thames) River following Endecott's raid and that the attack on Gardener's men in the cornfield occurred fourteen days later. He does not mention Mitchell and reports that no Englishmen were killed in the skirmish in the field, although one man was wounded by four arrows. It is possible that Winthrop was reporting an earlier incident not recorded by Gardener, but I think it more likely that he was misled by garbled, secondhand reports. Gardener's account is more believable. Even though he wrote some years after the event, he was an eyewitness. Furthermore, it does not seem at all likely that Gardener, persuaded that an Indian attack was

imminent, would have waited, as Winthrop represents him, for two weeks after the return of his men from battle with the Pequots before harvesting Fort Saybrook's corn crop. Clearly, given the anxieties he had expressed earlier about an Indian attack, Gardener had every reason to act promptly. Gardener does appear to be mistaken on one point. He believed that Mitchell was a clergyman from Cambridge. The records do not bear this out. Mitchell may have been an elder in the newly organized church at Wethersfield.

13. Lion Gardener to John Winthrop, Jr., November 7, 1636, *Winthrop Papers*, 3:319–21.

14. Gardener, "Relation," pp. 134–36.

15. Winthrop, *Journal*, 1:194; Underhill, "Newes from America," pp. 66–67; Gardener, "Relation," pp. 134–35; Israel Stoughton to John Winthrop, Jr. [June 1636], *Winthrop Papers*, 3:264–65.

16. Edward Gibbon to John Winthrop, Jr., September 29, 1636, *Winthrop Papers*, 3:323.

17. Gardener, "Relation," pp. 129–30.

18. Ibid., p. 130.

19. Ibid., pp. 130–31.

20. Ibid., pp. 131–32.

21. Ibid.

22. Ibid., pp. 132–33.

23. Underhill, "Newes from America," p. 61.

24. Gardener, "Relation," p. 133.

25. Winthrop, *Journal*, 1:265–66; Trumbull and Hoadly, eds., *Public Records of the Colony of Connecticut*, 1:19–20; Alden T. Vaughan, "A Test of Puritan Justice," *New England Quarterly* 38 (1965): 331–40.

26. Winthrop, *Journal*, 1:213; *Winthrop Papers*, 2:407–8; Mason, "Brief History," p. 18; Underhill, "Newes from America," p. 62; Vincent, "True Relation," pp. 100–101.

27. Underhill, "Newes from America," p. 63; Mason, "Brief History," pp. 18–19.

28. Johnson, "Wonder-Working Providence," pp. 105–6, 169.

29. Trumbull and Hoadly, eds., *Public Records of the Colony of Connecticut*, 1:9–10.

30. Ibid.; Palfrey, *History of New England*, 1:463. On Mason's career, see Louis B. Mason, *The Life and Times of Major John Mason of Connecticut, 1600–1672* (New York, 1935). For information about other Connecticut participants, see James Shepard, *Connecticut Soldiers in the Pequot War of 1637* (Meriden, Conn., 1913).

31. Johnson, *Wonder-Working Providence*, pp. 105–6.

32. Shurtleff, 1:192.

33. Winthrop, *Journal*, 1:213.

34. Ibid., 1:213–14.

35. Bradford, *Of Plymouth Plantation*, pp. 394–98.

36. Nathaniel B. Shurtleff and David Pulsifer, eds., *Records of the Colony of New Plymouth* (Boston, 1855), 1:60; Bradford, *Of Plymouth Plantation*, p. 295.

37. Winthrop, *Journal*, 1:197–99, 217, 240, 275–76; *A Short Story of the Rise, Reign, and Ruine of the Antinomians* (London, 1644), pp. 26–27. On the Antinomian Controversy, see Charles Frances Adams, *Three Episodes of Massachusetts History* (Boston, 1896); Emery Battis, *Saints and Sectaries: Anne Hutchinson and the Antinomian Controversy in the Massachusetts Bay Colony* (Chapel Hill, N.C., 1962); David D. Hall, ed., *The Antinomian Controversy, 1636–1638: A Documentary History* (Middletown, Conn., 1968); Edmund S. Morgan, "The Case against Anne Hutchinson," *New England Quarterly* 10 (1937): 635–49; Jasper Rosemmeier, "New England's Perfection: The Image of Adam and the Image of Christ in the Antinomian Crisis, 1634 to 1638," *William and Mary Quarterly*, 3rd ser. 27 (1970): 435–59; Lyle Koehler, "A Search for Power: The 'Weaker Sex' in Seventeenth Century New England and Female Agitation during the Years of Antinomian Turmoil, 1636–1640," *William and Mary Quarterly*, 3rd ser. 31 (1974): 155–78; Amy Schrager Lang, *Prophetic Women: Anne Hutchinson and the Problem of Dissent in the Literature of New England* (Berkeley, 1987); Kibbey, *Interpretation of Material Shapes.*

38. Shurtleff, *Records*, 1:125, 138, 146; Jack S. Rodabaugh, "The Militias of Colonial Massachusetts," *Military Affairs* 18 (1954): 1–18; Allen French, "The Arms and Military Training of Our Colonizing Ancestors," *Massachusetts Historical Society Proceedings* 67 (1944): 3–21; T. H. Breen, "English Origins and New World Development: The Case of the Covenanted Militia in Seventeenth Century Massachusetts," *Past and Present* 57 (1972): 68–87. For an overview of problems of military organization in colonial America, see John E. Ferling, *A Wilderness of Miseries: War and Warriors in Early America* (Westport, Conn., 1980).

39. "Petition of John Underhill to Governor and Assistants of Massachusetts, 1637," *Massachusetts Historical Society Collections*, 4th ser. 7 (1865): 175–76. Winthrop, *Journal*, 1:275–76. On Underhill's career, see Henry C. Shelley, *John Underhill: Captain of New England and New Netherland* (New York, 1932).

40. Underhill, "Newes from America," p. 67; Vincent, "True Relation," pp. 100, 106; Jonathan Brewster to John Winthrop, Jr., June 18, 1636, *Winthrop Papers*, 3:270–71.

41. Mason, "Brief History," p. 20; Underhill, "Newes from America," pp. 67–69.

42. Gardener, "Relation," p. 136.

43. Ibid.; Vincent, "True Relation," p. 101.

44. Underhill, "Newes from America," pp. 69–70; Gardener, "Relation," pp. 133–34.

45. Underhill, "Newes from America," pp. 69–70.

46. Ibid., pp. 71–73. For excellent analyses of this genre, see Slotkin, *Regenera-*

tion through Violence, pp. 94–148; Breitwieser, *American Puritanism and the Defense of Mourning;* Vaughan and Clark, "Introduction," *Puritans among the Indians,* pp. 1–28; and Roy Harvey Pearce, "The Significance of the Captivity Narrative," *American Literature* 19 (1947): 1–20.

47. Mason, "Brief History," pp. 21–23. Noting that Mason also mentioned that he regarded the original plan to attack at Pequot harbor as unduly hazardous for another reason, "which I shall forebear to trouble you with," Francis Jennings in 1975 charged that Mason's account concealed the real nature of the controversy over strategy at Saybrook in early May 1637 and that subsequent Puritan historians collaborated in a cover-up. Jennings believes that Mason actually proposed to avoid the concentration of Pequot warriors at Weinshauks and massacre unprotected women, children, and old men in the village at Fort Mystic instead. "Battle as such," Jennings writes, "was not his purpose. Battle is only one of the ways to destroy an enemy's will to fight. Massacre can accomplish the same end with less risk, and Mason had determined that massacre would be his objective. Gardiner and Underhill, hardened soldiers though they were, had opposed his plan." Mason, Jennings concluded, had won their reluctant approval only after the chaplain informed them that Mason's genocidal plan had God's blessing. "It strains credulity," Jennings writes, "that three proud and experienced military officers, even among Puritans, would ask a minister to decide the technical question whether to attack a fortified village from front or rear. Clerics are consulted on moral issues." Though Mason's own account does not support that charge, Jennings argues that to conceal what really happened Mason included in his history of the war a false report that Mystic had been reinforced by 150 warriors the night before the attack. He also presumably hid the real reason for allied Indian desertions during the march to Fort Mystic by accusing of cowardice warriors too decent to participate in a slaughter of the innocent (Jennings, *Invasion of America,* pp. 220–22). In light of what did transpire at Fort Mystic, Jennings's theory at first glance seems quite plausible. But it contains serious flaws. There is no evidence that Mason and his colleagues at Saybrook had any concrete information about the deployment of Pequot forces. Their war narratives testify that they were troubled by their lack of sound intelligence on the enemy. Archaeological excavations recently directed by Kevin McBride of the University of Connecticut confirm Puritan descriptions of Fort Mystic as a solidly fortified, palisaded settlement on a hill. It was obviously built to withstand enemy attack. It was by no means an unprotected village (McBride, "Historical Archaeology of the Mashantucket Pequots," pp. 98–99; Russell Bourne, *The Red King's Rebellion: Racial Politics in New England, 1675–1678* [New York, 1990], p. 69). Jennings supports his assertion that there were few if any warriors at Fort Mystic at the time of the Puritan attack only by the argument that, since the Pequots had guns, the absence of references to their use by the Pequot defenders at Mystic proves that the warriors were elsewhere. That is hardly conclusive evidence. The Pequot armory, as we noted earlier, contained

only sixteen muskets, and those weapons were of somewhat limited use in combat in close quarters in any case. The claim that Fort Mystic was in fact defended by warriors is found not only in Mason's war narrative but in the other contemporary accounts as well. It is highly unlikely that all of those references to their presence were contrived, as Jennings would have us believe, in order to conceal Mason's real intent. Finally, as for the role played by the chaplain, the Reverend Mr. Stone, the image of a Puritan commander asking a clergyman to seek the Lord's guidance before committing an act of genocide is a striking one, but contrary again to Jennings's assertion, Stone was not in fact consulted only on "moral issues." You will recall that earlier he had been asked to pray for a sign indicating that Uncas's Mohegans could indeed be trusted. There is nothing really exceptional in Mason's report that Stone was asked to pray that the commanders make a wise choice in their plan of battle. Military chaplains in the seventeenth century, as in later times, were frequently asked by commanders to implore the Almighty to grant success on the battlefield. They were seldom asked for advice about the morality of strategic plans. Jennings's assumption that some of the Puritans' Indian allies deserted to protest the intention to butcher noncombatants is also unfounded. There is no evidence that the Indians were privy to any such plan. We do know, however, that both the Narragansetts and the eastern Niantics were divided over the question of giving active support to the English in their confrontation with the Pequots. It is reasonable to assume that some continued to waver in their loyalties, even after Mason's army marched into Pequot territory. But we have no reason to believe that the plan of march had anything to do with the desertions. The Narragansetts had recommended to Roger Williams several weeks earlier the same plan of attack Mason devised. Jennings is, of course, correct in pointing out that the Puritans' Indian allies did not condone the massacre of women and children and were horrified by English actions at Fort Mystic. He is on shaky ground, however, when he claims that the atrocity was carefully premeditated by Mason at Saybrook, opposed for a time by Underhill and Gardener, and then blessed by the chaplain. The evidence available to us does not support that conjecture.

48. Mason, "Brief History," pp. 23–24.

49. Roger Williams to Governor Henry Vane or Deputy Governor John Winthrop, May 13, 1837, in Williams, *Correspondence*, 1:78–79.

50. Mason, "Brief History," p. 24.

51. Ibid., p. 25.

52. Ibid., pp. 25–26.

53. Ibid., p. 26.

54. Vincent, "True Relation," pp. 105–6. For a discussion of the impact of contact with Europeans on Indian warfare, see Patrick M. Malone, "Changing Military Technology among the Indians of Southern New England, 1600–1677, *American Quarterly* 25 (1973):48–63. Malone concludes that Indian adoption of European military technology postdated the Pequot War. "The Puritans and

their Indian allies crushed the poorly equipped Pequot tribe with little difficulty in 1637" (p. 51). See also Malone, *The Skulking Way of War: Technology and Tactics among the New England Indians* (Lanham, Md., 1991).

55. Mason, "Brief History," pp. 26–27. Underhill claimed the attack began some hours earlier, writing, "we set forth about one o'clock of the morning" ("Newes from America," p. 78). But as there is no reason for Mason to fabricate a story about oversleeping, I find his account more believable.

56. Mason, "Brief History," pp. 26–27.

57. Ibid., p. 28.

58. Underhill, "Newes from America," pp. 79–80. The Reverend Philip Vincent, in his brief tract on the Pequot War, accused Underhill of cowardice, a charge he hotly denied in his own war narrative. Vincent was not an eyewitness. He was an orthodox Puritan deeply opposed to Underhill's antinomian views. The story that Underhill hesitated before entering the palisade and had to be urged on by a subordinate may well have been fabricated to discredit a heretic. Mason, however, believed the story and attributed it to some of Underhill's men. His account, published after Vincent's and Underhill's, lends support to Vincent. See Vincent, "True Relation," p. 103; Underhill, "Newes from America," p. 80; Mason, "Brief History," pp. 29–30.

59. Underhill, "Newes from America," p. 80.

60. Mason, "Brief History," pp. 28–29.

61. Ibid.; Underhill, "Newes from America," pp. 79–80.

62. Mason, "Brief History," p. 29.

63. Ibid., p. 31; Underhill, "Newes from America," p. 81; Williams, *Correspondence*, 1:83–84.

64. Mason, "Brief History," p. 30.

65. Underhill, "Newes from America," p. 81.

66. Bradford, *Of Plymouth Plantation*, p. 296; Johnson, *Wonder-Working Providence*, p. 168.

67. Bradford, *Of Plymouth Plantation*, p. 29; Underhill, "Newes from America," p. 84.

68. Johnson, *Wonder-Working Providence*, p. 168; Underhill, "Newes from America," p. 82; Mason, "Brief History," p. 31; Gardener, "Relation," p. 137.

69. Underhill, "Newes from America," p. 82; Mason, "Brief History," p. 41. Mason (p. 31) claims that all the English Indian allies except Uncas's Mohegans deserted; but later (p. 33) he confirms Underhill's report that a number of Narragansetts accompanied the English forces to Pequot harbor on the Thames and were subsequently returned to their homeland by ship. I conclude, therefore, that while some of the Narragansetts returned by land on their own Mason exaggerated when he claimed that all of them "deserted."

70. Underhill, "Newes from America," p. 83. For a detailed analysis of this issue, see Hirsch, "Collision of Military Cultures."

71. Mason, "Brief History," pp. 31–32.

72. Ibid., p. 32; Underhill, "Newes from America," p. 84.

73. Mason, "Brief History," pp. 33–34; Underhill, "Newes from America," p. 86.

74. Mason, "Brief History," pp. 33–34; Daniel Patrick to John Winthrop, May 23, 1637, *Winthrop Papers,* 3:421.

75. Mason, "Brief History," pp. 33–34.

76. Ibid.; Underhill, "Newes from America," p. 85.

77. Mason, "Brief History," pp. 34–35.

78. Ibid., p. 36; Underhill, "Newes from America," p. 85; Vincent, "True Relation," p. 106; Roger Williams to John Winthrop, June 21, 1637, in Williams, *Correspondence,* 1:86; Winthrop, *Journal,* 1:225–26; Israel Stoughton to John Winthrop, c. June 28, 1637, *Winthrop Papers,* 3:435; Daniel Patrick to the Governor and Council of War in Massachusetts, June 19, 1637, *Winthrop Papers,* 3:430–31.

79. Gardener, "Relation," pp. 137–38.

80. Roger Williams to John Winthrop, July 3, 1637, in Williams, *Correspondence,* 1:90.

81. Winthrop, *Journal,* 1:225–27; Mason, "Brief History," p. 36; Gardener, "Relation," pp. 137–38. The Pequots also referred to the Owl's Nest *(ohomowauke)* as the hiding place *(cuppacommoch).* It is now called the Cedar Swamp and is located on the Mashantucket Pequot reservation near Ledyard, Connecticut. See Kevin A. McBride, "Prehistoric and Historic Patterns of Wetland Use in Eastern Connecticut," *Man in the Northeast* 43 (Spring 1992): 10–24.

82. Roger Williams to John Winthrop, June 30, 1637, in Williams, *Correspondence,* 1:88–89; Williams to Winthrop, July 19, 1637, ibid., 1:101–2; Williams to Winthrop, July 31, 1637, Ibid., 1:109; De Forest, *Indians of Connecticut,* p. 143. Williams adopted and reared a young Pequot boy captured during Stoughton's raid; see Williams, *Correspondence,* 1:88–89, 109.

83. Winthrop, *Journal,* 1:226; De Forest, *Indians of Connecticut,* p. 145.

84. Mason, "Brief History," pp. 37–38; Winthrop, *Journal,* 1:226–28.

85. Winthrop, *Journal,* 1:227–29, 260; Vincent, "True Relation," p. 107; Gardener, "Relation," p. 138; Roger Williams to John Winthrop, July 10, 1637, in Williams, *Correspondence,* 1:97; Ethel Boissevain, "Whatever Became of the New England Indians Shipped to Bermuda to be Sold as Slaves?" *Man in the Northeast* 11 (Spring 1981): 103–14; Karen Ordahl Kupperman, *Providence Island, 1630–1641: The Other Puritan Colony* (Cambridge, Mass., 1993), p. 172.

86. Mason, "Brief History," p. 40; Roger Williams to John Winthrop, September 21, 1638, in Williams, *Correspondence,* 1:182–89. The text of the Hartford agreement may be most conveniently consulted in Vaughan, *New England Frontier,* pp. 340–41.

87. Mason, "True History," pp. 40–43; Gardener, "Relation," pp. 138–39.

88. John Menta, "The Strange Case of Nepaupuck: Warrior or War Crimi-

nal?" *Journal of the New Haven Historical Society* 33 (Spring 1987): 3–17; De Forest, *Indians of Connecticut*, p. 175.

89. Johnson, "Some by Flatteries," pp. 233–40; Ceci, "Native Wampum," in Hauptman and Wherry, *Pequots in Southern New England*, p. 61.

90. The phrase "social harmony" is from Bourne, *Red King's Rebellion*, p. xiv.

91. Winthrop, *Journal*, 1:238, 271–72, 2:614–15; *Winthrop Papers*, 6:258–59; Gardener, "Relation," pp. 138–45; John A. Sainsbury, "Miantonomi's Death and New England Politics, 1630–1645," *Rhode Island History* 30 (1971): 111–23; Thomas, "In the Maelstrom of Change," pp. 69–71. For Roger Williams's efforts to defend Miantonomi and explain his behavior, see Williams, *Correspondence*, 1:119, 145–46, 183–84.

92. Winthrop, *Journal*, 2:74–76. On the later career of Wyandanch, see John A. Strong, "The Imposition of Colonial Jurisdiction over the Montauk Indians of Long Island," *Ethnohistory* 41 (1994):560–90.

93. Gardener, "Relation," p. 142. Gardener's account of Miantonomi's speech was written many years after the event and is not corroborated by the contemporary source materials. For a discussion of Indian oratory, see Kathleen J. Bragdon, " 'Emphatical Speech and Great Action': An Analysis of Seventeenth-Century Speech Events Described in Early Sources," *Man in the Northeast* 37 (1987): 101–11.

94. Winthrop, *Journal*, 2:131–34; *Declaration of Former Passages and Proceedings Betwixt the English and the Narragansetts* (Boston, 1645), pp. 2–3; Edward Winslow, *Hypocrisies Unmasked* (Providence, 1916), pp. 70–75; Sainsbury, "Miantonomi's Death," p. 118; Bradford, *Of Plymouth Plantation*, pp. 330–32.

95. Winthrop, *Journal*, 1:271, 2:134–35, 271; Gardener, "Relation," pp. 142–43; Johnson, "Some by Flatteries," pp. 121–39.

96. *Acts of the Commissioners of the United Colonies of New England* in David Pulsifer, ed. *Records of the Colony of New Plymouth in New England* (Boston, 1859), 1:127.

5. The War and the Mythology of the Frontier

1. Thomas Hooker to John Winthrop, May 1637, *Winthrop Papers*, 3:407–8.

2. John Higginson to John Winthrop, May 1637, *Winthrop Papers*, 3:404–5.

3. Mason, "Brief History," p. 44; Underhill, "Newes from America," pp. 49–50; Gardener, "Relation," pp. 139–41.

4. Johnson, *Wonder-Working Providence*, p. 170.

5. Pulsifer, ed., *Acts of the Commissioners of the United Colonies*, 1:83.

6. Increase Mather, *A Brief History of the War with the Indians in New England* (London, 1676), p. 1.

7. Cotton Mather, *Magnalia Christi Americana* (1702; New York, 1972), 1:24.

8. Hirsch, "Collision of Military Cultures," pp. 1199–2004, makes an excellent

case for the premise that neither side in the Pequot War anticipated a full-scale conflict. But while Hirsch may be correct in arguing that magistrates expected the Pequots to submit and were surprised by their resistance, he does not appreciate the depth of Puritan prejudice against "paganism" and "savagery," nor does he assess the long-range implications of that prejudice.

9. John Higginson to John Winthrop, May 1637, *Winthrop Papers*, 3: 403.

10. Johnson, *Wonder-Working Providence*, pp. 127–30, 147.

11. Slotkin and Folsom, *So Dreadful a Judgment*, provides an excellent analysis of the historiography of King Philip's War and reprints several key texts. Also useful is Charles H. Lincoln, ed., *Narratives of the Indian Wars, 1675–1699* (New York, 1913).

12. Increase Mather, *An Earnest Exhortation* (Boston, 1676).

13. Cotton Mather, *The Way to Prosperity,* reprinted in Plumstead, *Wall and Garden*, pp. 133–34.

14. Thomas Prince, *The People of New England Put in Mind of the Righteous Acts of the Lord to Them and Their Fathers and Reasoned with Concerning Them,* in Plumstead, *Wall and Garden*, pp. 205–6.

15. Daniel Gookin, "An Historical Account of the Doings and Sufferings of the Christian Indians in New England, in the Years 1675, 1676, 1677," *Transactions and Collections of the American Antiquarian Society* 2 (1836): 437–39.

16. Winthrop Jordan, *White over Black* (Baltimore, 1969), pp. 90–91.

17. Michael Paul Rogin, "Liberal Society and the Indian Question," in *Ronald Reagan, the Movie and Other Episodes in Political Demonology* (Berkeley, 1987), p. 137.

Index

215